Verification and Validation of Real-Time Software

Edited by W. J. Quirk

With 48 Figures and 3 Tables

Springer-Verlag
Berlin Heidelberg New York Tokyo

Editor

William J. Quirk
AERE, Harwell
Didcot, Oxon OX11 ORA
United Kingdom

ISBN-13:978-3-642-70226-6   e-ISBN-13:978-3-642-70224-2
DOI: 10.1007/978-3-642-70224-2

To the Reader

Real-time software poses serious problems. It fails too often and the failures can be both extremely troublesome and sometimes dangerous.

In this report, the techniques available for validation and verification of real-time systems software are reviewed. Material, which is at present scattered through conference proceedings, research notes and journal papers, is gathered together and presented in the context of practical usefulness. More detailed references are included wherever possible.

It is unrealistic and immodest to suppose that this report will solve all the real-time reliability problems that the reader may have. We hope, however, that it may be some help along the way.

W.J. Quirk, Editor.

Affiliations and Acknowledgements

The authors and their affiliations are given below. Although different chapters have been made the responsibility of different authors, all the participants have been actively involved in every chapter. It should be noted that any views expressed in this report are those of the authors as individuals and do not necessarily represent the views of the organisation to which they are affiliated, nor of the Commission of the European Communities whose funds from DG III/B/1 under contracts 009231-5 partly supported this project. We gratefully acknowledge this support and the interest of Mr. H. Fangmeyer, the project leader.

S.   Bologna
ENEA Casaccia.

W.D. Ehrenberger
GRS Garching.

P.   Puhr-Westerheide
GRS Garching.

W.J. Quirk
AERE Harwell.

J.R. Taylor
RISO Roskilde.

U.   Voges
KFK Karlsruhe.

Table of Contents

1 Introduction

W.J.Quirk

1.1 Real-time software and the real world

Real-time software and the real world are inseparably related. Real time
cannot be turned back and the real world will not always forget its
history. The consequences of previous influences may last for a long
time and the undesired effects may range from being inconvenient to
disastrous in both economic and human terms. As a result, there is much
pressure to develop and apply techniques to improve the reliability of
real-time software so that the frequency and consequences of failure are
reduced to a level that is as low as reasonably achievable.

This report is about such techniques. After a detailed description of
the software life cycle, a chapter is devoted to each of the four
principle categories of technique available at present. These cover all
stages of the software development process and each chapter identifies
relevant techniques, the stages to which they are applicable and their
effectiveness in improving real-time software reliability.

1.2 The characteristics of real-time software

As well as the enhanced reliability requirement discussed above, real-time
software has a number of other distinguishing characteristics. First,
the sequencing and timing of inputs are determined by the real world and
not by the programmer. Thus the program needs to be prepared for the
unexpected and the demands made on the system may be conflicting. Second,
the demands on the system may occur in parallel rather than in sequence.
This means that the processing pattern of a real-time system is typically
parallel, with either virtual or real concurrency, and there will be
some synchronisation aspects to be considered.

The third characteristic is that a real-time system must meet deadlines
in order to satisfy real physical time constraints. Mere functional
correctness is not sufficient. Finally, such systems typically have long
mission times. This implies that not only must the software deal correctly
with ordinary situations, but also that it must be able to recover from
some extraordinary ones.

1.3 Problems of real-time software

The characteristics discussed in the last section are responsible for
the problems associated with the production and validation of real-time
software. The lack of control over the input demands to the system
coupled with the time deadlines to be met make resource allocation and
control a critical feature of such software. Not only must deadlocks be
prevented but performance both in normal and overload situations must
be considered too. The long mission times imply that the software must
be able to continue in adverse conditions: hardware failure, interference,
synchronisation failure and even the presence of errors in itself. Full
recovery or fail-operational is the ideal, fail-safe may be the worst
acceptable. Designing software which is proof against its own design
shortcomings is very difficult indeed. The parallel demands on the system
may require the software to be reentrant, and this coupled with the long
mission time and failure recovery demands extra care over re-initialisation
and resource control. Various analysis techniques have to be applied in
areas such as these in order to demonstrate the adequacy of the design
chosen.

The alternative to analytic techniques is testing, but testing real-time
software is very difficult. The only real inputs to the system come from
the real world and it may be impossible or too dangerous to test the
system 'live'. Because timing as well as sequence are important in
governing system behaviour, it can be impossible to provide input data
with sufficient timing precision to guarantee reproducible test results.
In fact, apart from the sheer difficulty of performing tests with correct
timing, the aspects of parallelism, interrupts and time itself make
analysis, testing and understanding of real-time software much more

difficult than for strictly sequential programs. Similarly, the interpretation of test data is more of a problem, as what constitutes success and failure can be much less clear. Furthermore, even if testing reveals the presence of an error, it may do little or nothing to isolate it. Finally, the reliability requirements and mission times may be so high that testing on its own is insufficient to establish the software quality.

1.4 Experience to date

It would be wrong to throw a dark shadow over the rest of this report by painting too gloomy a picture of the performance histories of real-time software systems. However, experience has shown that even the best engineered systems can fail quite spectacularly. Everyone associated with real-time computing has their own 'favourite' horror story.

There seem to be two distinct areas of difficulty. The first is that the internal complexity of real-time systems is usually much greater than most people - even the system designers - appreciate. Problems that arise are often traced (after a prodigious effort) to some peculiarly subtle interaction. This is also shown by the extreme sensitivity exhibited by some systems to apparently minor changes. Possibly the most famous 'bug', the one that grounded the first flight of the NASA Space Shuttle, demonstrates precisely this problem /Garm81/. The second area of difficulty is that even if the system does what it was designed to do perfectly, it is still all too often inadequate. Its functionality may be insufficient or its interfaces, particularly with human operators, may be lacking. This was the case after the Three Mile Island accident, where the computer-based error logging system dutifully recorded thousands of lines of error messages (until it ran out of paper), presenting far too much unstructured information to an already overloaded operations staff.

The importance of these aspects is highlighted by data gathered and analysed by Bell Laboratories concerning their computerised telephone exchanges /Toy78/. This revealed that of complete system failures, only 20% were due to hardware. Software deficiencies accounted for 50% of the downtime while operations and maintenance errors accounted for the remaining 30%. Thus both software and people play a large part in the performance of real-time systems and as hardware becomes more and more reliable, this part becomes ever larger.

Validation and verification have traditionally been concerned with the former area of difficulty but the latter is now beginning to receive more attention. The importance of the operator and the man—machine interface with which he must interact is now realised, and this is part of the increasing awareness of the necessity of verifying requirements in the context of the whole system function. There is also growing recognition of the power of analytic techniques in the production of real-time systems. Unfortunately, many of the available techniques, especially in areas such as queuing and deadlock prevention, are insufficiently powerful to tackle realistic problems. In some cases, simplifying assumptions may be made to make the problem tractable but this can often invalidate the rigour of the technique.

1.5 Design for reliability

Although the topic of this report is the verification and validation of real-time software, two specific aspects of the production of real—time software should be mentioned. The first is that the verification and validation activities only check that the software has been produced to a satisfactory level of quality. No amount of testing can actually build in that quality. Furthermore, in order that the quality of the software may be satisfactorily assessed, it is necessary that the software be designed, implemented and documented with the verification activities in mind.

The second aspect is that the design for reliability may itself make verification harder. If systems are designed to mask faults and recover invisibly from errors, then that same design will hide faults in itself. This is a particular problem for later black-box testing. The redundancy built in for reliability may be rendered ineffective by undetected but masked errors within the system. This is an inherent conflict within real-time software: the desire to be able to mask out errors online but detect them offline. Thus there are even more stringent design requirements on redundant - and particularly diverse - software systems in order that these can be fully tested during verification while succeeding in their aims of increased online reliability, high availability and long survival time.

1.6 Outline of this report

The following chapters of this report deal with techniques aimed at both the areas of difficulty described in section 1.4, although much more work has been done on the former 'internal correctness' area than on the latter 'system acceptability'. Chapter 2 outlines the system life cycle and development environment. It describes the effects that high reliability demands and licensing have on the development process and how reliability is affected by the development process. Chapter 3 deals with the analytic techniques available. Chapters 4 & 5 deal with two different aspects of testing and discuss the effectiveness of these techniques and the influence the software structure has on this effectiveness. Chapter 6 deals with various aspects of simulation. The conclusions on the current 'State of the Art', the remaining problems and future developments are presented in chapter 7. In order to keep the chapters as self-contained as possible, a few topics are discussed in several places. This enables different aspects to be stressed in appropriate contexts and obviates inter-chapter jumping and referencing.

The aim in presenting this material is to increase the awareness of the reader about the techniques which are available to help in the production of good and safe real-time software systems. It is not intended as a prescription to be followed step-by-step. Nor is it intended to provide the full theoretical background for the techniques described, some of which are highly mathematical and merit books in their own right. A copious reference list is appended, and the interested reader is encouraged to continue studying from there. No such list could be complete; the authors apologise in advance for any important references which may have escaped their notice.

2 Software Reliability and the Software Life Cycle

S. Bologna and W. J. Quirk

Computer systems are planned or are already in use in a variety of areas involving online, real-time control. These areas include:

- flight control systems /AGAR82/ & /Hayn79/
- chemical plant control /OIL82/
- medicine /BaGa83/, /Kemb82/ & /Miko74/
- nuclear power /Gilb83/ & /StTh83/
- railway signalling /Ster79/ & /CrFu78/.

The single most important characteristic of any online control system is that its actions (or inactions) cannot be forgotten. Real time cannot be turned back. The effect that the system has on the real world may be desireable, inconvenient or disastrous: it is never inconsequential. Because of this, extra care and effort is involved in producing such systems in order to enhance their reliability. Some of the techniques for increasing reliability address technical aspects peculiar to real-time software. Others are more general but it is only economic to apply them in situations where reliability aspects are critical.

Each individual technique tends to be applicable to a single phase of the system development cycle and not to the whole cycle. However, any chain is only as strong as its weakest link. A lack of control or effort in any one phase of development may completely invalidate all the work done in other phases. This underlines the need to select a development methodology able to manage the complete system life cycle. It should direct each phase and suggest aids and tools for verification of the various phases and correct communication between them.

The central part of this chapter is in five sections. The first explores the relationship between the software life cycle and software reliability. The second examines what is currently practiced. The third looks in detail at the verification and validation aspects of the life cycle. The fourth section details what might be seen as an 'ideal' development environment, while the final major section gives some examples of the application of available development aids to achieve validated and verified real-time systems.

2.1 Real-time system development environments

In order to produce real-time systems to a satisfactory standard, it is necessary to amalgamate a number of development aids which will together increase the likelihood of achieving the required standard. If the system is to be licensed, even more is demanded: the development aids must assure that the required standard has indeed been achieved. This has implications for the development aids themselves which will be brought out later. For now, it is the real-time system itself which is of concern, and in particular how its development is affected by the available aids. To prevent any confusion between the real-time system to be developed and the tools assisting (hopefully!) in this development, the word 'aid' will be reserved for development tools, the 'development environment' will include all such aids together with the context of their application, and the word 'system' will be reserved for the target real-time system to be produced.

2.1.1 Real-time system life cycles

Many life-cycle models have been proposed for software systems. The purpose of this section is neither to compare these nor to select one as being 'right'. Rather, there are a number of points generally common to these models and which are significant (unfortunately they are often forgotten in the attempt to justify the detail of one particular model). There is also a slight problem between the use and meaning of two words: 'continual' meaning 'always happening, without cessation' and 'continuous' meaning 'unbroken, uninterrupted in time or sequence, not discrete' (both definitions from /COD76/). It may be a matter of philosophy whether human perception of a changing problem evolves continually or continuously: there is no doubt at all that a computer program cannot change continuously.

A very general life cycle is shown in figure 2.1. Three phases of the cycle are inception, working life and retirement. Inception starts with the first ideas about the functioning of a new system and continues until satisfactory commissioning has taken place. The working life takes over at commissioning and continues until the system is rendered unnecessary or replaced, at which point it becomes retired. It is not totally 'dead' in retirement however, because it may be kept as a back-up or standby for the new system, particularly for the early working life of the new system. This simple model is not meant to be interpreted in too great detail. Not only are some activities common to more than one phase, but the phase boundaries are not necessarily well defined in all cases. Figure 2.6 shows a more detailed model for safety related systems. A major revision of a system can be viewed either as a new system or as part of the working life of the old system: it depends on 'how major is major'. Indeed, it is probably true that the ideas for a new system spring mostly from experiences gained during the working life of other (similar) systems, as shown in figure 2.2.

The most important points of the life cycle are not details like these but rather the constraints and timescales associated with these details. Real-time systems are closely coupled to the real physical world, much more so than for example business systems. The plant to which a system is attached will itself be built to and operated around an understanding of basic physical processes and, except for highly advanced experimental equipment (such as fusion reactors), these processes will be well established. The capital cost of the plant is also usually high, so that the expected lifetime of the plant is correspondingly long. Thus we should expect that control procedures for the plant will be only slowly changing. This does not mean that the operational modes of the plant will not change, but rather that the normal and safe operating regimes of the plant are stable. With the physical processes themselves being established, this means that the control theory too is stable and hence that the control system function - and in particular its control algorithm - is not fast changing. Indeed while the requirements of commercial systems may change very rapidly, real-time systems may change only in response to secondary forces such as equipment obsolesence or plant accidents. Thus the life cycle has a long period.

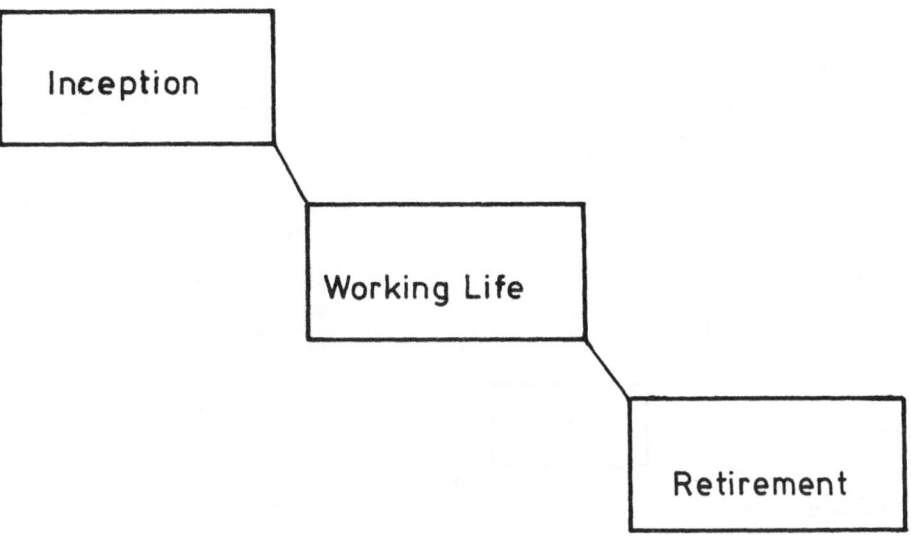

Fig. 2.1 System Evolution.

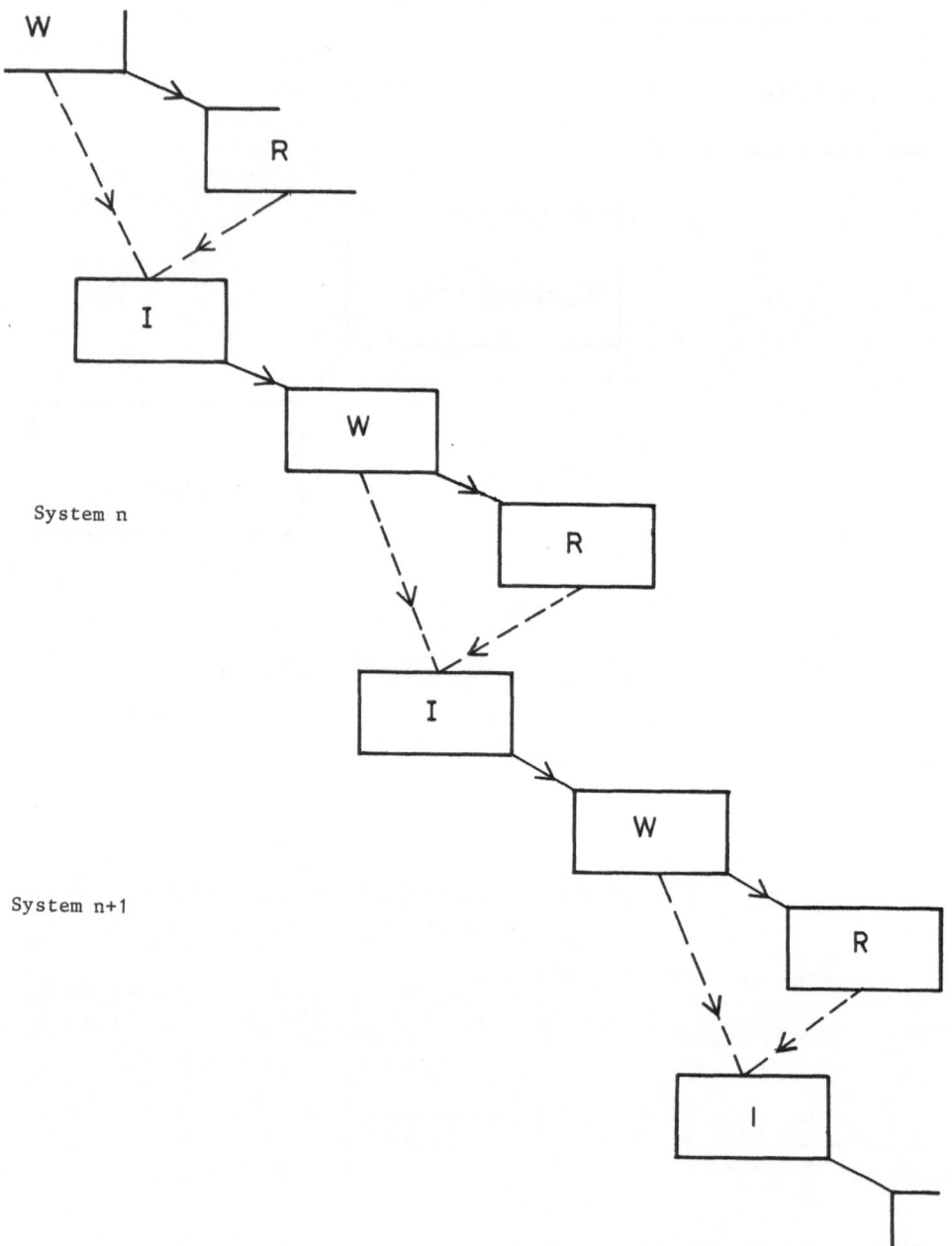

Fig. 2.2 System Evolution & Influence.

2.1.2 System life cycle and system quality

The reason for examining a system life cycle is to establish what errors occur and where development aids can best be introduced to enhance system quality. Currently, each of the recognised stages in the system life cycle is sufficiently large and complex to be in need of aids. Furthermore, errors can also be introduced by mistranslation or misunderstanding between the stages. Large numbers of aids have been produced /Mil179a/ & /SEAT82/, but most do not satisfy the particular needs of real-time software development.

The requirements of a system can be difficult to detail in an unambiguous manner. They can be hard to communicate to personnel with different backgrounds and are all to often inconsistent and incomplete. Furthermore, deficiencies in the requirements can go unnoticed until system validation, by which time much effort has been expended in producing an unsatisfactory system. Timing and sequencing requirements are especially difficult to understand and describe.

In the design stage, a failure to recognise resources - any part of the system which could be demanded by more than one other part of the system - and to provide adequate control mechanisms for them is potentially disastrous. Furthermore, the complexities of multi-processor asynchronous systems are still not fully comprehended. Such systems are necessary for real-time use because of the timing constraints and because of the need to tolerate failures. However the error recovery part of the system is itself prone to error and difficult to verify: Bell Laboratories have established that over one third of the catastrophic failures in computerised telephone exchanges are due to errors in attemping to recover from simple expected error situations /Toy78/.

Coding and verification generally depend on testing strategies to achieve their aims. But testing in real-time systems is especially difficult due to time-critical dependencies. This makes test cases difficult or impossible to repeat. Furthermore, systems designed to be error tolerant need special testing to unmask internal errors hidden by the inbuilt error tolerance.

All these aspects are most prominent in the inception or development phase of the system life cycle. However as we have already seen, real-time software has a long, stable working lifetime. As underlined in the next sub-section, this is made even more stable if licensing is involved. Consequently, there is a long period where maintenance may be necessary. Any change in the system involves some or all the activities discussed above but maintenance has its own characteristic problems. These are brought about by having to preserve an understanding of the system over a long period of time. As well as promoting this understanding, strict modularity, in the sense of independent modules, is necessary if changes can be undertaken easily and preserve the system quality. Consequently, the system design and coding must take this into account.

2.1.3 Licensing and the system life cycle

As stated in the introduction, practically all online control systems have a potential economic impact because failure of the system can lead to plant or equipment damage. With some systems, however, a failure could directly threaten personnel or public safety. For such safety-related systems, reliability considerations may outweigh all others. As well as the usual characteristics of real-time software, the responsibility for safety adds two further characteristics. First, the control or monitoring algorithms are not of great complexity. However, particular attention must be paid to the needs to detect and/or prevent unsafe process conditions, and to prevent the computer system itself from introducing unsafe conditions. Second, it has to be licensed before use. Traditionally, safety licensing has been carried out on a deterministic or probabilistic basis. With computer programs there are additional new problems because failures arise almost entirely from design errors. It is very difficult to prove the absence of design errors from a computer program. At the same time it is difficult to test a computer program so that its reliability can be verified with a high degree of confidence.

The object of all licensing procedures is to ensure that the system has attained a suitable degree of quality. However, as a recent speech by the United States Nuclear Regulatory Commission made plain, quality cannot be 'inspected in' /Pal181/. Licensing only checks that quality is already present: it does not actively provide or enhance quality. The effect of licensing on the life cycle, and hence on the support needed for it, is twofold. The first is that the long timescales involved in system evolution necessitate communication of information over these long times. It is very likely that the personnel involved with any system modification will not be the personnel involved with the system inception and commissioning. The second is that the licensing personnel need to be assisted throughout their long involvement with the system. At least part of the development environment must offer this assistance.

It is now realised that controlling the whole development process is not only the most economical way of producing systems but often the only way of producing such systems if they have to survive a licensing or quality control assessment. As a result, there has been much activity developing aids for all stages of system production. However the main thrust of these developments seems to have aimed at the commercial market and not at real-time systems. Consequently the State of the Art in this area is less advanced than might be hoped. Furthermore because few commercial systems are subjected to external licensing control, the methods developed have concentrated on aiding the developer, almost to the exclusion of the licensing assessor.

The need for certification, as to the safe operation of safety related computer systems, imposes strict requirements on the documentation for design visibility, implementation detail, proof of test cases executed, ease of modification etc. Documentation meeting these requirements is obviously useful throughout the life of a system from initial conception onwards. It is of crucial importance to Licensing Authorities and, because of this, section 2.3.5 will be devoted to it. The interested reader is referred to /FIPS76/, /EWIC81a/, and /IEEE83/ which are the result of international efforts in the direction of documentation standardization.

However, documentation is not the whole story. For while it is conceivable that licensing would merely entail testing of the completed system as a black box, this is very unlikely. Not only because system structure is of ligitimate interest in establishing system function, but also because it has a key impact on system behaviour under fault conditions. This aspect of behaviour may be impossible to check by testing, while yet remaining one of the most important licensable areas. Because of this, licensing authorities may well want to maintain an involvement with all stages of system development and not be satisfied merely with studying documentation later. Thus the development environment must support not only the developers but also the licensing personnel through all stages of the system development process.

It follows that if the system is to be the subject of a licensing procedure, the inertia to change will be further increased by three effects. First, any new ideas will probably be submitted for preliminary approval. This introduces an extra delay between idea conception and implementation and is also likely to lengthen the time taken to scrutinise ideas before submitting them for such approval. Second, although it is not suggested that the licensing authority should be involved only at the beginning and end of system development and not during the development phase, it will never-the-less be the case that an extra time delay for formal licensing approval will be introduced between implementation and commissioning. Finally, if the construction and licensing have been effective, the system should have less undesirable features than would otherwise have been the case and maintenance (in the sense of repairs or fixes) should be much reduced. Thus on all counts, one should expect the system to be stable, changing only infrequently.

2.2 Traditional system development phases

Requirements specification, design, implementation, integration and maintenance have been long held up as separate and recognisable stages in system production. As such, development aids have been produced to be used either within a single phase or at the interface between two phases. However in order to produce such aids, some formalisation of the application area had to take place and this generally revealed that the phase boundaries were really not clear and that often the different phases interacted. To a large extent, this interaction was modelled by 'feedback' loops; turning the whole system development activity into an iterative (and potentially endless) procedure. Furthermore, except in the strictest organisational regimes, such formal feedback processes did not accurately reflect reality. Design changes could be caused by, and happen concurrently with, implementation - especially if the designer and implementor were one and the same person. The conclusion drawn from this was that a strong organisation was needed to prevent such concurrency by making it impractical.

This conclusion is not necessarily valid however. It is not at all obvious that the real world is 'wrong' (in some sense) because it does not agree with some agreeable model of it! The current real world environment for real-time system production is clearly not ideal, but changes in this environment should be made to enhance the quality of systems and not to enshrine a convenient model of their production. The life cycle approach does have a small number of dissenters /McJa82/, /Glad82/ because of the growing awareness of unified development environments. However, to date, practical verification and validation studies have been most successful when tied closely to a life cycle model /Glas79/. A recent analysis of software errors during a six year life cycle is presented in /BaPe84/.

2.2.1 Requirements specification

The quest for more reliable software draws ever greater attention to the earliest phases of the software development cycle. The newest and least developed area of software reliability is that of requirements and specifications. An analysis of complete system requirements is made during the initial phase of software development. This is done to ensure that only those system requirements which can be accomplished realistically in software are allocated to software. Furthermore, it is necessary to gain the greatest possible confidence that these requirements are completely understood. There must also be some reliability target included in this software requirement. Whilst a large research effort in this area shows much promise, it is still very difficult to demonstrate results. Two examples of specification languages are included: PSL/PSA shown in figure 2.3, and SPECK shown in figure 2.4.

```
        PSA Version A4.2R1                                        84.270  15.34.44
                              BELUST   IDT/KFK   PSA V4.2

                                   Input Source Listing

Parameters:   DB=PSADB.DBF  INPUT=*  SOURCE-LISTING  NOCROSS-REFERENCE  UPDATE
DATA-BASE-REFERENCE

LINE  S T M T                                                             ID FIELD

   1 >/*PROCESSO-PROTEZIONE*/                                         < >00000100<
   2 >PROC  PROTECTION;                                               < >00000200<
   3 >DESC;                                                           < >00000300<
   4 >          DESCRIZIONE AL PRIMO LIVELLO DI ASTRAZIONE SISTEMA    < >00000400<
   5 >          DI PROTEZIONE W3XL;                                   < >00000500<
   6 >RCVS  INPUT-SIG;                                                < >00000600<
   7 >GENS  REACTOR-TRIP-SIG;                                         < >00000700<
   8 >SUBP  TRAIN-R, TRAIN-S;                                         < >00000800<
   9 >TRGD  PROTECTION-EVT;                                           < >00000900<
  10 >INTF  INSTRUMENTATION;                                          < >00001000<
  11 >DESC;                                                           < >00001100<
  12 >          ACQUISISCE LE VARIABILI NECESSARIE ALLA ELABORAZIONE  < >00001200<
  13 >          DEL SIGNALE DI PROTEZIONE;                            < >00001300<
  14 >GENS  INPUT-SIG;                                                < >00001400<
  15 >RCVS  PLANT-CONTROL-VARIABLES;                                  < >00001500<
  16 >INP   INPUT-SIG;                                                < >00001600<
  17 >GEND  INSTRUMENTATION;                                          < >00001700<
  18 >RCVD  PROTECTION;                                               < >00001800<
  19 >USED  PROTECTION DRV REACTOR-TRIP-SIG;                          < >00001900<
  20 >SUBP  INPUT-R-SIG,INPUT-S-SIG;                                  < >00002000<
  21 >OUT   REACTOR-TRIP-SIG;                                         < >00002100<
  22 >GEND  PROTECTION;                                               < >00002200<
  23 >RCVD  ATTUATOR;                                                 < >00002300<
  24 >SUBP  TRAIN-R-TRIP-SIG,TRAIN-S-TRIP-SIG;                        < >00002400<
  25 >COND  PROTEC;                                                   < >00002500<
  26 >          TRUE WHILE;                                           < >00002600<
  27 >          TRAIN-R-TRIP-SIG AND/OR TRAIN-S-TRIP-SIG AND/OR MANUAL-TRIP-SIG  < >00002700<
  28 >          AND/OR SAFETY-INJECTION-TRIP-SIG COMBINED IN THE BREAKERS LOGIC;  < >00002800<
  29 >          BECOMING TRUE IS CALLED PROTECTION-EVT;               < >00002900<
  30 >INTF  ATTUATOR;                                                 < >00003000<
  31 >DESC;                                                           < >00003100<
  32 >          ESEGUE L'AZIONE DI PROTEZIONE COME CONSEGUENZA        < >00003200<
  33 >          DI UN REACTOR-TRIP-SIG;                               < >00003300<
  34 >GENS  ATTUATOR-ACTIONS;                                         < >00003400<
  35 >RCVS  REACTOR-TRIP-SIG;                                         < >00003500<
  36 >/*PROCESSO-TRENO-R*/                                            < >00003600<
  37 >PROC  TRAIN-R;                                                  < >00003700<
  38 >DESC;                                                           < >00003800<
  39 >          DESCRIZIONE AL SECONDA LIVELLO DI ASTRAZIONE DEL SISTEMA  < >00003900<
  40 >          DI PROTEZOINE W3XL CON PARTICOLARE RIFERIMENTO ALLA   < >00004000<
  41 >          SUBBOPARTE TRAIN-P;                                   < >00004100<
  42 >PART  PROTECTION;                                               < >00004200<
  43 >SUBP  MANUAL, NEUTRON-FLUX,PRIMARY-COOLANT,PRESSURIZER,         < >00004300<
  44 >          STEAM-GENERATOR,SAFETY-INJECTION,TURBINE,SOLIDE-STATE;  < >00004400<
  45 >RCVS  INPUT-R-SIG;                                              < >00004500<
  46 >GENS  TRAIN-R-TRIP-SIG;                                         < >00004600<
  47 >TRGD  BY TRAIN-R-EVENT;                                         < >00004700<
  48 >INP   INPUT-R-SIG;                                              < >00004800<
  49 >PART  INPUT-SIG;                                                < >00004900<
  50 >RCVD  TRAIN-R;                                                  < >00005000<
  51 >USED  TRAIN-R DRV TRAIN-R-TRIP-SIG;                             < >00005100<
  52 >SUBP  MANUAL-SIG, NEUTRON-FLUX-SIG, PRIMARY-COOLANT-SIG,        < >00005200<
  53 >          PRESSURIZER-SIG,STEAM-GENERATOR-SIG,SAFETY-INJECTION-SIG,  < >00005300<
  54 >          TURBINE-SIG,SOLIDE-STATE-SIG;                         < >00005400<
  55 >COND  TRAINR;                                                   < >00005500<
  56 >          TRUE WHILE;                                           < >00005600<
  57 >          MANUAL-TRIP-SIG OR NEUTRON-FLUX-TRIP-SIG OR           < >00005700<
  58 >          PRIMARY-COOLANT-TRIP-SIG OR PRESSURIZER-TRIP-SIG OR   < >00005800<
  59 >          STEAM-GENERATOR-TRIP-SIG OR SAFETY-INJECTION-TRIP-SIG OR  < >00005900<
  60 >          TURBINE-TRIP-SIG OR SOLID-STATE-TRIP-SIG;             < >00006000<
  61 >          BECOMING TRUE IS CALLED TRAIN-R-EVT;                  < >00006100<
  62 >OUT   TRAIN-R-TRIP-SIG;                                         < >00006200<
  63 >PART  REACTOR-TRIP-SIG;                                         < >00006300<
  64 >GEND  TRAIN-R;                                                  < >00006400<
  65 >SUBP  MANUAL-TRIP-SIG,NEUTRON-FLUX-TRIP-SIG,PRIMARY-COOLANT-TRIP-SIG,  < >00006500<
  66 >          PRESSURIZER-TRIP-SIG,STEAM-GENERATOR-TRIP-SIG,        < >00006600<
  67 >          SAFETY-INJECTION-TRIP-SIG,TURBINE-TRIP-SIG,SOLIDE-STATE-TRIP-SIG;  < >00006700<
  68 >/*PROCESSO-PRIMARY-COOLANT*/                                    < >00006800<
  69 >PROC  PRIMARY-COOLANT;                                          < >00006900<
  70 >DESC;                                                           < >00007000<
  71 >          DECSRIZIONE AL TERZO LIVELLO DI ASTRAZIONE DEL SISTEMA DI  < >00007100<
  72 >          PROTEZIONE W3XL CON PARTICOLARE RIFERIMENTO ALLA VARIABILE  < >00007200<
  73 >          PRIMARY-COOLANT;                                      < >00007300<
  74 >PART  TRAIN-R;                                                  < >00007400<
  75 >SUBP  OVERTEMP,OVERPOWER,LOW-FLOW,UNDERVOLTAGE,UNDERFREQUENCY;  < >00007500<
```

Fig. 2.3a: An example of specifications stated in PSL

```
        PSA Version A4.2R1                            84.270  15.34.44
                       BELUST  IDT/KFK   PSA V4.2

                       Formatted Problem Statement

Parameters:   DB=PSADB.DBF  FILE=PSATEMP.PSANAME  NOINDEX  NOPUNCHED-NAMES  PRINT  EMPTY
   NOPUNCH  SMARG=5  NMARG=20  AMARG=10  BMARG=25  RNMARG=70  CMARG=1  HMARG=40  NODESIGNATE
   ONE-PER-LINE  DEFINE  COMMENT  NONEW-PAGE  NONEW-LINE  NOALL-STATEMENTS
   COMPLEMENTARY-STATEMENTS  LINE-NUMBERS  PRINTEOF  DLC-COMMENT

    1 OUTPUT                           MANUAL-TRIP-SIG;
    2     /*   DATE OF LAST CHANGE -   84.270, 15.34.44 */
    3     PART OF:     TRAIN-R-TRIP-SIG;
    4
    5 OUTPUT                           NEUTRON-FLUX-TRIP-SIG;
    6     /*   DATE OF LAST CHANGE -   84.270, 15.34.44 */
    7     PART OF:     TRAIN-R-TRIP-SIG;
    8
    9 OUTPUT                           PLANT-CONTROL-VARIABLES;
   10     /*   DATE OF LAST CHANGE -   84.270, 15.34.44 */
   11     RECEIVED BY:  INSTRUMENTATION;
   12
   13 OUTPUT                           PRESSURIZER-TRIP-SIG;
   14     /*   DATE OF LAST CHANGE -   84.270, 15.34.44 */
   15     PART OF:     TRAIN-R-TRIP-SIG;
   16
   17 OUTPUT                           PRIMARY-COOLANT-TRIP-SIG;
   18     /*   DATE OF LAST CHANGE -   84.270, 15.34.44 */
   19     PART OF:     TRAIN-R-TRIP-SIG;
   20
   21 OUTPUT                           REACTOR-TRIP-SIG;
   22     /*   DATE OF LAST CHANGE -   84.270, 15.34.44 */
   23     GENERATED BY:  PROTECTION;
   24     RECEIVED BY:  ATTUATOR;
   25     SUBPARTS ARE:  TRAIN-R-TRIP-SIG,
   26                    TRAIN-S-TRIP-SIG;
   27     DERIVED BY:   PROTECTION
   28      USING:      INPUT-SIG;
   29
   30 OUTPUT                           SAFETY-INJECTION-TRIP-SIG;
   31     /*   DATE OF LAST CHANGE -   84.270, 15.34.44 */
   32     PART OF:     TRAIN-R-TRIP-SIG;
   33
   34 OUTPUT                           SOLIDE-STATE-TRIP-SIG;
   35     /*   DATE OF LAST CHANGE -   84.270, 15.34.44 */
   36     PART OF:     TRAIN-R-TRIP-SIG;
   37
   38 OUTPUT                           STEAM-GENERATOR-TRIP-SIG;
   39     /*   DATE OF LAST CHANGE -   84.270, 15.34.44 */
   40     PART OF:     TRAIN-R-TRIP-SIG;
   41
   42 OUTPUT                           TRAIN-R-TRIP-SIG;
   43     /*   DATE OF LAST CHANGE -   84.270, 15.34.44 */
   44     GENERATED BY:  TRAIN-R;
   45     SUBPARTS ARE:  MANUAL-TRIP-SIG,
   46                    NEUTRON-FLUX-TRIP-SIG,
   47                    PRIMARY-COOLANT-TRIP-SIG,
   48                    PRESSURIZER-TRIP-SIG,
   49                    STEAM-GENERATOR-TRIP-SIG,
   50                    SAFETY-INJECTION-TRIP-SIG,
   51                    TURBINE-TRIP-SIG,
   52                    SOLIDE-STATE-TRIP-SIG;
   53     PART OF:     REACTOR-TRIP-SIG;
   54     DERIVED BY:   TRAIN-R
   55      USING:      INPUT-R-SIG;
   56
   57 OUTPUT                           TRAIN-S-TRIP-SIG;
   58     /*   DATE OF LAST CHANGE -   84.270, 15.34.44 */
   59     PART OF:     REACTOR-TRIP-SIG;
   60
   61 OUTPUT                           TURBINE-TRIP-SIG;
   62     /*   DATE OF LAST CHANGE -   84.270, 15.34.44 */
   63     PART OF:     TRAIN-R-TRIP-SIG;
   64
```

Fig. 2.3b: Formatted Problem Statement Report

```
+--PROCESS--+
I          I
IPROTECTION I
I          I     .                         +--OUTPUT---+                              +---INTF----+
+-GENERATED-+     .                         IREACTOR-  I                              I          I
                  .....................     ITRIP-     I..............................I ATTUATOR  I
+--PROCESS--+     .                         ISIG       I                              I          I
I          I     .                         +----------+                              +-RECEIVED--+
IPROTECTION I                                    .
I          I                                     .
+--DERIVED--+                                    .
                                                 .
                                                 .
                                                 .
                                                 .
                                              .     .
                                             .       .
                                            .         .
                                           .           .
                                   +--OUTPUT---+ +--OUTPUT---+
                                   ITRAIN-    I ITRAIN-    I
                                   IR-        I IS-        I
                                   ITRIP-SIG  I ITRIP-SIG  I
                                   +-SUBPARTS--+ +-SUBPARTS--+
```

Fig. 2.3c: Picture Report with the flow option in effect

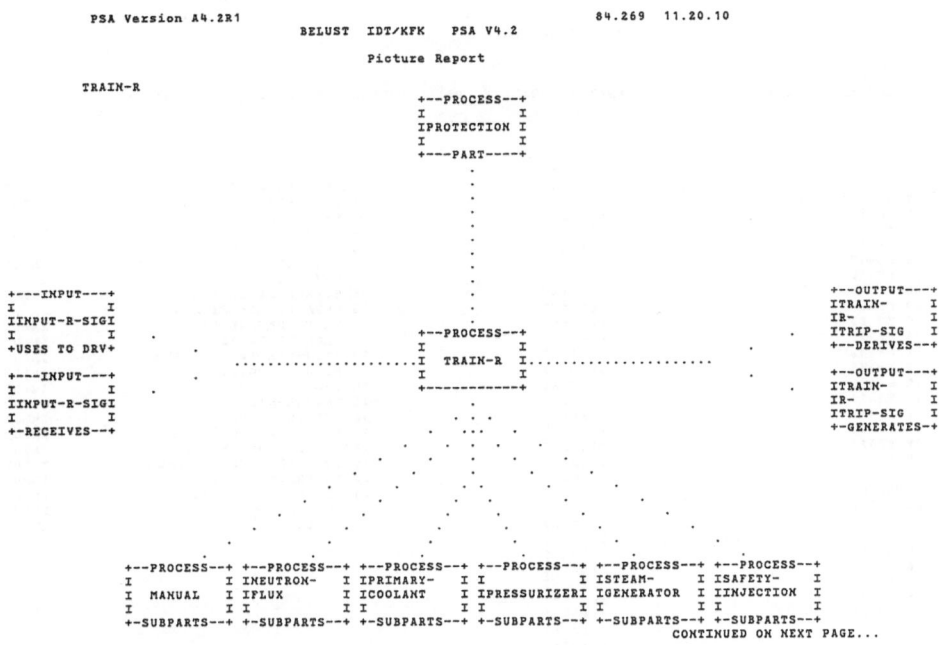

Fig. 2.3d: Picture Report with the structure option in effect

```
        PSA Version A4.2R1                               84.270  13.17.03
                              BELUST  IDT/KFK   PSA V4.2

                             Contents Analysis Report

Parameters:   DB=PSADB.DBF  FILE=PSATEMP.PSANAME  PRINT-MATRIX  CONTAINED  EXPLANATION


        Row Names                                   Column Names

    1 AB01                     ELEMENT         1 FLUX-RATE-SIG               INPUT
    2 AB02                     ELEMENT         2 LOW-PRESSURIZER-SIG         INPUT
    3 AB03                     ELEMENT         3 P-13-SIG                    INPUT
    4 AB04                     ELEMENT         4 P-6-SIG                     INPUT
    5 AB05                     ELEMENT         5 OVERTEMP-SIG                INPUT
    6 FB417                    ELEMENT         6 P-10-SIG                    INPUT
    7 FB418                    ELEMENT         7 P-7-SIG                     INPUT
    8 FB419                    ELEMENT         8 SOURCE-RANGE-SIG            INPUT
    9 FB427                    ELEMENT         9 UNDERFREQUENCY-SIG          INPUT
   10 FB428                    ELEMENT        10 UNDERVOLTAGE-SIG            INPUT
   11 FB429                    ELEMENT        11 HIGH-LEVEL-SIG              INPUT
   12 FB437                    ELEMENT        12 HIGH-PRESSURIZER-SIG        INPUT
   13 FB438                    ELEMENT        13 HIGH-SETPOINT-SIG           INPUT
   14 FB439                    ELEMENT        14 P-8-SIG                     INPUT
   15 FB510                    ELEMENT        15 MANUAL-SIG                  INPUT
   16 FB511                    ELEMENT        16 OVERPOWER-SIG               INPUT
   17 FB520                    ELEMENT        17 LOW-FLOW-1-OF-3-SIG         INPUT
   18 FB521                    ELEMENT        18 LOW-FLOW-2-OF-3-SIG         INPUT
   19 FB530                    ELEMENT        19 LOW-FEEDWATER-FLOW-SIG      INPUT
   20 FB531                    ELEMENT        20 INTERRANGE-SIG              INPUT
   21 LB498                    ELEMENT        21 LOW-SETPOINT-SIG            INPUT
   22 LB507                    ELEMENT        22 LOW-WATER-LEVEL-SIG         INPUT
   23 LB508                    ELEMENT        23 AB-E1                       INPUT
   24 LB517                    ELEMENT
   25 LB518                    ELEMENT
   26 LB527                    ELEMENT
   27 LB528                    ELEMENT
   28 LB537                    ELEMENT
   29 LB538                    ELEMENT
   30 NC41P                    ELEMENT
   31 WWW                      ELEMENT
```

```
        PSA Version A4.2R1                               84.270  13.17.03
                              BELUST  IDT/KFK   PSA V4.2

                             Contents Analysis Report

                      THE ROWS ARE CONTAINED IN THE COLUMNS WITH *S



                                11111111112222
                            12345678901234567890123
                            +---------+---------+---+
                         1  :**       :         :   :
                         2  :*  **    :         :   :
                         3  :   ******:         :   :
                         4  :         :****     :   :
                         5  +----******----**---+---+
                         6  :         :     **  :   :
                         7  :         :     **  :   :
                         8  :         :     **  :   :
                         9  :         :     **  :   :
                        10  +---------+-----**--+---+
                        11  :         :     **  :   :
                        12  :         :     **  :   :
                        13  :         :     **  :   :
                        14  :         :     **  :   :
                        15  +---------+--------*+---+
                        16  :         :      *: :   :
                        17  :         :      *: :   :
                        18  :         :      *: :   :
                        19  :         :      *: :   :
                        20  +---------+--------*+---+
                        21  :         :      *  :   :
                        22  :         :      *  :   :
                        23  :         :      ** :   :
                        24  :         :      *: *   :
                        25  :         :      *: *   :
                            +---------+---------+---+
```

Fig. 2.3e: Contents Analysis Report

PSA Version A4.2R1   84.270 13.17.03
                           BELUST IDT/KFK   PSA V4.2

                        Data Process Interaction Report

Parameters: DB=PSADB.DBF FILE=PSATEMP.PSANAME PROCESS DATA-PROCESS-INTERACTION-MATRIX
   DATA-PROCESS-INTERACTION-ANALYSIS PROCESS-INTERACTION-MATRIX PROCESS-INTERACTION-ANALYSIS
   EXPLANATION

   THE ROWS ARE DATA NAMES, THE COLUMNS ARE PROCESS NAMES.

      Column Names   Row Names

    1 LOW-FLOW   PROCESS   1 AB-E5   INPUT
    2 MANUAL   PROCESS   2 AB-E3   INPUT
    3 NEUTRON-FLUX   PROCESS   3 MANUAL-SIG   INPUT
    4 OVERPOWER   PROCESS   4 FLUX-RATE-SIG   INPUT
    5 OVERTEMP   PROCESS   5 INTERRANGE-SIG   INPUT
    6 PRESSURIZER   PROCESS   6 LOW-WATER-LEVEL-SIG   INPUT
    7 PRIMARY-COOLANT   PROCESS   7 OVERPOWER-SIG   INPUT
    8 PROTECTION   PROCESS   8 OVERTEMP-SIG   INPUT
    9 SAFETY-INJECTION   PROCESS   9 REACTOR-TRIP-SIG   OUTPUT
   10 SOLIDE-STATE   PROCESS   10 INPUT-SIG   INPUT
   11 STEAM-GENERATOR   PROCESS   11 TRAIN-R-TRIP-SIG   OUTPUT
   12 TRAIN-R   PROCESS   12 INPUT-R-SIG   INPUT
   13 TRAIN-S   PROCESS
   14 TURBINE   PROCESS
   15 UNDERFREQUENCY   PROCESS
   16 UNDERVOLTAGE   PROCESS

        PSA Version A4.2R1   84.270 13.17.03
                           BELUST IDT/KFK   PSA V4.2

                        Data Process Interaction Report

   DATA PROCESS INTERACTION MATRIX

   (i,j) value   meaning
   -----------   ---------------------------

        R   Row i is received or used by column j (input)
        U   Row i is updated by column j
        D   Row i is derived or generated by column j
                     (output)
        A   Row i is input to, updated by, and output of
                     column j (all)
        F   Row i is input to and output of column j (flow)
        1   Row i is input to and updated by column j
        2   Row i is updated by and output of column j

                              1111111
                       1234567890123456
                       +----+----+----+-+
                    1 :   : R :   : :
                    2 :   : R :   : :
                    3 :   : R :   : :
                    4 :   : R :   : :
                    5 +----+-R--+----+-+
                    6 :   : R :   : :
                    7 :   : R :   : :
                    8 :   : R :   : :
                    9 :   : D :   : :
                   10 +----+--R-+----+-+
                   11 :   :   : D : :
                   12 :   :   : R : :
                       +----+----+----+-+

   Fig. 2.3f: Data Process Interaction Report

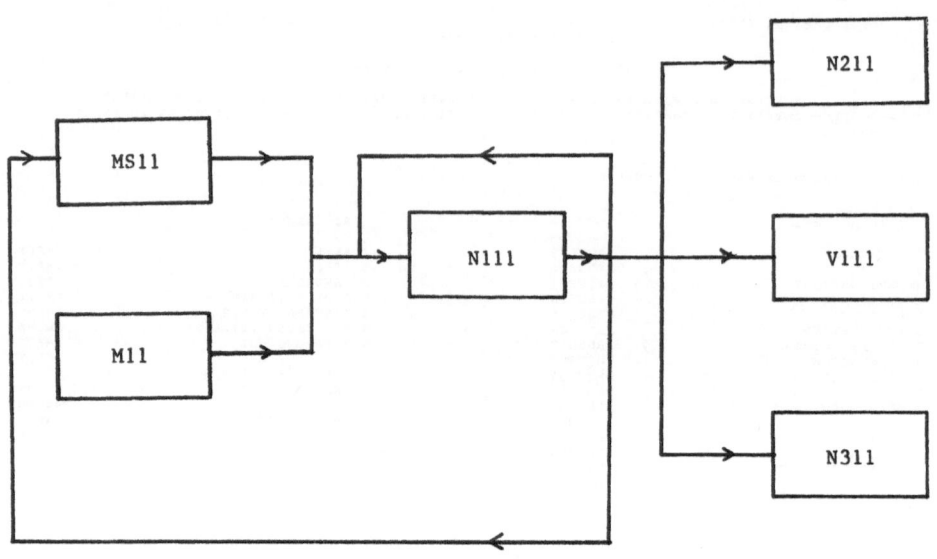

```
MODULE NAME, MODULE TYPE
      N111,      PROCESS
 TIMESET, EARLIEST END, LATEST END
   TA11,            4,          6
SENDNAME,EARLIEST DATA,LATEST DATA
    M11,            0,          0
   N111,            1,          1
   MS11,            1,          1
TIMESET,  TMAX,   TMIN
   TA11,    51,     49
SOURCE,   SINK,  TYPE,  LBND,  UBND, EDATA, LDATA
  N111,  N311, ASYNC.    0,    0,    1,    0
  N111,  V111, SYNCH.    0,    0,    0,    0
  N111,  MS11, ASYNC.    0,    0,    0,    0
  N111,  N211, SYNCH.    0,    0,    1,    1
  N111,  N111, SYNCH.    0,    0,    1,    0
   M11,  N111, SYNCH.    0,    0,    0,    0
  MS11,  N111, SYNCH.    0,    0,    1,    1
```

Fig. 2.4 Typical SPECK Graphic and Formal Specification Output.

As well as all the well-appreciated benefits that a good requirements specification give to any project, there are extra pay-offs for real-time systems. A lack of functionality or a logical inconsistency in the requirements which can lead to a deadlock situation could be catastrohic in a control system. Furthermore, one needs to recognise the high degree of interaction between various parts of the system and the effect that these may have on system timing performance, so that suitable design steps can be taken commensurate with the complexity of the problem.

The traditional view of requirements specification is that it produces a document in natural language which acts as an interface between a customer and a supplier. Although some interaction may preceed the production of the document, it is largely taken as the 'signing on' point for the software producer.

2.2.1.1 Specification as a description

The customer issues a specification so that suppliers can provide the customer with what the customer wants. As such, the customer sees the document largely as a description of the system he would like to have. In principle, it should describe both what the system should do and what it should not do. In practice, it is usually tacitly assumed that the system should do what is detailed in the specification and should not do everything else. Herein lies the major problem with the description view of a specification. It assumes that the customer already knows exactly all that the system should and should not do: an assumption which is often far from true. Moreover, it further assumes that the customer has completely tranfered this knowledge to the specification document. Regardless of the formality or otherwise of the document, regardless of its self-consistency, a description is rather like a painting of a scene: there is no way of detecting from it whether any item or area has been completely left out.

2.2.1.2 Specification as a prescription

The supplier views the specification document as ingredients to be put
together in order to solve the customer's problem. This prescriptive
view is affected not only by the difficulties of a descriptive document
(as described above) but also by information which intentionally or
unintentionally preempts or limits the supplier's freedom. (The difficulty
in separating result from method, function from algorithm, specification
from design will be considered in more detail later.) In general, the
information contained in the prescription will match not one but a whole
class of systems and the supplier will attempt to select one such system,
probably a minimal one with respect to some metric (cost, effort,
material availability etc.).

2.2.1.3 The contractual methodology

Within this customer-description - supplier-prescription framework, the
specification is seen as a formal separation between the parties. To the
customer, it represents the minimum acceptable while to the supplier,
it represents the maximum required. The contract is offered and accepted
at system inception and is fulfilled after system commissioning when the
customer accepts the system as meeting his minimal requirements /Cohe81/.
It offers no scope of interaction during system production, even if the
supplier suspects that what is prescribed is unlikely to be what the
customer really wants. Since no reputable supplier would be likely to
keep silent in such circumstances, it is clear that to be a realistic
model of real system production, the continuing interaction must be
included.

This model also ignores the role played by the producer's application
engineers. All systems producers have personnel whose job it is to
interact with the customer on the details of the system required. Many
organisations pride themselves on being able to advise, guide and even
correct customers in matters pertaining to the system specification.
Moreover, many customers rely heavily on this service, especially when
the application area is new to them. Outwardly, these personnel can be
seen as stimulating and formulating the customer's descriptive

specification. Internally however, these personnel may become 'customer
substitutes' and the system produced will be closer to the perception
of these substitutes than that of the real customer. Rather than
continually referring to the real customer with detailed queries (and
maybe thereby appear inept to him), such details are provided by the
substitute on hand. Being internal, there may well be no formal interface
for such exchanges of information. Thus the real customer's specification
may be translated but not documented both before and during later
production phases.

2.2.1.4   Specification as a model

Recent, more rigorous treatments of specification treat it as a model
of the system. Freed from the design constraints, such a model should
predict the system performance which will be observed if the system is
subsequently designed to meet this specification. Providing that the
underlying semantics of the model are sufficiently tightly established,
such a specification provides an unambiguous statement of the requirement.
This is invaluable for future validation and verification stages.

Suitable models also provide for automated consistency checking and
other prediction analyses which ensure that design is not proceding for
a system which is inherently incapable of satisfying its requirement
/Alfo77/, /Quir78/, /Quir83/. Zave develops the idea of executable
specifications /Zave82/ & /Zave84/, one of the fastest growing areas of
interest. In this approach, the specification is built up from application
independent structures which can then be interpreted. This is very
closely related to rapid prototyping, which is considered in more detail
in chapter 6. Recent work by Balzer, Lehman, Stavely and others is
reported in the Rapid Prototyping Workshop proceedings /RPW82/. A number
of formal approaches to this are described by Smoliar in the same
workshop. Such formal methods are now seen as parts of more unified
production environments, which are dealt with in section 2.4. This view
of a specification is strongly recommended. Because of the complexity
of real-time software, the best automated techniques should be used to
help in assuring the required degree of quality.

2.2.2 Software design

Software design may well be the portion of the software life cycle least amenable to tools and methodologies and most desperately in need of them. Design is a thought-intensive task. As such, it is difficult to define approaches to design which are applicable to a broad spectrum of software builders. Design is the process of converting a hopefully rigorous problem statement into a plan for an algorithmic-specific or computer-specific solution. The designer looks at a problem from the viewpoint of solution techniques played against the realities and capabilities of computing machines and software technology.

The design phase is critical as regards quality and reliability of the end product. It may be possible to produce a poor implementation from a good design, but it is seldom possible to produce a good implementation from a poor design. Because design is preceeded by requirements definition and specification, the designer should have a fairly firm problem definition to work with and be able to concentrate on methods of solution rather than methods of problem definition. But in practice, this is often not the case. Those who have a problem to solve are often unaware of the detailed problem specifics, and the entire cycle of requirements – specification – design is all too commonly an iterative process.

The design of real-time systems poses its own characteristic set of problems. Clearly, timing performance is one of them. Achieving performance targets requires not only that efficient algorithms be selected to provide the necessary functional processing, but also that the various asynchronous parts of the system synchronise so as to provide the various functional units with the necessary inputs in a timely manner: quick algorithms are no use if they are kept waiting for data. The recognition and proper handling of resources is another key design problem. Parts of the system which may not even be recognised as being resources in batch situations can become crucial in systems based on parallel processing. Where resources have been recognised, their control can be significantly more difficult in multi-processor systems: solutions which work for a single processor implementation may fail in these situations. The dynamic nature of real-time systems pose another set of problems. Resources in general, and such things as buffers in particular, cannot be allocated statically. Consequently provision has to made not only for their control but also for coping with unavailability on demand. Process priorities must be considered similarly, as these can be affected by demands - sometimes conflicting - on the system. Finally, long mission times and the consequent reuse of software mean that extra care must be taken in re-initialisation of variables and resetting of resources: code which works once-through may well not work iteratively.

Some design techniques are suggested in the open literature which should help the designer during the design process. They all are conceptual tools that impose an engineering way of thinking and a design representation language. Amongst the better known are JSD /Jack82/, JSP /Jack75/, MASCOT /MASC80/, SADT /SADT76/ and SREM /Alfo77/. There are also a number of design support and documentation systems, such as PSL/PSA /TeHe77/ & /ISDOS/ which support one or more of these techniques. However, in the area of real-time systems, it is our belief that all of these techniques are too immature and there is a continuing large effort being expended in the search for better techniques and tools to support them. A recent Study Report /ASDM81/ identified a total of 36 development methodologies and examined 21 of these in detail in the context of real-time system designs in an ADA environment. Technical Committee No 7 of the European Workshop on Industrial Computer Systems (EWICS TC7) has produced a guideline /EWIC81b/ which should help to produce software which is as error-free as possible from the very beginning and which can easily be verified. The suggested general approaches are based on experience in developing safe and understandable software.

It is one thing to conceive a design in the mind. It is quite another to write it down in such a way that it is useful. Understandability is one of the key issues here, and since the design must be communicated between the designer, design reviewers and eventually implementors, the representation of the design becomes important. There is world-wide effort and interest in this area. However it is still unclear at this point in the design description technology whether the same medium that is appropriate for detail-level description is also appropriate for top-level description.

Among the design representation techniques we mention:

- flowcharting, which is now under serious attack /RaAt83/.

- decision tables (figure 2.5), which have their highest applicability in logic-oriented programs.

- program design languages (PDLs), which are evolving as the latest favourite and which will be dealt with here.

A Program Design Language provides a framework for representing the structure and control of a computer program. Some controversy has arisen around the degree of formality that should be used in specifying a PDL. Advocates of formality cite rigour and automated consistency checks as advantages of their point of view; opponents cite the constraints of formality on the mental processes. As a result, PDLs vary from extremely well defined, formally specified languages such as SREM /Alfo77/, through graphic descriptions, as described in /YoCo79/, and to others which are English-like /DeMa78/. Although the concept of a PDL is well understood, there are few well-defined PDLs to choose from and thus the designer wishing to use a PDL may need to define his own. Pseudocodes offer examples of program design languages /CaGo75/ & /Palm82/.

2.2.3 Coding

In the last ten years many coding techniques have been suggested whose chief value is claimed to be increased productivity or maintainability of the final product. Some of these have had an impact on software reliability, however, including high-order languages, structured programming and detailed programming standards. As with design, though, these techniques are too general for safety related software developments, where more restrictive rules are needed.

There are not so many coding problem areas specific to real-time programs. One - the necessity to reinitialise variables - has already been mentioned. There is also the closely related problem of module reentrancy or pure code. This latter aspect is also strongly affected by the choice

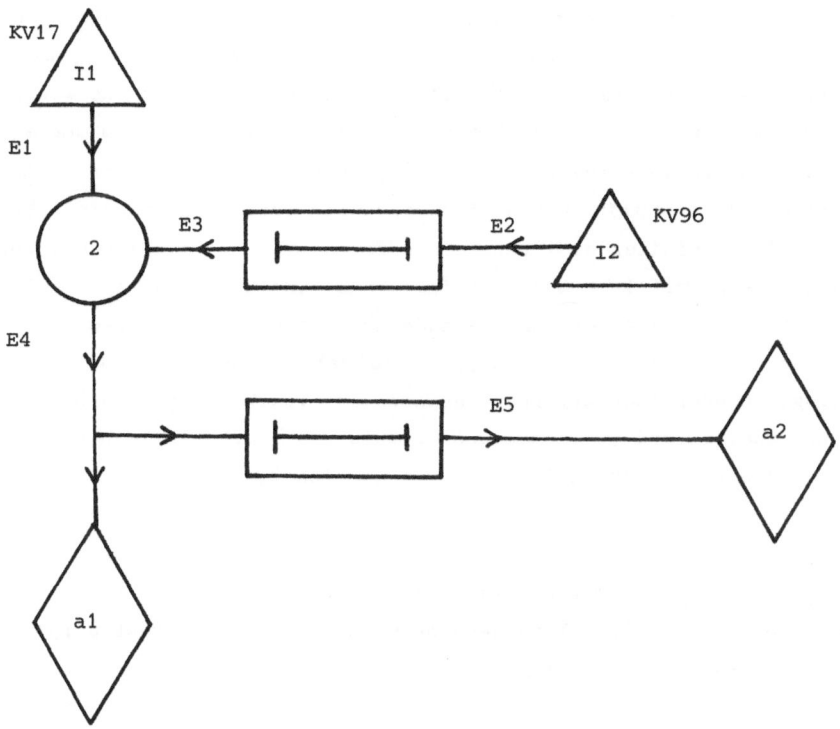

Fig. 2.5a Logic Diagram derived from System Requirements.

```
E1=I1                         TABLE COMPLETE & NON-REDUNDANT
E2=I2
E3=-E2
E4=E1.E3                                            1 2 3
E5=-E4
A1=E4                     I  1  KV17                 1 - 0
A2=E5                     I  2  KV96                 0 1 0

ACTIONS
A1  BIT11 ALL.BIANCO  :   A  1  BIT11 ALL.BIANCO    X . .
A2  NESSUNA AZIONE    :   A  2  NESSUNA AZIONE      . X X

INPUTS                    MISSING RULES
I1  KV17:                 NONE
I2  KV96:                 REDUNDANT RULES
END                       NONE
```

Fig. 2.5b Input to CERLTAB   Fig. 2.5c Decision Table for
from Logic Diagram above.   Logic Diagram above.

Fig. 2.5 Example Formal Language for Software Design Specification.

of language. The more modern high-level languages, such as ADA, do provide primitives for synchronisation, process control and, more generally, non-interruptible instruction sequences. While in one sense, this only pushes the problem back from the programmer to the language support system, it does mean, for example, that the problems associated with forgetting that certain instruction sequences must be uninterruptible are removed. (A similar assistance is offered by macro facilities, but this is not as powerful because the individual instructions are still available to the programmer and the code must be checked to ensure that only macros have been used.) This is a valuable aspect. It is worth commenting, however that all these aspects are in the grey area between design and coding, and it is because of this that emphasis is placed on more unified development environments in section 2.4.

The design guideline /EWIC81b/ mentioned in the previous section also gives some recommendations for programming languages and coding techniques suitable for high reliability developments, and the interested reader is again referred to this document.

2.2.4 Integration

Integration of the hardware and software can be considered as part of the final system checkout before it is handed over to the customer. The quality control activities which should accompany this integration are, however, a mixture of testing (continued from the code verification) and the overall system validation exercise. Notice that integration requirements should have been drawn up at an early stage in the life cycle.

2.2.5 Maintenance

Maintenance is the term used for all activities after the system has been accepted by licensing authorities. It also includes the implementation of approved software revisions. Significant cost, and therefore significant importance, is attached to the maintenance process. But because of its lack of glamour, little research and tool development has been done in this area. However, some results are beginning to appear.

The best kind of maintenance is, of course, no maintenance at all. It can be attained by preventive maintenance. Preventive maintenance is also the use of techniques to make maintenance more comfortable, easier, and safer. Some of those techniques are the same as those used to improve reliability. Among them we mention:

- modularity
- parameterization
- data structuring
- program structuring
- good documentation.

Notice that all these are static techniques of good software engineering, however, and not specific to real-time applications.

Software errors emerge from all phases of the software life cycle and error reporting is a very important part of software maintenance. It must be supported by a suitable error reporting procedure which can:

- record all the relevant error information
- ensure that errors are corrected, not forgotten
- ensure that all corrections are approved before changes are made
- enable the measuring of error correction progress.

As discussed in previous sections, the maintenance phase may be extended over a long period of time. If the quality of the software was originally high (and if any licensing process has been effective) then the rate of error occurence will be low. However, a low incidence of sporadic errors may occur which are difficult to classify or characterize. Because of this diversity of errors, their sources, the subtlety of the conditions under which they occur, and the various methods of detection, the error reporting system must be capable of maintaining an error log over a long period of time. It must also be correlated with any system changes that occur, and must contain as much information as possible about the complete system state when the error was detected. Because of the subtlety of conditions which stimulate such errors, it is vital that error detection occurs very soon after the error occurence, and the

software itself must log all the relevant information. Substantial
detective work and processing of this log may be required to determine
the cause and location of the error.

It is also very important that, from the beginning, a well defined
procedure is established to be followed when correcting errors and
testing the corrected software.

2.3 Verification and validation

As shown in figure 2.6, the activities of verification and validation
have an essential part in the overall software life cycle. The verification
process is closely tied to the individual steps in the software
development. Verification is defined /EWIC83/ to be the comparison at
each stage of the software life cycle to determine that there has been
a faithful translation of that stage into the next one. Each verification
activity applies techniques which have proved effective in detecting
errors commonly made in that step of the development process /Glas79/.
After the functional requirements have been established, verification
must check the adequacy of these in fulfilling the system requirements
assigned to the software in the System Requirements Specification. After
the design phase, verification addresses the adequacy of the software
design in meeting the software functional requirements. Likewise, after
coding, verification checks the compliance of the coded software with
the design derived in the Software Design Specification. The importance
of the life cycle is shown clearly here, because the proper placing of
these verification activities can only be made with close reference to
the cycle. Auditing throughout the life cycle is described in /BrSi82/.

Verification activities must be carefully planned before starting with
the project and the Verification and Validation (V&V) Plan will constitute
the most relevant section of a document that must be produced before
starting with the project: the Software Quality Assurance Plan (SQAP).
Besides the Software Verification and Validation activities, the SQAP
will also define the management organization, standards and documentation,
practice and convention used, review and audit activities to be conducted,

33

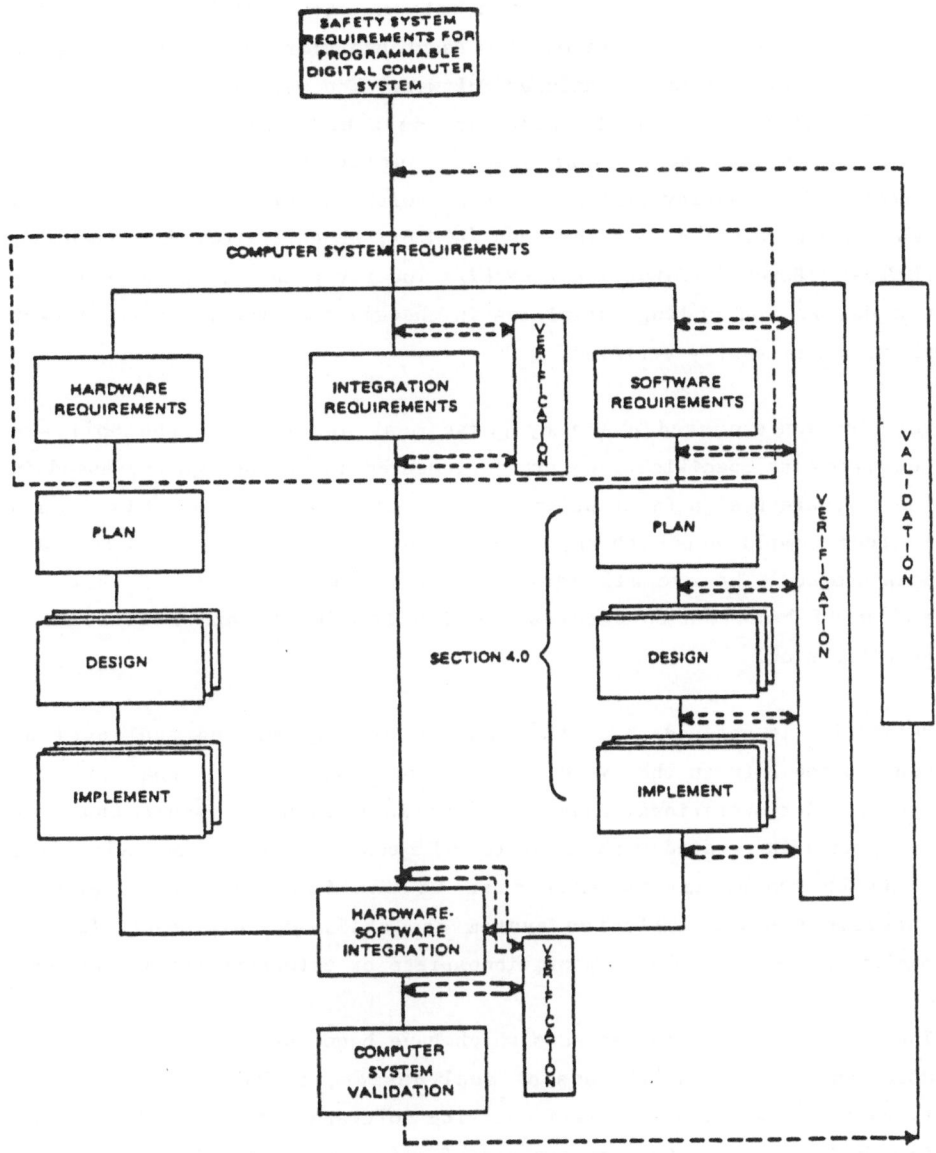

Fig. 2.6 Development, Verification & Validation Activities
for Safety Related Systems.
(From ANSI Standard ANS-4.3.2.)

problem reporting and corrective action, etc. /MILS74/ & /IEEE81a/.
Preparation of the Software Quality Assurance Plan is a vital step in
the production of Safety Related Software. The verification activities
must be undertaken by a separate team, detached from the development
team, which will be responsible for quality and reliability-related
concerns. This activity will not be dealt with in this report; interested
readers are referred to references /ACM78/, /Boeh78/, /Chin80/, /EWIC83/,
/EWIC84/, /Howd82/, /IEC81/ & /Tayl82/. The V&V plan will also influence
the design and coding activities in the way that the products of each
phase can be easily verified.

Verification executed phase by phase must assure that the Software
Requirements Specifications are implemented in the design expressed in
the Software Design Description and further into the code. This should
include compliance with any standards or codes of practice which have
been adopted. The overall verification process determines that the
software behaves in accordance with its Functional Requirements
Specification.

Validation is defined to be the process of determining the level of
conformance between the system requirements and an operational software
system under operational conditions. Validation will assure that the
code, when integrated with hardware and executed in the system environment,
meets the requirements expressed in the Software Requirements
Specification. A validated system can still exhibit unsatisfactory
performance, however, due to poor, incomplete or erroneous specifications.

There are several other aspects which have been investigated. One of the
more controversial is the use of dual design, functional diversity,
redundant programming and self-checking software. Some reference to this
is made in chapter 5. Current methods of software reliability assessment,
about which much has been written /MuOk83/, /Goel81/, /RADC79/ & /Glas79/
are equally controversial. Some software specialists feel that the use
of such traditional reliability concepts as "mean time between failure"
are meaningless for software (because when software fails, it is always
an inherent design/implementation failure, never a fatigue failure).
Others believe there is value in these traditional measures. Chapter 5

develops some of the models for software reliability prediction. The distinction between the achievement and demonstration of reliability and the assessment of reliability should be stressed, however, and this report concentrates on the former. Software Metrics, first introduced in /Hals77/, should be mentioned here. There have been many attempts to correlate software metrics and software reliability, but none has proved very convincing. Recently, a switch in emphasis has been made to correlate software complexity with program maintenance /HaMa82/ and overall development effort /AlGa83/.

Each of the production phases has its own associated verification phase, and the development process finishes each cycle with an overall system validation. The details of these techniques are described in the other chapters of this report. Here we mention briefly the most important aspects of these processes.

2.3.1 Requirements specification verification

The verification of the software requirements specification (elaborated by the system designers) against the system requirements specification (elaborated by plant engineers) is necessary to avoid an incorrect interpretation of the system requirements by the system designers. Such an eventuality would be extremely dangerous because it could imply common mode failures in the final system. It is desirable that Software Requirements Specification document be prepared in formal language so that it can be checked for:

- completeness, by eliminating arbitrary assumptions or undefined concepts,

- consistency, by emphasizing contradictions present in the document,

- ambiguity, by avoiding unclear function definitions.

Verification of requirements during this phase will also ensure that all requirements, documented in the requirements specification, are traceable to the system specification and that the requirements are clear, complete, correct and testable. Testable requirements are those which are specific and unambiguous, with a clearly identifiable result when they are met: for example, specify that accuracy should be "within $\pm$ 1" rather than "sufficient to meet mission requirements".

2.3.2 Design verification

The design review is an analysis of the design of a computer program. It is conducted to determine if the proposed implementation is capable of meeting the specified performance and verification requirements. The design review is made by people who have not participated in the design activities. A design review is required for each phase of the design.

The aim of the preliminary design review is to guarantee that all the functional requirements have been fully mapped into the preliminary design according to the established methodology. The preliminary design description is reviewed for completeness and consistency.

The aim of the detailed design review is to verify the detailed design description for completeness, unambiguity and consistency (both internal consistency and consistency with the description of the result of the preceding phase). Reviews and analyses conducted to verify the design include the following:

- reviews of all external functional interfaces (interfaces with the rest of the system),

- reviews of all internal functional inferfaces,

- analysis of critical timing requirements of the system as they apply to the software to ensure that the proposed computer program design will satisfy them,

- reviews of the structure of the program as a whole with emphasis on allocation of requirements to components, storage requirements and peripheral devices, operating sequences, and design of any associated data base.

The design review methodology normally adopted is that the designer issues a written design document prior to the review, and the reviewers submit written comments which are dealt with at the review.

Most important, the success or failure of a design review is dependent on people. The people who attend must be skilled and knowledgeable in the specific problem area. This is due above all to the lack of any specific technique for design review. For these reasons some efforts have been made in the direction of automated design checkers. An automated design checker is a computer program that accepts a design representation as input, analyses that design, and prints out a list of flaws in, and other descriptive information about, the design. Two things are immediately obvious; the design representation must be computer-readable, and the analysis performed cannot progress much beyond an analysis of the form and structure of the design, as opposed to its content. A few checkers of relatively general applicability are now available in the software marketplace: see section 2.5 on current practice for details.

2.3.3 Code verification

The code produced for the system is inspected to ensure that it correctly implements the design and has not introduced any errors. Commonly mentioned techniques include 'eye-balling' (or desk checking), walk-through, structural analysis and program proving. All these techniques are static and do not involve execution of the code. Some dynamic techniques exist including further analysis, symbolic execution and, most importantly, testing.

Verification accomplished by testing should demonstrate that the result of executing each logic branch, each input/output statement, and each logic segment in general satisfies the specification requirements. A good test will require the development of a Test Plan to define all levels of testing. In general several levels of testing will be required: unit testing will be conducted to verify that individual components have been properly coded and that they satisfy corresponding software design requirements; various degrees of integration testing will be conducted to verify that software/software interfaces between computer program components and with the executive program are satisfied.

Test activities are also concerned with the adequacy of the test cases, the conformance of test conduct and test results with test procedures, the control of the configuration tested, the timely reporting and correction of all software deficiencies, and the tracking of corrective action. The test plan is reviewed to ensure that the planning and test case definition are adequate and that appropriate levels of testing are planned. The test plan should identify the schedules, test methods, and success criteria as well as all required support facilities, equipment, software and personnel. It should include plans for testing in both normal and extreme conditions.

The details of Test Plans, testing techniques and automated verification tools are complex and too voluminous for inclusion here. The reader who is specially interested in this topic is referred to /Mil177a/ for a general discussion, and to /EWIC83/ for real-time specifics.

Independently from which testing techniques are used, a test coverage analyser should be used to find out the percentage of code elements covered by testing. A test coverage analyser is a computer program which, when applied to another computer program (the "subject program"), produces information on each occurrence of the execution of each logic segment of the subject program.

Normally, a so-called test driver is required to do a unit test. This is a computer program developed to enable the testing of another computer program. The driver enables the inputting of sufficient data to test the components and the printing of the resulting component outputs. Drivers are essentially "throwaway" code, similar from this point of view to the stub used in the top-down approach. Chapter 6 discusses how simulators can also be used in system testing.

The problem of building an adequate set of test cases is nontrivial. A test data generator is a computer program that automatically and systematically constructs test cases. This can be done from an analysis of the requirements specification, from a structural analysis of the code or from programmer-inserted test case generation clues. It should be appreciated that automation is not always possible. Paths through the software may be sensitive to real time dependencies and correlations between the input parameters, which may be difficult to identify and even more difficult to generate without sophisticated test generators or simulators.

A radically different concept of testing by data selected to be similar to operational input data is Symbolic Execution. This involves the algebraic execution of the symbolic version of a program upon symbolic input data. A fuller discussion is included in chapter 4. Program proving techniques and fault tree analysis can also be applied at this stage, as described in chapter 3. With all these techniques, skillful personnel aided by sophisticated automated tools are required if there is to be much hope of success.

2.3.4 System validation

After system integration, system testing will be conducted to demonstrate that the system meets the performance and design requirements of its specifications. In such areas as real-time software, where the interfacing of the software with some external device must be tested, it is particularly useful to do this with the help of a System Environment Simulation. However, the requirement of an environment simulator to represent the external world faithfully may, indeed, make the simulator more complicated than the program or component being tested. This approach is dealt with in more detail in chapter 6.

One interesting variant of the environment simulator is the instruction-level-simulator (ILS), a system that allows one computer to simulate another, instruction by instruction. This can be very helpful in cases where the target machine is unavailable, for some reason, when the software is ready for testing. If an ILS for that computer exists which runs on some other computer, the software may be tested there. However, because getting one computer to behave like another at the instruction level is a laborious process, this type of simulation is usually resorted to only when there is no alternative.

2.3.5 Verification and validation documentation

The documentation of all verification and validation activities is extremely important, especially for systems which must be licensed. The scope of these documents is to provide a record of these activities carried out at each stage of the software life cycle, starting with the requirements phase and ending with the integration testing and system validation phase. The following subsections give a broad indication of the contents of each document, but the lists should not be thought of as exclusive or limiting. Any other relevant information should be included.

2.3.5.1 Software requirements specification verification report

This document provides a record of the verification of the software requirements specification against the system requirements. It will report on the verification of the following:

- the software functional requirements
- the software safety and reliability requirements
- the external and internal interface requirements
- compliance with particular solution constraints.

The report will include:

- a description of the analysis procedure adopted.

- a list of discrepencies (if any) found between the software functional requirements and the system functional requirements.

- a record of any inconsistencies, redundancies or incompleteness discovered in the software requirements specification.

2.3.5.2 Software design verification report

This document provides a record of the verification of the software
design against the software requirements specification. It reports the
results of:

- verification of functional capabilities
- verification of interface capabilities
- verification of testability
- verification of compliance with particular design standards.

The report will include:

- a description of the analysis procedure adopted
- any items which do not conform to the software functional requirements
- any items which do not conform to the design standards
- data structures and algorithms poorly adapted to the problem.

2.3.5.3 Code verification report

This document provides a record of the testing of individual modules and
of functionally related groups of modules. It contains verification
reports of:

- the functional capabilities
- the performance capabilities
- the interface capabilities
- compliance with particular code standards.

The report will describe:

- the test environment in which the tests were executed
- the test procedure adopted
- the test equipment used (both hardware and software)
- the acceptance criteria adopted
- the error detection strategy and corrective action procedures.

It should also include:

- input test listing
- output test listing
- additional data regarding timing, sequence of events and special cases
- an error log characterizing any errors detected and remedies taken.

2.3.5.4 System validation report

This document provides a record of the validation of the system software in the total system environment. It covers both functional and performance aspects. It should contain:

- a description of the equipment used
- the results obtained
- a description of the modification procedure to be followed if necessary
- a list of any items not in compliance with the system requirements
- any necessary corrective items.

2.4 Unified system development environments

We have established in the previous sections that successful system production requires the close and prolonged interaction of three groups of people with different system perceptions, different technical outlooks and different concerns and responsibilities:

- customers
- producers
- licensers.

The producers can be further subdivided (at present) into different technical classes (analysts, programmers etc.) and management classes (project control, finance, quality assurance etc). This is shown in figure 2.7. We have also seen that the interest in any single system is likely to extend beyond any individual's membership of an interested group. Finally, we have suggested that while current practice does not

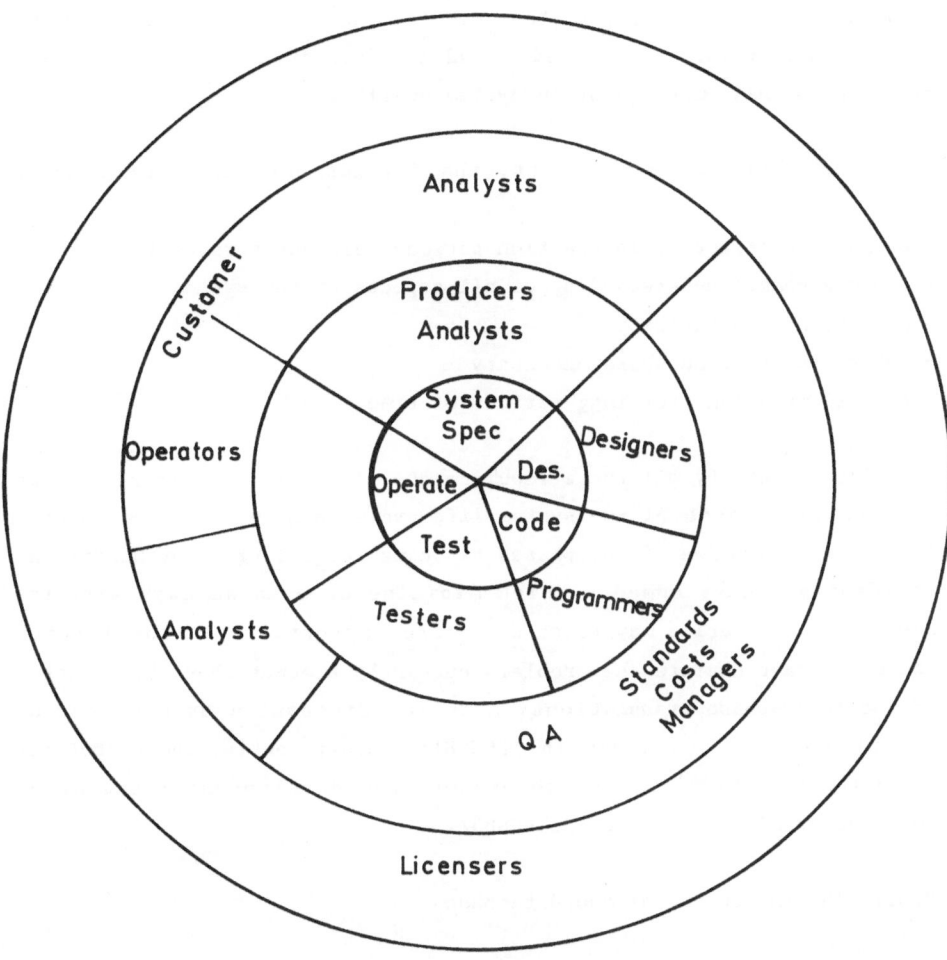

Fig. 2.7 Components of the System Production Environment.

conform to many development phase models, there is as yet little or no indication that these idealised - and to some extent naive - models represent a real improvement in system quality.

To achieve such an improvement, the development environment must:

- promote constructive interaction between relevant personnel
- enhance common understanding of all aspects of the system
- promote maintainability
- enforce protection where necessary
- be self managing over long periods of time.

In order to satisfy all these requirements, it would seem desirable to support all phases of the system life-cycle in a more unified manner. Indeed, the separation of the phases has come about largely by historical accident and environments which minimise or even do away with the separating boundaries may be seen as more appropriate in the future. These at least obviate the problems currently brought about by mistakes in the inter-phase translations. A fuller discussion by a number of contributors is contained in /PENV81/. More recently, the US DoD has initiated its STARS program to promote the development integrated, tool-supported environments /STARS83/.

2.4.1 The importance of the data base

Even without considering the technical aspects of a system, dealing with its associated files and their modifications over any protracted period of time poses a major logistical problem. Furthermore, practically all of the points made in the previous section point to the desirability of a data base to support the development environment. Data base management systems form the ideal basis for both the protection of information and its properly authorised modification and maintenance. The provision of the data base also eases the problem of eliminating out-of-date documentation: in a properly designed system, all personnel involved with the system can be informed automatically of changes relevant to their area of responsibility. Conversely, the consequences of any proposed modification can be made much more apparent and at an early stage. Of course, all this is not achieved without careful design of the support system but the technology to produce such a system already exists and should be put to use in this direction. Work in this area was reported in /BaGo79/ & /GoWi79/ and more recently, some systems utilising this approach have been announced, including the PLASMA system produced by Triumph-Adler /Balz81a/, the PROMOD system from GEI and the TOOLPACK research project /Oste83/. Further work specifically relating to real-time systems is continuing at Harwell.

2.4.2 A formal basis for production environments

In order that the complete lifecycle can be adequately supported, it is necessary to ensure that equal rigour and coherent access is provided to all phases of the software production process. Rigour is the usual argument in support of formality. But coherence is just as important, especially in support of large groups of people with complex interactions. It should be noted that a formal basis for the production environment does not necessarily imply that highly formal languages must be used at any stage in the production. Nor is formal synonymous with mathematical: all programming languages are formal but some, especially non-procedural ones such as PROLOG, are not mathematical.

2.4.2.1 For and against formality

There is still much disagreement about the advantages and disadvantages of formal languages. There is no doubt that formal techniques allow higher degrees of confidence in the consistency and completeness of systems to which they are applied. Most of the disagreement stems from whether or not the human interfaces to formal systems can be made sufficiently 'friendly' that the advantages of the formality are not overtaken by the difficulties in communicating and applying them.

An analogy with programming languages is instructive here. Programming languages, both high level and low level, are formal. A relatively large number of people can successfully communicate and manipulate the high level languages, even though their semantics are often difficult to establish formally. The low level languages are easier to define semantically but less easy to use. To overcome the problem, automated aids - compilers - are provided to translate the high level to the low level. If the high level is sufficiently high, then it can also be read as an informal text. As such, it will suffer from all the ambiguity of meaning that any informal text suffers. However if it is communicated informally and then recompiled, a suitable comparison of the low level languages will show whether or not the meaning has been maintained. Furthermore, by a back-translation method, a formal meaning can be given to the high level program treated as an informal text. This is one possible way of bridging the gap between formal languages and human understanding.

2.4.2.2 Formal languages to preserve information over time

While data base systems are a good vehicle for maintaining and manipulating data, they do not of themselves help in the interpretation of that data. Because of the extended lifetimes involved, the problems of promoting common unambiguous understanding are compounded by the fact that informal terms may change their meaning over the lifetime. This is yet another reason for using formal language.

2.4.2.3 Predictive power of formal mathematical models

A major benefit from formality stems not from the uniqueness of interpretation, but from the prediction of consequence. By basing the formal method on a mathematical model and then exercising the model, facets of system behaviour can be exhibited which would not otherwise become apparent until a much later stage. This has already been demonstrated in specification systems and is currently being explored in design aids /Quir80/.

For real-time software, predictions of the real-time performance, freedom from deadlock and resource utilisation (especially processor and memory loadings) may be obtained. Time critical processing paths can be highlighted before they become bottlenecks. The degree of redundancy in systems which must be fault tolerant can also be established, showing both areas with insufficient redundancy and areas with overkill.

2.4.2.4 Formal language as enforcer of separation of concerns

A further advantage of formal language is that it can be used to limit
the areas that it can describe. This should not be seen as restricting
design freedom, however, but rather as guiding the designer and focussing
the design ideas on the relevant areas. Thus by separating the relevant
concerns of different design areas and phases, and providing a suitable
language for each, it becomes possible to enforce the proper separation
of concerns through the different stages of system development. This is
crucially important for verification, licensing and maintenance.

2.4.3 Abstraction as the unifying basis of system production

Formal languages provide the vehicle to support conceptual abstraction.
Just as in program design, where abstract data types have been recognised
as a powerful concept, so too is abstraction important in system
specification and design /GuHo78/. Starting from the earliest stages of
system requirements specification, one can view the development process
as one of abstraction. The functional requirements specification abstract
out all the system details except what the system is to do. With a
suitable abstract 'functional' machine, the specification could itself
be run. Since no suitable machine exists, various concepts concerning a
lower level of abstraction have to be integrated with the functional
specification to produce a high level design. The process continues
until the abstraction level reaches a point where the abstract machine
needed to run the conceptual model exists (or can be built). At that
point the design is complete and once the necessary machine is available,
the system production phase is complete too. Thus the whole production
cycle can be seen as a process of filling out abstractions until a real
physical level exists.

2.4.3.1 Theoretical basis for abstraction-based development environment

There are two key aspects which underpin formal specification techniques
for real-time systems: modelling and abstraction. The important concepts
to be dealt with in the specification have to be abstracted from the
real system. Typically these are concerned with aspects of what it is

the system should do, and not with details of how the system is to carry out these operations. It is not always a clear-cut distinction however. For example, a functional decomposition of a system requirement can in some sense be seen as a partial design. Typical concepts, as used in the SPECK system /QuGi77/, include events, processes, subsystems and communication channels.

Having identified the concepts, their interaction and inter-relations must be modelled in a formal mathematical sense. It is this modelling which fixes the semantic meaning of a specification built up in terms of the concepts involved. Furthermore, and just as important, it is the model detail which will govern the power of any analyses which can be applied to such a specification.

It should be noted too that the concepts on different levels may be related /Quir80/. Design decisions on one level may be constrained by the relations in previous higher levels. By describing these restrictions and constraints when the levels are defined, it is possible to keep a formal and automatic check on various aspects of the design consistency.

Real-time systems are naturally dynamic: their behaviour depends on the physical world to which they interface. Thus it is natural to try to develop dynamic analyses to mirror the behaviour of the system. Conceptually, many different processes may be active at any time in the real-time system. Thus the model should be capable of handling concurrent processing aspects reflected in the terms abstracted for the specification. (This is the "Cognitive Model" referred to in /BaGo79/.) As another example, the time taken for the system to respond to events in the real world, and indeed some guarantee that the system will respond to events as required, are of crucial concern in real-time systems: hence the model should be able to handle such details. The purely algebraic specification of a stack structure may well yield a provably correct model of a stack, but in a real-time system, one is just as interested in proving that the stack will not overflow. Completeness of input space and freedom from deadlock are also of critical interest.

2.4.3.2 Abstraction as the separator between specification and design

A particular result of the abstraction view described in the previous
section is that one can use it to separate formally specification and
design levels. This is achieved by deciding in advance which abstractions
belong to which level. Thus loosely, a functional specification must
only contain concepts related to 'what' is to be achieved and not 'how'
it is to be achieved.

The abstractions are important for other reasons too. Information hiding
is a valuable technique for helping to guarantee freedom from unwanted
interactions and side effects - especially critical in multi-processor
real-time systems - and also to aid long term maintainability.

2.4.3.3 Level limiting by abstraction content in top-down approaches

A second result is that some control can be maintained over a top-down
specification or design approach. Again this is achieved by deciding in
advance the hierarchy of relevant concepts and then enforcing each level
to use only abstractions at the correct level in this hierarchy.

It is in this enforcement role that the formal language is important,
for as described in 2.4.2.4 it allows concepts to be recognised and thus
classified as being relevant or not to the design level under
consideration.

2.4.3.4 Viewpoints as orthogonal abstractions

In dealing with a unified system production environment, it must not be
forgotten that the development will require the interaction of numbers
of different personnel with differing requirements. Each group will have
interests not just in given areas of the system, but also in different
aspects of given areas of the system. For example, one group may be
interested in the control flow aspects of part of the system while
another is concerned with the data flow. Or again, one group may be
concerned with software partitioning while another is interested in the
colour of the cabinets to house the equipment. Each of these groups has

its own view of the system. This view will encompass some concepts of the system while ignoring others as being irrelevant.

The important point is that any reasonably well defined concept in a viewpoint must be represented by some associated abstraction of the real system. By suitable data base techniques, it is possible to automate to some degree this association. Consequently, even if the details of such an association have to be provided by human intervention, the validity of these associations and their completeness can be checked by machine. Some degree of consistency checking may also be possible if there are discernible restrictions between the valid associations between a number of abstractions.

While not completely unassociated with each other, various viewpoints may well exist independently (eg. data flow and control flow). It follows that the mappings from the system itself to these viewpoints may also be independent and in this case, the abstractions involved are said to be orthogonal.

2.4.4 Recommendations for the development environment

Errors in the production of real-time software come from within the individual stages and from the necessity to translate between these stages. By unifying the development environment, the problems associated with the translation between stages can be largely eliminated. As explained earlier, the allocation of errors, when discovered, to particular stages can be difficult. This would seem to indicate that the various stages should be brought closer together if possible. By making full use of the possibilities for computer support of the development cycle, much of the administrative drudgery can be automated, and the simple errors due to forgetfulness and mistyping can largely be eliminated.

The importance of formality and rigour throughout the system life cycle is becoming increasingly recognised. Not only for specification /HeMc83/, /RaKe83/ (and the many others already discussed), but increasingly for design and verification /NeHa83/, /ChYe83/ and documentation and

maintenance /YaGr81/. Even the bases of static analysis /Niel82/ and
testing /Gour83/ are being questioned. The necessity of unity of the
development environment encompassing the whole life cycle is also
becoming more apparent, with the first results of many projects now
starting to appear /Oste83/. The importance of including the Verification
and Validation activities in this can hardly be overstressed for safety
related systems /StTh83/. Finally, a formally-based development
methodology /Cohe82/ offers great potential for avoiding performance
problems which currently only come to light late in the production cycle
and are costly to overcome.

2.5 Current real-time application examples

2.5.1 Use of Formal Requirements Specifications

Several pilot experiments have been carried out to study the advantages
resulting from using formal languages as requirements specification
languages. Among them we mention:

- Research Project 961 "Validation of Real-Time Software for Safety
Applications" funded by the Electric Power Research Institute (EPRI).
The following institutions were involved in the project:

    - Electric Power Research Institute
    - University of California at Berkeley
    - Babcock and Wilcox
    - Science Application Inc
    - General Research Corporation.

The formal language used was RSL with its related automatic working
analyser REVS as part of the SREM Methodology developed from TRW for
BMDATC /DoSt78/, /StFe78/ & /RaBa81/.

- the Casaccia project, in which the PSL/PSA system was used on a pilot
project for requirement specification of a PWR protection system /Abba81/,
/Bolo82/ & /Bolo83/.

- the Harwell project, in which a software system for formal requirements specifications, SPECK, has been developed and used in the specification of complex real-time systems /QuGi77/, /Quir78/ & /Quir83/.

- the Karlsruhe project conducted at Institut fur Datenverarbeitung in der Technik, Kernforschungszentrum, Karlsruhe. This project started studying the applicability of PSL/PSA to describe real-time software systems and finally produced both a new language, PCSL, and a new system, ESPRESO, for specifications and their analysis /Lude81/ & /Trau81/.

- the Halden project, in which a formal language, X, based on the existing RSL language, has been developed for the specification of computer programs /DaIs80/.

- PWS 5.22 project on software reliability. This is a joint research program involving Westinghouse Electric Research and Engineering for Atomic Systems Incorporated (WEREAS), Framatome, CEA and EDF. A specification language, Z, with associated support for analysis was developed within the project and was later applied to a pilot experiment /Abri80/, /ChNe80/ & /HeMe80/.

A very interesting experiment funded by Naval Research Laboratory, Washington DC, USA, had a slightly different topic. The objective was not to demonstrate the feasibility of the use of formal language and automatic tools for the specification of a real-time complex systems but rather to try to answer the questions of how a good requirement document should be made, what it should contain and what it should not contain. The project has been conducted by redesigning and rebuilding the Operational Flight Program (OFP) for the Navy's A-7 Aircraft. The document of A-7 Software Requirements makes extensive use of special notation and tables in order to present a large amount of information both concisely and precisely and is so organized as to facilitate the rapid answering of requirements questions /HeKa78/, /PaHe80/ & /BaWe80/.

The use of modelling and simulation as a software requirement and design aid has been also investigated. A preliminary study has been conducted by the System Reliability Service and EWICS TC7 members for the EEC. The results are reported in /SRS81/.

2.5.2 Use of Program Design Languages and Design Checkers

To date, we know only a very few pilot applications of conceptual tools with associated formal representation languages and automated design checkers in the design of Safety Related Systems. These are:

- the SREM methodology and associated RSL language, which has been used in the preliminary design phase within the Research Project 961 funded by EPRI, USA /StFe78/.

- the MASCOT approach to developing real-time systems, which has been used in several applications in the United Kingdom. Initially developed by the Royal Signals and Radar Establishment (RSRE) within the Ministry of Defence, a MASCOT Suppliers Association was formed in 1977 to transfer the MASCOT technology from RSRE into a broader environment /MASC80/. Recently a software development system called CONTEXT, based on the MASCOT approach, has been developed and marketed by System Designers Limited /CONT79/.

- a graphic language tool, called Structured Analysis and Design Technique (SADT), which facilitates system design and development and has been developed by SofTech Inc. and marketed /SADT76/. A pilot experiment, meant to demonstrate its applicability in the field of safety and safety related systems, has been conducted within the Babcock and Wilcox Company /ThRe80/ & /Thom81/.

2.5.3 Use of Verification Techniques and Automated Tools

Much experience has been gained in the past years related to the use of techniques and tools for verification and validation of computer programs which must achieve the highest safety standards. Two papers have been produced inside EWICS TC7 which, starting from the results obtained in practical experiences, define a guideline for complementary activities of program verification and validation strategies /EWIC83/ and of program testing /Tayl82/. Among the studies that have been conducted we mention:

- the Casaccia project, in which complementary testing techniques have been used to verify the code of a safety system /BoAg79a/ & /BoAg79b/.

- the computerized safety system for the Brunsbuttel reactor. This is one of the very few cases we know in which the program has been completely analyzed by hand. Successively, it has been tested and some statistical approaches have been applied practically to assess reliability figures /Ehre76/, /EhPl78b/ & /EhPu79/.

- the distillation plant project at Grindsted, Denmark, in which fault tree techniques were used to verify the specification and coding of the sequential control system /TaJu82/.

- the Karlsruhe project for the Reactor Safety System called BESSY. The team thoroughly tested the program with the help of an automatic test system which consists of static analysis of the code, dynamic analysis of the code and automatic test data generation /Voge76/ & /GmVo79/.

- the Halden project. In this project, a dual programming technique has been used, together with random testing, program analysis, artificial error insertion and quantitative reliability assessment /DaLa78/ & /DaLa79/.

- EPRI Project 961. The code was verified first using a checklist approach. Then, to determine adherence to the programming standards, the code was subjected to a structured walk through. Finally, it was verified according to Test Plan and the test results obtained been used as input for a reliability growth model /DoSt78/, /StFe78/ & /RaBa81/.

2.6 Conclusions

There are three major potential contributors to achieving the highest
reliability in real-time software:

- the use of an integrated system development environment

- the use of formal methods for the different system development phases

- the adoption of planning guidelines covering the whole life cycle.

The use of an integrated system development environment provides the
developers with a uniform set of tools and techniques covering the whole
life cycle. Ideally, this allows the software requirements to be
transformed into an implementation with sufficient continuity to guarantee
that the semantics of the problem are preserved throughout. It obviates
many of the traditional problems at the interfaces between the various
development phases and also helps with product maintenance. The
development of unified environments is currently proceeding very actively,
coupled with practical developments in relational databases and
knowledged-based systems.

Formal methods open up the way for powerful analysis at each stage of
the software development process. These can give increased confidence
in the correctness, safety, reliability and acceptability of the final
product. They also assist any licensing process which must be a part of
the development process.

Unfortunately, the current state-of-the-art does not make these generally
available for complex projects, although they are coming very near now.
The development efforts at universities and research institutes has
shown very clearly what can be achieved. However, their application
requires skilled practitioners and what automated tools are available
also require much skill to use. There is much current effort into moving
these techniques into less specialist environments and providing tools
to render the formality less obtrusive.

Until these techniques are more mature and widely available, planning guidelines offer the best practical solution to achieving high reliability. Such guidelines define exactly the project structure, standards, tools and organisation in such a way as to develop the software in a well controlled method with good and timely documentation, quality control checks and a high standard of software engineering. The key organisational roles of Quality Assurance, Verification & Validation and Configuration Management should be identified, together with any other areas of the organisation involved with the product reliability. The communication problems between all these organisations may be severe in large projects, however, and the development of Integrated System Development Environments and Formal Methods remain very necessary if the very highest standards of reliability are to be regularly achieved.

3 Structural Analysis and Proof

J.R.Taylor, U.Voges, P.Puhr-Westerheide and W.J.Quirk

3.1 Structural analysis

3.1.1 Simple techniques

There are many techniques which can be used to analyse programs, and to demonstrate program properties, which do not require any form of program execution. These techniques fall into two groups:

- those which prove that a program satisfies certain criteria, or that it performs according to a given specification
- those which carry out some form of structural analysis, to show some structural property of the program.

These techniques can be used to show that some (or all) aspects of a program are implemented correctly. Only rarely can they be used to identify errors in incorrect programs.

Simple structural analysis techniques treat control flow and data flow in programs. In control flow analysis, each program statement is represented by a node in a graph. Arcs in the graph represent the possible flow of control between two statements. Statements such as IF statements, which lead to branching in programs, provide double or multiple arcs leading from a statement node.

Control flow graphs can be inspected to show that:

- all parts of a program can be reached
- there is an exit or termination for all parts of a program.

This kind of check can be automated by using programs for plotting reachability trees. Further discussion can be found in /ClEm81/ and /YaCh80/, which deals with concurrency problems in particular.

In data flow analysis, a graph is constructed which represents not only individual statements (in the form of nodes) and control flow (arcs) but also, for each statement, indicates which variables are defined, which are assigned to and which are referenced. By tracing all paths in a program, it becomes possible to detect:

- paths along which a variable is referenced or assigned to, before it is defined
- paths along which a variable is referenced before it is assigned to
- variables which are never referenced
- variables which are defined several times.

Numerous systems for data flow analysis have been described, including /OsFo76/, /Alle76/, /FoOs76/, /Kodr78/, /BaJa78/, and /TaOs80/. The checks provided by these forms of analysis are not perfect. It is not possible to determine whether all elements of an array have been assigned before referencing, for example. Also, a program path which 'breaks one of the rules' may in fact turn out to be logically imposible, when the values of variables in branching conditions are taken into account. A technique called Sneak Circuit Analysis, primarily developed for detecting obscure transient hardware malfunctions /Rank73/, can also be applied to software to detect flow anomalies /Sidl77/ & /Goen78/. A formal basis for data flow analysis has been described recently in /Niel82/.

The number of errors found by these techniques in any one program are usually low. Nevertheless they are very useful, especially in large program systems with many programmers, since it is often very hard to detect unassigned variables in complex program structures. The methods can be applied automatically, and so put very little load on the programmer.

For real time programs, similar kinds of analysis can be applied to identify cases where shared resources are requested but not released, referenced before they are requested, or are requested in the wrong order. This last form of check can be used to enforce Havender's technique for preventing deadlock /Have68/. This involves ordering resources (partially). Resources are then requested by all programs in this order.

It is then impossible for a program to request a low number resource
while possessing a high number resource, and therefore impossible for
it to wait indefinitely while the possessor of the low number resource
waits for the high number resource.

Control flow analysis can be used for timing analyses of programs, to
ensure that all programs can meet their deadlines, for example. This is
discussed in detail in the next section, where one of the most advanced
techniques of timing analysis, SPECK, is described.

Simpler forms of static analysis can be applied to programs to ensure
that they obey fixed rules, such as the rules of structured programming,
of ISO FORTRAN, or of dynamically relocatable or reentrant assembler
code programming. A related possibility is the production of variable
and subroutine cross reference lists, which can be a very useful aid in
the initial steps of program debugging.

3.1.2 The SPECK Specification Model and its Analyser.

SPECK is the name of both a formal mathematical technique for analysing
real-time system specifications and also for the suite of computer
programs which implements this analysis and aids the creation, manipulation
and presentation of such specifications. The formal model which underlies
the technique is based on a timed data-flow representation of real-time
system behaviour. SPECK's particular power lies in its ability to handle
real time explicitly, even in complex asynchronous systems. This is
often crucial in real-time systems, where responding within the correct
time frame is no less important than responding functionally correctly.

The SPECK model is based on just three fundamental concepts:

-    PROCESS
-    CLOCK (referred to as TIME SET in /QuGi77/)
-    CHANNEL

A process is responsible for calculating a single entity from inputs provided internally by other processes or externally by the real world. As well as being defined in terms of the function it carries out and the data it uses, the temporal behaviour of the process must also be specified. This extra time-related data includes the total time the process takes to complete a calculation and the times during a calculation at which it accesses the input data. Each process is controlled by a CLOCK, and different processes may share a common clock. In this case the various processes are said to be synchronised. Finally in order that data can be communicated between the processes in a system, the processes are joined together as necessary by CHANNELS.

This model is considered to operate as follows. When a clock ticks, a new instance is created of every process controlled by that clock (regardless of whether or not previous instances of those processes are still active). Each instance is active until it completes its calculation, at which point it ceases to exist. If the duration of a process instance is greater than the the time between instances, then multiple instances of that process may be simultaneously active in the system but at different stages of execution. Because each process instance is new and separate from any previous instance, a process can have no memory. If a process needs data from any other process instance, including any of its own previous instances, this must be detailed explicitly in that process description and a corresponding channel must be defined. Thus although the channels are represented as joining processes, they actually transfer data between process instances. A process may access the data produced for any finite back history of any processes in the system and the channels have the responsibility of storing and managing this data. The terminating action of each process is to write the data it has just calculated to its channel, and notice that it has no knowledge of which other processes in the system may use this data in the future. Processes which are synchronised may demand data corresponding to particular instances and, if this data is still being calculated, they may have to wait for this data to become available. No such waiting is permitted for communication between asynchronous processes: the most recent data available is supplied by the channel without any waiting.

Some aspects of this behaviour may seem obscure at first sight, but as a result of them, a complete separation in time and space is enforced on the process instances. That is to say, the only interactions which the model allows are those data transfers necessary for system operation. Thus the model accurately represents a perfect implementation of the system free from all unnecessary design constraints. Two aspects are worthy of particular note. The first is that there can be no invisible 'side effects' in the system because all the data flows are explicit and the computation pattern depends only on this explicit data. The second point is that the model assumes that there are always sufficient resources to meet the processing demands. It is this perfect behaviour which can now be analysed by the computer to check internal consistency both in time and data flow. And of course, if the behaviour of such a perfect system is incorrect, there is no way in which any real implementation could be correct.

There is no suggestion that in the final implementation of the system, there should be a one-to-one correspondance between the SPECK processes and any computer processes: many of the former may be implemented by one of the latter. Similarly, the channels may be data managers, named variables (local or common) or any other implementation that fulfills the functional needs of the system. It will also be part of the design procedure to ensure that sufficient real resources are available in the system so that it can meet its processing deadlines. Part of the SPECK analysis gives the total active process profile of the system, but the actual number of processors needed in the implementation will depend on the details of the association between processes and processors which results from the design.

The SPECK modelling philosophy is as follows. The top level of the functional requirements specification represents the system as a single black box. The system function is named (but not normally defined) and its inputs and outputs identified. The acceptable scan rate for inputs and overall response characteristics should also be identified. The next level of decomposition is achieved by identifying key data which must be derived by the system from the inputs but is not just a system output. Typically, such data will have a strong significance to the physics or engineering of the plant associated with the system: for example, the total coolant flow derived from an integration of individual flows or a mean temperature derived as an average of several available measurements. These newly identified data items become the inputs and outputs of subsystems which are treated as systems in their own right. Thus we get a sequential decomposition into subsystems with decreasing functional complexity until a level is reached where each subsystem has a simple transformation to produce a single output under the control of a single scheduling event. This is the process level and this is where the decomposition ceases.

Although not a fundamental concept, subsystems are allowed in the SPECK model as a structuring mechanism. The only constraint currently enforced on their structure is that different subsystems cannot be synchronised. That is to say, if two processes are synchronised, then they must be in the same subsystem. This restriction is necessary to separate the behaviour of different subsystems and to allow some of the detailed analysis on complex systems to be carried out without the need to expand the complete system down to the lowest level. Notice too that when redundancy is necessary for whatever reason, the total system may contain many identical subsystems whose performance need only be evaluated once.

The consistency analyses carried out by SPECK are detailed in /Quir78/, and cover several areas. SPECK is an interactive program which carries out its analysis in two parts: local and global. At a level which corresponds to the syntax checking of an ordinary compiler, each descriptive statement entered is checked at the time of entry. This ensures that the database assembled by SPECK contains only syntactically correct statements. Some items of gross temporal misbehaviour are also trapped at this stage; in particular any conditions which could allow the data items identified in the system to become badly ordered in time. Such behaviour can sometimes be observed in message switching systems where, because of routing algorithms which attempt to balance traffic densities, the individual packets making up a message may be shuffled on arrival at their destination and need to be sorted. This implies, for example, that each packet must contain some explicit sequencing information which would be unnecessary if the timing constraints on the whole network were tightened to the point that such mis-ordering could not occur.

Once a potentially complete system has been specified, the global analysis can be carried out. This has four phases. First the data flow between the various processes is checked for consistency, in the sense that the data required by a process will actually be provided by the relevant channel. It checks further that all the processes in the system do contribute to the system behaviour, and that the interfaces between this system and other systems (including the external world) are properly defined and matched. This corresponds approximately with the completeness and consistency requirements of specifications in general. However, because the process specification includes the details of the time history profile of data required, this particular aspect, peculiar to real-time systems, is checked here.

Second, the whole system is checked for deadlock. Because of the semantics of the model behaviour, there is only one general condition which has to be evaluated: that there does not exist any closed loop of processes all waiting on data from each other. Although a single condition, a significant amount of work is necessary to determine that the system is well formed in this respect. Experience shows that while simple examples of such a deadlock condition do not often occur, systems requiring much data feedback (for example, to establish correlations in time) or including many interlocks are more prone to this problem. Adding such interlocks after the primary specification has been completed can also lead to this problem, which highlights the need for careful re-analysis after any change in the specification.

The third phase probes the system topology and ensures that there is no partition of the system into disjoint, non-interacting parts. Although such a partition is not a logical inconsistency per se, it may well indicate that some area of the requirement, which should bridge the partition, has been completely overlooked.

Finally in the fourth phase, the effects of internal timings on the data flow characteristics are determined: this amounts to determining the ability of the system to have a guaranteed response to transient events. The importance of this characteristic varies with the detailed system requirement. In some cases, the inertia of the plant may mitigate the necessity to respond to transients in some measured parameters. In others, it may be crucial to guarantee response to any transient of duration greater than some specified value.

It is important to notice that the time to respond to a transient or change in input state is not the same as the minimum time duration of such a transient. Again, the inertia of the plant may allow a relatively long time to elapse between the detection of the change and any subsequent control or safety action. The response time to any particular input depends on the subsequent data flow details, process functions and their rates of instantiation. The SPECK analyser provides the facility to trace these response times through the system from any process within it. It will detect if there is no response path to another process and whether or not any process along a response path needs to latch in order that the path is guaranteed. All this needs the assumption that each process along the path does respond to the input change on the first instance which 'sees' that input change. The facility could be extended so that processes (or to be more accurate, their functions) can be defined in terms of their response and latching profiles, thus allowing this assumption to be relaxed.

This final stage of analysis also yields details of the system activity, in terms of the maximum number of process instances active at any time and the total quantity of data flowing within the system. If the requirement is to be implemented as a distributed system - as is almost certainly the case for reliability reasons - then these figures can be used early in the design to evaluate the processor power needed for any particular partition of the system and the bandwidth of the necessary data interconnections. Table 3.1 shows typical SPECK analysis output.

As well as these analytic packages, there is an associated simulation package /Quir83/. This simulator provides a user with the facility to put together a model of the system at a very early stage and demonstrate it running in simulated real-time. All the control and data flow is handled by the simulator; the user has only to provide code to implement the processes or subsystems making up his system. The level of detail in the simulation is determined by the complexity of this code. This has important uses. It allows a re-presentation of the system to the customer, so that he can see whether or not any important functional area has been completely overlooked. (It is not possible to detect such a complete missing area by analytic techniques.) If a complex algorithm is to be included in the system, it can be tested in the simulator in an environment close to its final real environment. Indeed, real recorded data could be input to simulator to test the real-time response of such an algorithm. If the system involves significant user interaction, then the user interface could be simulated to a great level of detail to assess its suitability. In principle, but not yet in practice, it is possible to simulate a system at a subsystem level until an 'interesting' event occurs, and then replace the high level subsystem by its more detailed system simulation to adduce further information about the system behaviour. All these aspects are dealt with more fully in chapter 6.

The simulator also make it possible to study the behaviour of systems whose processing pattern is not regular enough to permit analytic treatment. In this case, some of the clocks of the normal SPECK model are replaced by event generators. When the system is being simulated, a suitable scenario of events must be provided. Various sources are catered for, including on-line generation, pre-recorded data files and human intervention. By analysing the observed behaviour, some statistical measure of system load and performance can be derived, the accuracy of which depends on how closely the event scenario generated matches that of the real target environment.

Needless to say, the results obtained from the analytic sections of SPECK are inherently more reliable than those obtained statistically from the simulator. However, together they form a powerful combination and allow the consequences of timing constraints to be explored before a commitment to design is undertaken.

```
ANALYSIS PHASE 1
DATA CONSISTENCY CHECKS

THE FOLLOWING DATA INCONSISTENCIES HAVE BEEN DETECTED
CHANNEL NAME       MODULE DATA      CHANNEL DATA EXPECTED
SOURCE,  SINK,     EDATA, LDATA,      EDATA, LDATA
  STAT,  LRPD,       0,     0,          1,     0
MODULES WITH UNUSED OUTPUTS
                       T23

ANALYSIS PHASE 2
SYSTEM CONNECTIVITY CHECK

THE FOLLOWING MODULES FORM A DISCONNECTED SUBSYSTEM
MODULE NAME
        T22
        T21
        T23

ANALYSIS PHASE 3
SYNCHRONOUS LOOP DETERMINATION CHECK

THE FOLLOWING MODULES CONTAIN A SYNCHRONOUS LOOP
MODULE NAME
        T22
        T21

ANALYSIS PHASE 4A
ASYNCHRONOUS CHANNEL LOSS CALCULATIONS

CHANNEL SOURCE,  SINK, DATA LOSS
          T22,   T23,        1

ANALYSIS PHASE 4B
DATA REPETIION
THE FOLLOWING DATA CHANNELS REPEAT DATA ITEMS
SOURCE,  SINK, REPEATS
   T21,   T22,       1
  LRTM,   STAT,      1
  UDTM,   STAT,      1
  STAT,   CHNG,      2
  STAT,   LRTM,      1
  STAT,   UDTM,      1
   T22,   T23,       1


ANALYSIS PHASE 4C
CONCURRENT PROCESS DETERMINATION
THE FOLLOWING PROCESSES HAVE CONCURRENT INSTANCES
PROCESS, INSTANCES
   T23,         2

*
*SYSTEM CONTAINS EVENT-DRIVEN PROCESSES*
*ANALYSIS INCOMPLETE
*
```

Table 3.1   Typical SPECK analysis output.

3.1.3. Petri Nets

Although it is not yet possible to define formal primitive properties of the characteristic real-time features, there are two main aspects to be used for an informal description of a real-time system:

- One is that a real-time system is a stimulus-response (or cause-consequence) system of elements where time constraints exist besides the stimulus-response relations.
- The other is that such a system consists of a combination of events where several of them may occur in any order.

Even if such a system is partially ordered by the stimulus-response relations, it is not possible to define a total order in most cases. However, a specific execution will order it totally. It makes sense to distinguish between two classes of real-time systems:

- One class contains physical real-time systems as environments to the control systems or processes. In regard to their interactions with the processes or control systems it is desirable to describe the interesting real-time environment features in a formal way. In many cases, these features are given from outside and are unchangeable.
- The other class concerns the processes or control systems. As these are man-made, it is possible to alter their design.

There is a need to model the real-time environment features to get their relevant properties. Formalized models of real world systems allow several kinds of conclusions to be drawn. The results must, however, be checked against the real system, in order to validate them. Another need to model real-time systems comes from the necessity to describe real-time features in the software requirements definition phase. This is of interest under the following aspects:

- To show whether that model meets the environment's requirements,
- to check if the model is consistent and can be realized by at least one technical system,
- to determine subsystems which may run concurrently on distributed hardware to achieve optimal execution times.

The last point is related to concurrencies that are introduced by the design. This kind of concurrency is not an inherent system property.

It is desirable to use real-time models that have both good formal properties and are conveniently understandable. It turns out that the main difficulty in handling real-time systems arises from the unknown order of events that causes many problems in the field of resource allocation and, therewith, deadlocking. Although the timing problems are not trivial, they may be regarded as a subclass of the problem of the unknown event order, as will be outlined later. A number of formalisms exist for modelling the properties of real-time systems. The modelling systems may be ordered hierarchically by their modelling power as shown in fig. 3.1 (from Pete 81/).

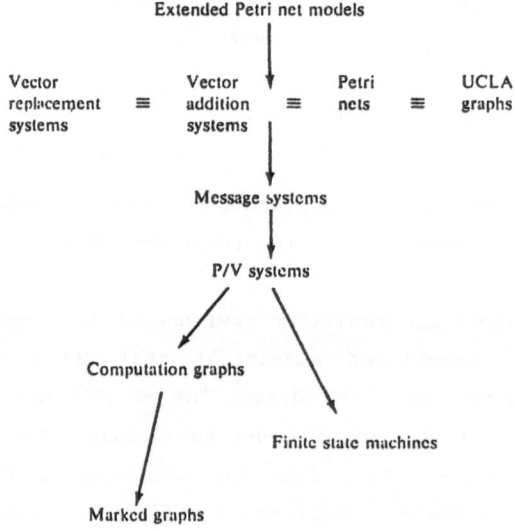

Fig. 3.1 The complete hierarchy of models of parallel computation
          (from Pete 81/).

Various examples exist for the different models showing their limitations, as e.g. the cigarette smokers problem for Dijkstra's P/V
systems /Parn75/, or the Kosaraju and Agerwala problem of a particular
producer-consumer system with priority restrictions for non-extended
Petri nets /Kosa73/.

Although all these models can be depicted by use of graphics, some of
them rely particularly on net models, including the UCLA system, Petri
nets, Computation graphs, Marked graphs and Finite state machines. All
these systems are either equivalent or subsystems of Petri nets, as
outlined in /Pete81/. From the engineers' point of view, a completely
self-explaining graphical representation is desirable. Petri nets are
very well intellegible even though simple Petri nets may hide a more
complicated formalism.

3.1.3.1   Modelling with Petri nets

The development of software subsystem requirements for real-time purposes contains the system's operating rules in terms of conditions and
events. These two primitive concepts, on the other hand, are also the
fundamentals of Petri nets.

The occurrences of events, i.e. actions in the system, depend on the
system state, which can be expressed as a set of conditions. The occurrence
of an event is enabled when certain conditions are fullfilled. These
conditions are called the preconditions of an event. As a result of the
occurrence of an event, certain other conditions will hold that are
called the postconditions.

In Petri nets, events are called transitions and are depicted as bars in
the Petri net graphs. The preconditions of an event are called its input
places and are depicted as circles in the graph, tied to the transition
by directed edges. The postconditions of an event are called its output
places, depicted by circles to each of which lead directed edges from
the transition as shown in fig. 3.2.

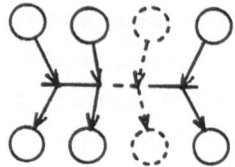

Fig. 3.2. A petri net transition and its input/output places

The petri net topology rules claim that a directed arc must connect a place to a transition or vice versa; a place with input and output edges represents an input condition as well as an output condition. The formal characterisation of a Petri net is given in /Pete 81/.

In the Petri net graph, a marking is a set of tokens depicted as dots which reside in the place. One or more tokens in a place mean that the represented conditions holds. The set of tokens in the place of the net defines its state; it is represented by the marking vector μ_i of the net. The occurrence of an event in a Petri net graph means that all input places of a transition must contain at least one token (i.e. all input conditions hold) and from each input place one token will be removed and to each output place one token will be added (i.e. all output conditions will become 'true'). The occurrence of an event is called a firing of a transition. A marking μ_1 will change into μ_{i+1} by firing a transition.

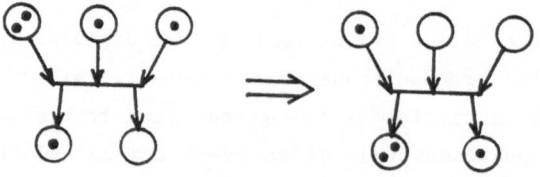

Fig. 3.3 Firing a transition

An important property of Petri nets is that there exists no inherent measure of time as the Petri nets deal with cause-consequence relations only[1], and firings take 'zero time'. By that definition, there is also no simultaneous firing.

Petri nets do have non-deterministic properties. Whenever the input conditions of several events hold in a particular state, the Petri net will not give any information on which event will occur next; in this case, the sequence of firing is not determined. Thus, the sequence of firings is not totally ordered but by a partial order.

All possible markings based on an initial marking are depicted in the reachability tree of a Petri net.

The introduction of fixed execution times into Petri nets (thus leaving the strict Petri net model) results in reachability trees that are always subtrees of the appropriate Petri net reachability trees.

The reachability tree is the basis for most of the Petri net analyses.

3.1.3.2   Analyses techniques for Petri nets

The main analysis tasks for Petri nets deal with the following items:

- Safeness, i.e. the maximal number of tokens per place does not exceed one for any firing sequence.

- k-boundedness, i.e. the maximal number of tokens per place does not exceed a finite number k for any firing sequence.

  These two properties are related to the problem fo finite number of resources and to queue bounds.

---

[1] Petri nets extended by time properties are described in /Ramc74, Sifa79/.

- Liveness. A Petri net is said to be live if each of its transitions is live; a transition is live if for any arbitrary marking there exists a firing sequence such that the transition will be enabled. There are several definitions of degraded liveness which are outlined in /Pete81/. This property is related to deadlock problems.

- Reachability. A marking μ' is reachable from a marking μ if there exists a firing sequence that goes from μ to μ'. This property is related to the question: Given a particular state of the net, is there a firing sequence to another particular state? The reachability relations of Petri nets are of crucial importance for the analysis of boundedness and liveness.

- Equivalence. Two Petri nets are said to be equivalent of they possess the same reachability tree. A dual definition exists for firing sequences. This topic is important when performing optimisation works.

An analysis method based on the topology of unmarked nets has recently found attention (e.g. in /AzBe80, Chez79/). It is based on the matrix view of Petri nets, and its aim is to show the existence of two invariants, one of which is the necessary but not sufficient condition of a net to be conservative, and the other os the necessary but not sufficient condition to be deadlock-free.

The base for classical Petri net analyses is the elaboration of the reachability tree. An algorithm for that purpose is given in /Pete81/. The reachability tree is the ordering structure of the net's states that are depicted by the marking vectors μ_1. The partial order mirrored by the reachability tree results from the stimulus-response relations.

As there is no inherent limit to the number of tokens residing in any place of a Petri net, it is obvious that reachability trees may become infinite. A finite representation, however, can be achieved by using the following notation. The symbol ω is allowed as a component in a marking vector which stands for a positive integer that can be made arbitrariliy large. Here, the reachability trees containing ω are called degenerate reachability trees. If a degenerate reachability tree is re-arranged so that all nodes of the same content are collapsed, a directed graph with forks, joints and loops results reflecting the overall behaviour of the underlying non-sequential system, having more than shallow similarities to the control flow graphs of sequential systems that are depicted by directed graphs as well. This is useful for the investigation of the properties of the degenerate reachability graph by using all of the well-known analysis techniques for sequential flow graphs, but will not solve all problems.

Problems will also occur similar to the infeasible path problem. A node for which a successor exists in the degenerate reachability graph topology may become a terminal node during dynamic execution. This makes an essential difference to sequential control flow graphs where a node with successor can never be a terminal node.

3.1.3.3   An example of modelling with Petri nets.

In order to get an impression of how systems may be modelled and analysed by use of Petri nets, a small example will be outlined in the following.

A system of two independent processes, one of which is a message-producer PR1 ('writer'), and the other a message-consumer PR2 ('reader'), use an independent, concurrent third process PR3 ('box') to co-ordinate the appropriate message handling. Fig. 3.4 shows the basic structure of the system.

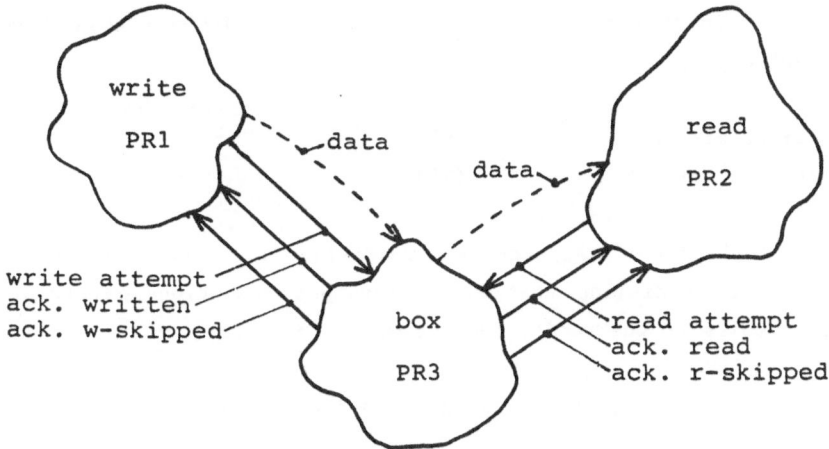

Fig. 3.4   An example system

The message itself and its transport is not considered. Although the process PR3 ('box') is passive, in the sense that it has to perform the desired tasks on request of PR1 of PR2 only, it is only the actions of this process which are of interest here.

In terms conditions (characterized by a leading 'C') and events (characterized by a leading 'E') that will happen if their preconditions hold, the following can be formulated concerning the process PR3 ('box'):

- Cread_attempt & Cfull → Eread   (1)
- Eread → Cempty & Cack_read   (2)
- Cwrite_attempt & Cempty → Ewrite   (3)
- Ewrite → Cfull & Cack_written   (4)

These expressions illustrate the basic actions of process PR3. Further, for all states it is claimed that Cempty is never true when Cfull holds and vice versa.

For the acknowledgement of unsuccessful write and read attempts, the following supplementary expressions have to be considered:

- Cread_attempt & Cempty →Eskip_read   (5)
- Eskip_read → Cack_r_skipped   (6a)
- Cwrite_attempt & Cfull → Eskip_write   (7)
- Eskip_write → Cack_w_skipped   (8a)

There are two input events that result in the conditions read-attempt and write-attempt:

- EI_1 → Cread_attempt   (9)
- EI_2 → Cwrite_attempt   (10)

The events read, write, skip-read and skip-write flow into corresponding acknowledgement conditions that are the output conditions representing the message going to the reader and the writer process:

Cack_written, Cack_read, Cack_w_skipped and Cack_r_skipped.

Because modelling by use of Petri nets influences the preconditions of an event, it is necessary to complete the expression 6a and 8a, as the conditions empty and full shall still hold after the occurence of the events skip_write and skip_read respectively:

-   Eskip_read → Cack_r_skipped & Cempty   (6)
-   Eskip_write → Cack_w_skipped & Cfull   (8)

It is not claimed that the above written relations give a complete formal description of the example, but they illustrate it well.

This sample has a total of six events and eight conditions, representing their preconditions and postconditions. Now the Petri net topology is set up corresponding to the expressions 1 to 10:

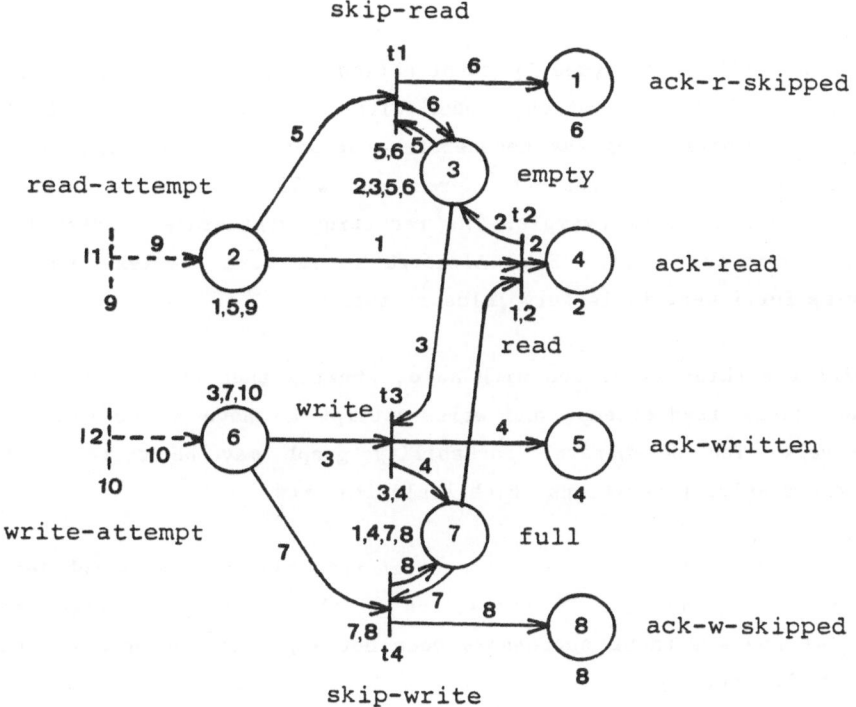

Fig. 3.5 The Petri net topology of the example.
          The numbers labelling the arcs, transitions and nodes refer
          to the description expressions in the description.

The numbers labelling the arcs, places and transitions give the expressions where the elements are used. Note that each place has as many numbers as arcs are connected to it, and that a transition has a pair of numbers, referring to the precondition- and postcondition expression, except for I_1 and I_2 that have no preconditions as they are the input links to the outside world.

To achieve better model properties, the dashed transitions I_1 and I_2 and the linked two arcs will be omitted. To preserve the cut-off properties in the remainder of the net, enough tokens must be put into the places read_attempt and write_attempt; enough in the sense that for the system's mission time there will be one token for every read_attempt and write_attempt respectively. This has the advantage that the four remaining transitions each have the same number of input-arcs as output-arcs; so, the net has the property of token-conservation: No tokens are ever produced or consumed within the net, i.e. the number of tokens in the net is constant.

Now the net will be analyzed by construction of the degenerate reachability tree. After elaboration, nodes with the same content will be merged, thus constructing the degenerate reachability graph. Instead of using the symbol ω, the correct expressions will be inserted which is easy to derive in this example. The resulting degenerate reachability graph is depicted in fig. 3.6. Although it is more complex than the underlying Petri net, it is very illustrative.

The initial marking is signed with an α, showing that the box is empty and the places read_attempt and write_attempt do have a and b tokens respectively. The degenerate reachability graph may be traversed by firing the enabled transitions which lable its arcs.

It is emphasized that the use of the degenerate reachability graph leads to a loss of information in comparison to the reachability tree; the absense of nodes without successors does not imply the absense of dead states of the net.

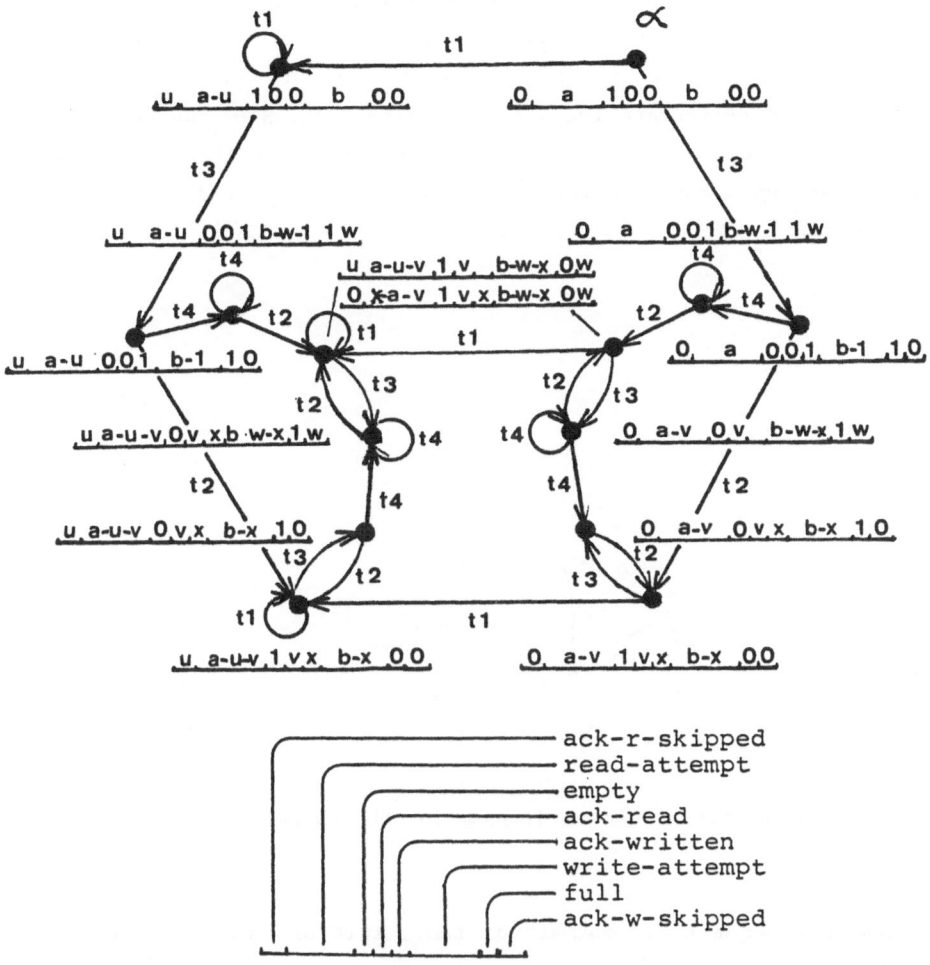

Fig. 3.6 The degenerate reachability graph of the example

From fig. 3.5 and fig. 3.6, it is obvious that the tokens of the places read_attempt and write_attempt migrate to the output places during the net's execution; if there is a finite number of tokens at the net's initialisation, only a finite number of firings may occur. When all of these tokens rached the output places, the net has reached a dead state. But as we claimed to have enough tokens for every read_attempt and write_attempt, this property is not relevant. Here, we refine the definition of liveness to the following: If a mission is defined by a certain finite number of firings, a system is said to be partially live in its mission if no dead state can occur for that number of firings.

With this definition the example is partially live in its mission, but
there exists a finite sequence of firings that leads to deadlock when the
tokens in the places read_attempt and write_attempt have expired. An
inspection of the degenerate reachability graph (fig. 3.6) show that the
sequences of possibel firings are less complex than it might be thought.
Fig. 3.7 shows the transition sequence diagram that is found to hold for
the example Petri net during its mission.

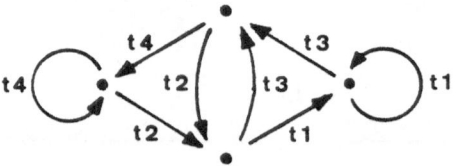

Fig. 3.7 The transition sequence diagram for the example.

The following gives a brief summary of the result of an analysis of the
example Petri net:

- The net is token-conservative; this is obvious form the net topology
  where for each transition the number of in-arcs equals the number of
  out-arcs.
- the net is (at least) k-bounded, where k is the sum
  $k = a+b+1$
  this follows from the initial number of tokens and the conservation.
  Furthermore, the place ack_read and ack_skipped are a-bounded, the
  places ack_written and ack_w_skipped are b-bounded, and the places
  empty and full are one-bounded or safe as can be seen from the degenerate reachability graph.
- The net is live for its mission, This results from the transition
  sequence diagram where each arc is in a loop containing the initia-
  lization point.

By the admission of multiple arcs in Petri nets, the given example of a queue process with one member only can easily be extended to a system with a deeper buffer, even if the degenerate reachability graph and the transition diagram will blow up. This is a general problem of analyzing Petri nets: even for simple nets there may a combinatorial explosion of the reachability tree.

3.1.3.4 Constructive design approaches

To keep the properties of sequential system simple, the technique of structured programming was introduced, and similar methods should be introduced for the design techniques of real-time systems.

To circumvent the previously mentioned problems of functional complexity, constructive approaches from the real-time software requirements definition phase on should enforce the rule: keep it simple. The synthesis of a system by use of easily analyzed components will lead to more transparent results. One approach to this goal is to start with a primitive net whit desired properties and to extend it by constructs preserving these properties. Some of these problems are discussed in /GeLa79/ for modified Petri nets, the so-called bipolar synchronization nets.

A simple but widely used class of concurrent processes results from certain constraints that are valid in many sequential systems, as listed below:

- A sequential process is divisible into sequential partial processes which do not interact mutually.

- The partial processes, once triggered simultaneously, will finish in finite time (or, in terms of Petri nets, after a finite sequence of firings).

- The whole process is terminated when all partial processes have ended.

- Before the termination of the whole process, its re-triggering is excluded.

So, the partial processes are incomparable as the sequence of their execution is meaningless, they are coherent in triggering and termination, and they are non-reentrant.

Although non-reentrancy in general is a simpler quality than reentrancy in computer systems, it is the opposite in Petri net modelling where the rejection or skip of tokens is difficult to model. The structuring of a system by determination of its incomparable, coherent, and non-reentrant components plays an important role for the distribution of tasks in distributed systems. Unfortunately, as non-reentrancy is a condition in this approach, it is only of limited benefit for general real-time-problems.

Whenever an item-consuming process has a lower consumption rate than the producing rate of the preceeding item-producing process, and no item shall be lost, there is a need of buffering. Every kind of buffer is a real-time memory, as its contents reflects a part of the system's history that may influence the next steps. Therefore, it is of importance to structure a real-time system into components of clear bounds that either represent reentrant or non-reentrant parts. Reentrant parts are difficult to understand and should be limited to minimal configurations. A simple example of such a structuring is shown in fig. 3.8.

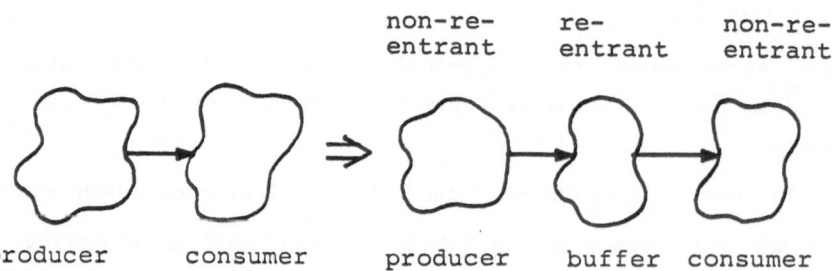

Fig. 3.8 Structuring a system in reentrant and non-reentrant parts.

The careful elaboration of this kind of structuring also prevents problems of unintended rejection of items. Every non-reentrant section my be replaced by a primitive subnet C_{ps}, consisting of an entry place, an exit place, and a transition in between. Its unique sequence is the firing of the transition as shown in fig. 3.9.

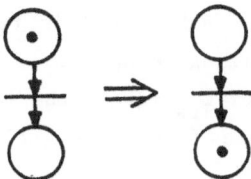

Fig. 3.9 A primitive subnet and its execution

Note that its non-reentrancy has to result from outside the subnet. To make non-reentrancy a subnet quality, it must be implemented separately, e.g. by use of a semaphore as shown in fig. 3.10.

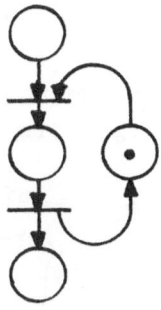

Fig. 3.10 The enforcing of non-reentrancy in Petri nets.

When initializing place 3 in fig. 3.10 by one token, the places 2 and 3 are safe (non-reentrant), but not the places 1 and 4, which have to be made either reentrant in their realisation or are safe by outside contraints in which case enforcing of non-reentrancy becomes meaningless.

A top-down design approach, for example, may start by structuring a system in reentrant and non-reentrant parts, the latter being modelled by primitive subnets. During the refinement process, every primitive subnet C_{ps} may be substituted by a subnet C_{rs} characterized by the following:

- Whenever the precondition of a subnet C_{rs} is true, its postcondition will be true after a finite firing sequence.
- The final marking of the subnet C_{rs} equals the initial marking, except for its entry- and exit-place (i.e. the real-time-memory is time-invariant).
- It must be initialized appropriately.

A subsequent substitution of C_{ps} or C_{rs} by C_{rs} - subnets results in a system having the same properties as listed above.
Note that it may happen that the property of safeness of the exit place will be lost during the refinement process. In general, this property may be achieved by use of buffers only. It is not a trivial task to model a buffer capable of absorbing every token from its input place by a Petri net construct as it is not possible to deduce a sequence of firings for several enabled transitions.
Finally, a rough draft of a refinement process by the successive replacement of subnets is shown in fig. 3.11.

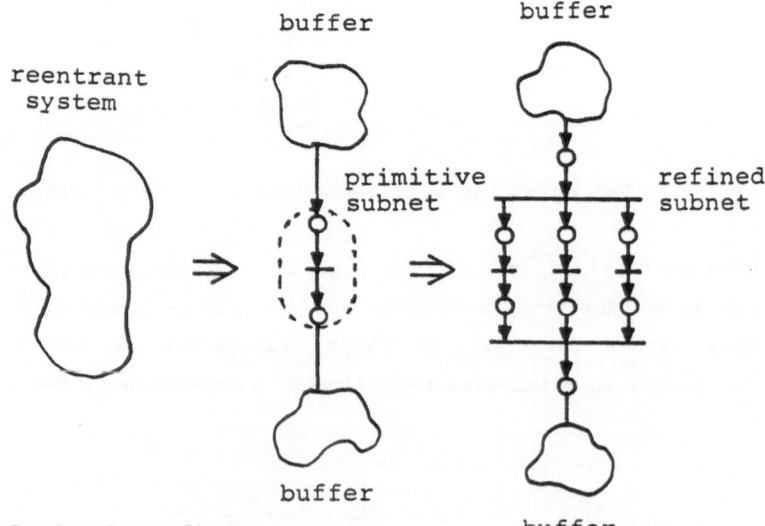

Fig. 3.11.   Draft of a refinement process

3.1.4   Other net models

There are several net models that are of the same or a lower modelling power as shown in fig. 3.1 and as the Petri net model is quite universal and found in many theoretical works, it is now accepted as a standard for real-time modelling. Recently, however, some alternative models have been introduced that are slightly different from Petri nets.

/YoGi80/ has suggested a net model as powerful as the Petri net model where the property of bipartiteness was eliminated. In this model, the tokens do not reside in the places but in the arcs of the net, and some branch and join node categories exist where tokens are either propagated to all out-arcs of a node (thus creating parallelism) or to one of the out-arcs as is usual in sequential systems.

Another model mentioned previously is the bipolar synchronisation graph model /GeLa79/ where tokens may have binary values 'busy' or 'not busy' and reside in the arcs as well. This allows a better control of the number of tokens, but changes their meaning. Fig. 3.12 shows an IF... THEN...ELSE construct of a bipolar synchronisation graph, where an alternative branch comes out with one token 'busy' for the branch to be performed and one token 'not busy' for the branch to be skipped.

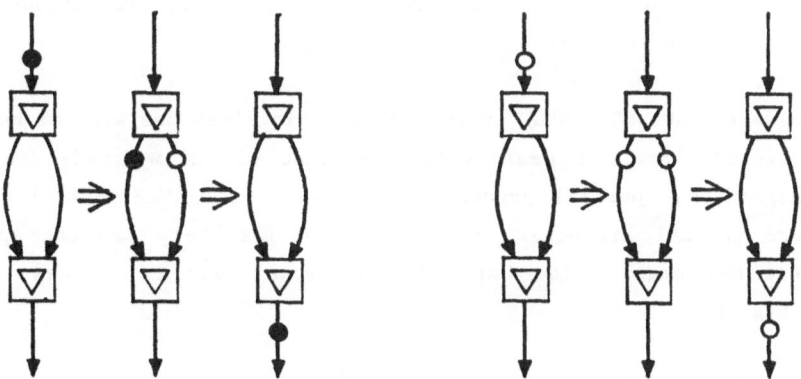

● busy
○ not busy

Fig. 3.12 An IF...THEN...ELSE construct in a bipolar synchronisation graph.

Subcategories of Petri net models were introduced that have restricted properties; an example is the original model of Petri in which a transition was enabled only for its postconditions not to hold (this can be seen as a feedback that does not exist in general Petri nets). This kind of model now is regarded as a subclass of general Petri nets with enforced safeness.

Liveness is decidable for some restricted class of net, but not for arbitrary Petri nets. It is strongly related to certain topological invariants, as outlined in /AzBe80/. Hack /Hack72/ showed this for free choice nets, where a free-choice net is one that does not contain the structure shown in fig. 3.13. Liveness is also decidable for bounded Petri nets. Another example is a net such that all transition are live for an initial marking, and the initial marking is reachable from every state. This is the case when in the transition sequence diagram at least one loop contains every transition.

Fig. 3.13 Non-permitted and permitted conflicting transitions in free-choice nets.

The well-known SREM/SREP system /Alfo77/ involves the kind of concurrency mentioned above. It deals with the class of incomparable coherent and non-reentrant partial process. Fig. 3.14 shows a SREM/SREP R-net detail where partial processes may execute in parallel, and the appropriate Petri net model. Also here, the non-reentrancy is defined by outside constraints.

The SARA software design system is partially based on the UCLA graph model /CaEs78/ that is also as powerful as the Petri net model (see fig. 3.1). Finally it should be mentioned that, in the author's opinion, the formalism of Petri net models is more or less equivalent to the formalism of other real-time models, but the way of representing a system's execution and the system's states is the most convenient from the engineers point of view. Petri nets and similar net models give an easily understandable impression of a systems basic functions, although the more refined properties have to be elaborated by a large amount of work.

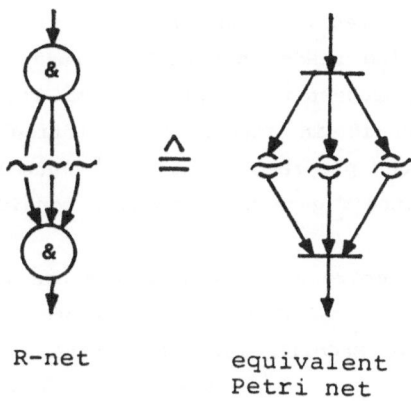

R-net   equivalent
                     Petri net

Fig. 3.14 R-net construction for a class of concurrent processes and its Petri net equivalent.

3.2 Proving Techniques

The idea behind program proving is that one can specify the task to be carried out by a program, or some properties of the results of a program. One can then implement the program. There should be some logical relationship between the program and its specification. This relationship is expressed by the semantic rules or axioms of the programming language statements. Given a program and a specification, it is possible to use the axioms to construct a proof. The reader should be warned at this point that, in practice, the proving process is rather complex. For one thing, obtaining a correct specification is in itself very difficult, and involves much interaction between the programmer and the eventual user of the program. Secondly, the proof itself generally requires considerable manual effort.

The method of proving correctness of programs has its origins deep in the history of computing. Some of the first proofs were carried out by von Neumann /Neum56/ and J. McCarthy /McCa60 , McAb62/, whose work on Lisp has proof as one of its goals. The ideas were first seriously proposed as a field of development by Floyd /Floy67/, but the main wellspring of the enormous amount of current research is a paper by Hoare /Hoar69/.

3.2.1 Hoare's approach to proving program correctness

The main idea underlying Hoare's techniques for proving program correctness is that after execution of any particular statement in a program, it is possible to make an assertion about the values of variables in the program. For example, after the statement

    x := 1

the following assertions could all be made

    x > 0

    x ≠ 0

    x = 1

In general, what is true after execution of a program statement will depend on what is true before execution. We can write

P {S} Q

This means that if P is true before execution of a program statement S, then Q will be true afterwards.

Hoare's axiom for assignment is very simple

P[x/E]   {x := E}   P

This means that if P is true after execution of the assignment, then P with every instance of x replaced by expression E must be true before the assignment. This axiom holds in general only if evaluation of E does not modify any variables (has no side effects). Also, x must be free in P.

The composition rule allows proofs about sequences of statements. It is

$$\frac{P \ \{S_1\} \ Q \ , \ Q \ \{S_2\} \ R}{P \ \{S_1 \ ; \ S_2\} \ R}$$

This reads

- if it can be shown that if P is true before execution of S_1 results in Q being true after execution of S_1, and if it can be shown that if Q is true before execution of S_2, then R is true after execution of S_2, then it can be deduced that if P is true before the execution of S_1 followed by S_2, then R is true after the execution.

Actually, the interpretation is more general than this, since deductions can be made both in the forward and backward direction.

Integers

A1 $\qquad$ $x + y = y + x$

A2 $\qquad$ $x * y = y * x$

A3 $\qquad$ $(x+y) + z = x + (y+z)$

A4 $\qquad$ $(x*y) * z = x * (y*z)$

A5 $\qquad$ $x * (y+z) = (x*y) + (x*z)$

A6 $\quad$ $y \leqslant x \Rightarrow (x-y) + y = x$

A7 $\qquad$ $x + 0 = x$

A8 $\qquad$ $x * 0 = 0$

A9 $\qquad$ $x * 1 = x$

Program Execution

DO $\quad$ $|-$ $\qquad$ $P_o \{x := f\} \ P$ $\qquad$ where $\qquad$ $P_o = P [x/f]$

D1 $\quad$ $|- P \{Q\} \ R$ $\quad$ and $\quad$ $|- R \Rightarrow S$ $\qquad$ then $\qquad$ $|- P \{Q\} \ S$

$\qquad$ $|- P \{Q\} \ R$ $\quad$ and $\quad$ $|- S \Rightarrow P$ $\qquad$ then $\qquad$ $|- S \{Q\} \ R$

D2 $\quad$ $|- P \{Q_1\} \ R_1$ and $\quad$ $|- R_1 \{Q_2\} \ R$ $\quad$ then $\qquad$ $|- P \{Q_1 ; Q_2\} \ R$

D3 $\quad$ $|- P \wedge B \{S\} \ P$ $\qquad\qquad\qquad$ then $\quad$ $|- P \{\text{while } B \text{ do } S\} \ \overline{B} \wedge P$

The symbol $|-$ means "it can be proved that".

Table 3.2 $\quad$ Hoare's basic axioms

The 'if then else rule' is

$$\frac{P \ \& \ B \ \{S_1\} \ Q \ , \ P \ \& \ \bar{B} \ \{S_2\} \ Q}{P \ \{IF \ B \ THEN \ S_1 \ ELSE \ S_2\} \ Q}$$

and for the while statement, the rule is

$$\frac{P \ \& \ B \ \{S\} \ P}{P \ \{WHILE \ B \ DO \ S\} \ P \ \& \ \bar{B}}$$

A complete set of rules is given in table 3.2. These deduction rules can be put together to construct an overall proof. Axioms of a similar flavour for other program constructs such as declarations, functions and goto statements can be found in later joint work with Clint /ClHo72/ and Wirth /HoWi73/.

The following example is taken from /Hoar69/.

The simple program for division by successive subtraction is

$$d := 0$$

$$r := x$$

while $\quad r \geqslant y$

do $\quad r := r-y \ ; \ d := d+1 \quad$ od.

The formal specification for this is

$$x \geqslant 0 \ \& \ y \geqslant 0 \ \{program\} \ d \cdot y + r = x \ \& \ 0 \leqslant r < y$$

The second assertion here expresses the definition of a division function. The first expresses the two conditions for the program to work.

The first assertion is termed a precondition, the second is termed a postcondition.

We begin the proof by considering the contents of the while loop.

$$(d+1) \cdot y+r = x \quad \{d := d+1\} \quad d \cdot y+r = x \ \& \ 0 \leqslant r < y \ \& \ 0 \leqslant r < y$$

Here, two of the post conditions turn out to be identical, and can therefore be amalgamated.

$$(d+1) \ y+r-y = x \quad \{r := r-y\} \quad (d+1) \ y+r = x \ \& \ 0 \leqslant r < y$$
$$\& \ 0 \leqslant r-y < y$$

These two statements are made using the assertion rule, and can be put together using the composition rule.

We can recognize the expression

$$y \geqslant 0 \ \& \ r \geqslant 0 \ \& \ (d+1) \ y+r-y = x \equiv d \cdot y+r = x \ \& \ r \geqslant 0 \ \& \ y \geqslant 0$$

as a candidate for the role of P in the proof rule for the while statement. It is a so-called loop invariant i.e. if $d \cdot y+r = x \ \& \ r \geqslant 0 \ \& \ y \geqslant 0$; true after an iteration of the loop, it was true before that iteration. The term $r \geqslant 0$ applies provided $y \geqslant 0$.

We can now apply the rule for while statements. If we write

$\bar{B} \equiv r < y$, so that $B \equiv r \geqslant y$, we have

$$y \geqslant 0 \ \& \ d \cdot y+r = x \ \& \ r \geqslant 0 \ \{while \ \ldots\} \ d \cdot y+r = x \ \& \ 0 \leqslant r < y$$

We now have only to prove the first term in this. Applying the assignment rule

$$y \geqslant 0 \ \& \ d \cdot y + r = x \ \& \ x \geqslant 0 \ \{r := x\} \ r \geqslant y \ \& \ d \cdot y + r = x \ \& \ r \geqslant 0$$

Applying the assignment rule again

$$y \geqslant 0 \ \& \ x = x \ \& \ x \geqslant 0 \ \{d := 0\} \ x \geqslant y \ \& \ d \cdot y + r = x \ \& \ x \geqslant 0$$

Applying the composition rule three times the proof is now complete.

Note that considerable logical manipulation was performed during the course of this proof. Strictly, we need a rule to allow this, the rule of consequence.

3.2.2 Proof of termination

Hoare's logical scheme can be used to show that programs satisfy a specification <u>provided that the program terminates</u>.

Dijkstra /Dijk75/ proposed the concept of 'weakest preconditions'. These are the weakest (most general) statements which will guarantee that a program both terminates and that the result will satisfy a given postcondition. This allows much stronger, so-called 'total' proofs to be made. This formulation of weakest precondition rules is oriented especially towards nondeterministic programs which make it rather specialized.

Yeh and Basu have given a version of weakest precondition rules appropriate to more conventional programming language constructs /YeBa75/. These formalisms allow the problems of termination to be stated explicitly as theorems to be proved. However, they do not in themselves solve the problems – they lead to theorems which involve sequences, existence relations or infinite series, and which often require induction arguments in their proofs.

3.2.3 Treatment of arrays

From the proof rule for assignment it will be obvious that the rule cannot be applied directly to arrays. Several approaches have been suggested to the treatment of arrays including Hoare, /Hoar72/ and Dijkstra /Dijk76/. Most ran into difficulties when general expressions are allowed as subscripts.

One of the neatest solutions to the problem is that suggested in much earlier work by McCarthy and Painter /McPa67/. That is, to treat any array as a complete object, and to treat assignments to an array element as an assignment to the array as a whole.

We introduce two functions which apply to arrays.

ACC is a function defined so that ACC(A,E) returns the Eth value of the array.

UPD is a function which returns as its value an array which is defined as follows:

UPD(A,E,V) is the array which is obtained by replacing the Eth value in A by V.

We have the following algebraic relation for UPD and ACC

ACC(UPD(A,E,V),E) = V

This axiom can be used in simplification of the complex formulae which can arise as preconditions in proving programs.

We then have the following Hoare style axioms

P[A/UPD(A,E,V)]   {A[E] = V} P

and

P[x/ACC(A,E)]   {x = A[E]} P

More recent discussions can be found in work by Reynolds /Reyn79/ and by Suzuki and Jefferson /SuJe80/.

3.2.4 Theorem proving in general

Use of the Hoare/Floyd approach to proving correctness of programs
(consistency with input/output specifications) requires a considerable
amount of theorem proving. Given a precondition for a given program
statement, it is possible to derive a postcondition, using the Hoare rules
more or less directly. However, the desired postcondition, needed to allow
the final program output condition to be proved, may have a completely
different form. The two chief problems are finding invariants for loops and
the simplification of long expressions. In order to perform the proofs,
help from automatic theorem proving programs is invaluable. The simplest of
such theorem provers are the expression simplifiers described later. These
reduce any theorem to be proved to a so-called 'canonical form', that is, a
single form which expresses in a unique way the theorem. If the theorem can
be proved, the canonical form has the value TRUE.

Such simplifier theorem provers are generally inadequate in ordinary program
proving, firstly because the canonical forms can be very bulky, and secondly
because the theorem itself is seldom a basis for generating its own proof.
Additional statements, or 'lemmas' are needed.

A typical advanced theorem prover takes a statement to be proved and negates
it. It then transforms the theorem logically into a number of 'cases', which
are the alternatives. Each such (negated) case must be proved false, if the
theorem is to be proved true.

London /Lond77/ describes a number of examples, including a rework of the
previous division program example demonstrating the use of such lemmas.
This article is also an excellent and realistic review of the whole area and
is a good further source of references and examples.

The deduction rule which is mostly (though not always) used in such programs
is resolution. This is a rule which generalises the simple implication rule
of logic. It will be illustrated here by an example.

Expressions are first transformed to disjunctive normal form, and sorted so
that negated terms come after positive terms,

e.g.

$$A \ \& \ B \ \& \ C \ \& \ \bar{X} \ \& \ \bar{Y} \ \& \ \bar{Z}$$

Another expression might be

$$X \ \& \ Y \ \& \ \bar{W} \ \& \ \bar{S}$$

These two expressions can be resolved, by eliminating the matching terms $X, \bar{X}, Y, \bar{Y}$ giving

$$A \ \& \ B \ \& \ C \ \& \ \bar{Z} \ \& \ \bar{W} \ \& \ \bar{S}$$

This kind of process will be repeated many times during the course of a proof, aiming always to make matches which shorten the expressions, and which ultimately reduce the value to false. The deduction process will be repeated for each case in the theorem to be proved.

The algorithms developed by Bledsoe /Bled74/ and Shostak /Shos77/ deals with Presburger arithmetic only /Pres29/, that is arithmetic with plus, minus and multiplication by a constant as its only arithmetic operations. Logical and inequality operators are also allowed. This turns out to be adequate for by far the majority of program proofs in practical real time programming. It is sufficient to treat assignments and IF statements in a standard way. It is insufficient for WHILE statements because of the difficulties of selecting or generating invariants - no algorithm exists which can do this.

Recent surveys and criiques of the Hoare approach can be found in the work of Apt /Apt81/ and O'Donnell /ODon82/.

3.2.5 Proving timing properties

The method of Hoare can be extended to deal with real time programs. One of the early attempts at this was proofs about a very small operating system by Taylor /Tayl74/. The principle here was to use the Hoare axioms as 'predicate transformers' to make deductions through the structure of a program. The other principal step was to introduce temporal logic into the predicates. These then took the form

$$P_t \quad \{S\} \quad P_t'.$$

Proofs of program properties could be carried through using this system, but the problems of complexity arising from the combination of the program code complexity, the use of parallelism, and the considerations of timing, make the effort impracticable without the aid of support tools and a multilevel approach. Temporal logic is being increasingly used: see, for example, the work of Bochmann /Boch82/ and Schwart, Melliar-Smith & Vogt /ScMe83/.

3.2..6 Proofs of parallel programs

Gilbert and Chandler /GiCh72/ describe a finite state machine approach to investigating parallel programs. Code is divided into 'sections'. These are pieces of code between process interactions. The 'state' of a process describes which section the process currently is in. The state of a set of processes is described by the state of each process, and by the value of variables addressed by the processes. The possible states of the system are described implicitly by rules of the form

$$(p_1, p_2, \ldots, p_n) \quad (v_1, v_2, \ldots, v_m)$$

$$\Rightarrow (p_1', p_2', \ldots, p_n') \quad (v_1', v_2', \ldots, v_m')$$

where the p's are process sections and the v's are the variables.

Given a set of rules of this kind, it is possible to trace state maps, which describe all of the state transitions which the system can make.

If a set of 'forbidden states' for a system can be found E, then it is possible to formulate

$$E \cap \text{Reachable } (T, S_o) = \emptyset$$

as a correctness condition for programs.

Reachable(T, S_0) is the set of program states which can be reached from the initial program state. It is defined by

$$\text{Reachable } (T, S_0) = \{S_t \; Q \mid S_0 \Rightarrow^* S\}$$

where Q is the set of possible states of the set of processes and $\Rightarrow^*$ is defined by

$$S \Rightarrow^* S' \equiv S \Rightarrow S' \quad \text{or} \quad S \Rightarrow S'' \quad \text{and} \quad S'' \Rightarrow^* S'$$

This is a simple formalism, but to apply it to any practical system involves an enormous amount of work. In practice, partial state transition rules are used

$$(- - - P_1 - -)(- - - V_j - - -)$$
$$\Rightarrow (- - - P_i' - -)(- - - V_j' - - -)$$

where the hyphens in the rules mean 'don't care'.

To derive the state map, different rules for elaborating partial state transition rules can be made, e.g.

No simultaneous "activity"

1. Fill out partial rules with all possible combinations of other process states in initial state, and copy these values across to the final state of the rule.

alternatively

deterministic simultaneous activity

2. combine rules pairwise, triplewise, etc. (so that two or more states change simultaneously), but avoiding pairs which change the same variable simultaneously. Fill out these rules with all possible combinations of states in the don't care positions and add these in.

non—deterministic
simultaneous
activity

3. As for Case 2 but where the same data values are changed by two partial rules, include two new sets of rules with both possible target values of the data.

The various rules lead to different degrees of complexity in the state maps. In practice such state analyses can become enormous, and techniques such as this one are only really applicable to some aspect of a parallel program system rather than to a complete system.

These rules are interesting in a wider context than the work of Gilbert and Chandler, since they express some of the fundamental characteristics of interrupts and parallel systems. It is those very characteristics which so complicate the proof of parallel programs. For example, rule 3 expresses true multiprocessor parallelism with no synchronisation between the processors.

An alternative method using a variant of interpreted Petri nets has been suggested by Keller /Kell76/. These follow normal Petri net conventions except that each transition is associated with both a program action and an algebraic condition, and the transition can only fire when the condition is satisfied. This representation models many aspects of parallel programs. Keller shows how to implement semaphore operations in his system and how to prove the implementation correct.

Owicki and Gries extended Hoare's axiomatic approach to parallel programs in two papers /Owgr76a/ and /Owgr76b/, and gave a number of examples. They provide two parallel program statement types.

cobegin $S_1 // S_2 // \ --- \ // S_n$ coend

await B then S

The axiomatic definitions are

$$P \,\&\, B \,[S] \,Q \,\mid- \; P \,\{\underline{\text{await}} \; B \; \underline{\text{then}} \; S\} \; Q$$

and

$$P_1 \,\{S_1\} \,Q_1 \;, \; P_2 \,\{S_2\} \,Q_2 \;,\ldots, \; P_n \,\{S_n\} \,Q_n \;, \; S_1 \,\ldots\, S_n$$
$$\text{are interference free}$$

$$\mid- P_1 \,\&\, P_2 \,\&\, \ldots \,P_n \,\{\underline{\text{cobegin}} \; S_1//S_2// \; \ldots \; //S_n \; \text{coend}\} \; Q_q \,\&\, Q_2 \,\&\, \ldots \,Q_n$$

Interference free means here that each parallel statement S_j does not disturb the conditions which are required in the proofs about all the other S_K.   This can be stated more precisely.

Given a proof P {S} Q and another statement T with precondition R, then T does not interfere with R <u>if</u>

a) $\mid- Q \,\&\, R \,\{T\} \,Q$

b)   let S' be a statement within S, but not within an <u>await</u>.   Then

$$\mid- (S') \,\&\, R \,\{T\} \,S'$$

The extension of this to a set of statements is straightforward.

In most formulations of this kind of problem, such interference between programs arises through access to shared variables.

Compared with the earlier two methods, this axiomatic approach makes more use of manual organisation of proofs, and much less use of state tracing. As such it can potentially treat much larger systems, but the need to prove non-interference means that software must be very well structured to keep the proof work to a minimum. There are good grounds for making use of syntactic devices, such as the concept of data classes or monitors, to limit the amount of program text with access to shared variables.

There are a large number of other concurrent program—proving formalisms which have been used largely for small experimental demonstrations, or as exercises in developing the theory. They can be divided into two groups, those which trace states in a system explicitly, and make induction proofs about state traces; and those which use axiomatic approaches with predicates describing states at specific points in programs (rather than in state graphs).

Recently there has been an extension by Hoare and his colleagues /Hoar78/ to Communicating Sequential Processes /Hoar78/. These are particularly appropriate for dealing with distributed program systems which send messages to each other via communication channels. The theory is an axiomatic one which allows proofs to be built up gradually based on program text, rather than on full program structure.

3.2.7 Practical application of the techniques

By far the major part of work on proving program correctness has been academic in orientation, and, more recently, in applications requiring verified secure operating system kernels /Mill76/ & /Mill49b/. This is even more true of real time systems. What practical work has been done has to a large extent been classified. One published exception is the verification of the SIFT fault tolerant flight control system /MeSc82/. The work on the Tapiro reactor shutdown system /BoAg79a/,/BoAg79b/, /TaBo77/ is closely related to proof.

Systems to assist in proving have been constructed which have been the subject of thorough experimentation.

Gypsy   U. of Texas /Good82/, /GoCo79/

HDM/SPECIAL   SRI International /RoRo77/

FDM/Ina Jo   Systems Development Corp. /Gerh80/, /Muss80/

AFFIRM   U. of Southern California /SuTh82/

These have been especially used for demonstrating security properties of software for military and intelligence purposes.

100

3.3 Fault tree analysis

Fault tree analysis is a technique which was developed during the 1960's for hardware failure analysis. It is one of the most widely used techniques for hazard identification in risk analysis of complex systems. It can take many forms and involve many different kinds of reasoning /Tayl79/. The most relevant of these for software analysis is the form in which disturbances are traced in process plant components.

For use with software correctness investigations, formalised and preferably automated analysis techniques are preferred, because of the large amount of work involved in thoroughly examining even reasonably small computer programs.

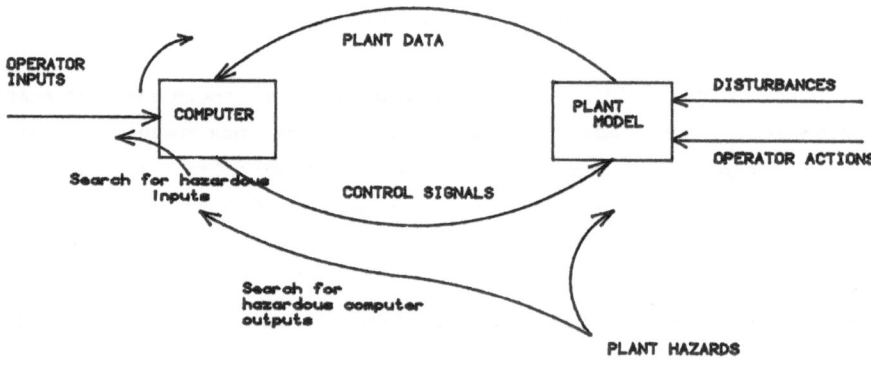

Fig. 3.15 Combined fault tree analysis for plant and computer programs

The overall process of analysis is shown in fig. 3.15. Plant hazards are identified by use of various (well developed) heuristic techniques. Conventional fault tree techniques are used within the plant structure to identify potential erroneous operator actions, component failures and process disturbances, which could cause the hazards. Software fault tree analysis is used to identify potential causes of hazardous computer outputs. Note that a plant hazard may well arise as a result of a combination of program errors and plant disturbances or operator errors. Fault tree notation provides an ideal method of representing such combinations (fig. 3.16).

Automated fault tree analysis of process plant makes use of plant component models which are very much like predicate transformers used in program proving or path testing. Each component is described by means of a set of statements, termed fault tree fragments, of the form:

"if x occurs at the input to a component, and if the state of the component is Y then x' will occur at the output of the component, and the new component state will be Y'."

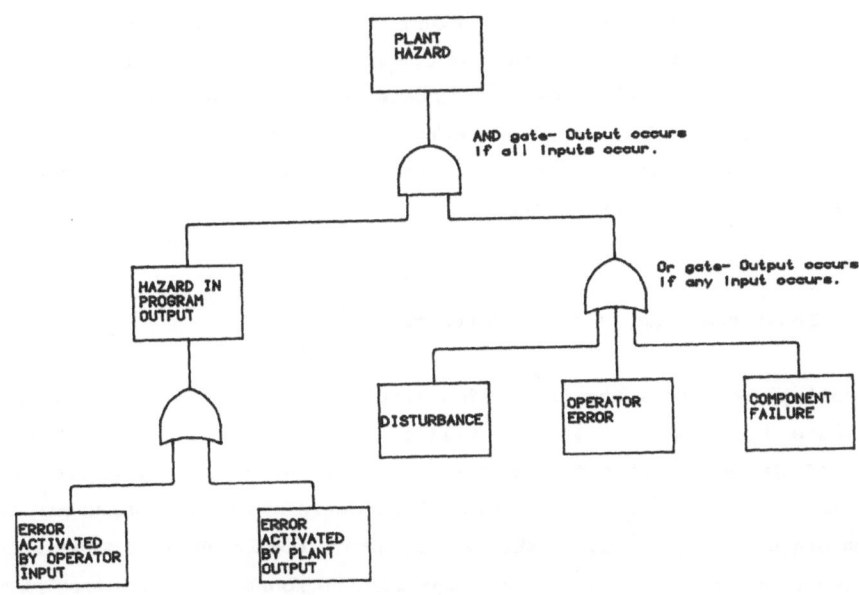

Fig. 3.16 An example of a fault tree, summarising some possible plant hazard combinations

In building up a fault tree a "top event" is chosen within a component, generally some undesired event, such as an explosion or crash. This event is matched to output events of mini-fault trees for the component, and any matching mini-fault trees are added to the overall fault tree for the system. If there are several matching mini-fault trees, they are connected into the overall fault tree via an OR gate.

Each match indicates a "first level" cause of the top event, as either an input event or internal state change event X within the component. Having found an initial match, causes of this event are then sought. If X is an internal state change event, mini-fault trees with X as a resulting event are sought for. If X is an input event, mini-fault trees providing a cause for X are sought in the components connected to that in which X occurs.

This process is iterated, building up chains of events backwards in time. The chains branch via an AND gate whenever both an event X and a state Y are required for an event X' to occur. The chains branch via an OR gate whenever there are two or more potential ways in which an event X occurs (fig. 3.16). The process of building up an event chain terminates when either a "spontaneous" event is found (that is one for which no specific further cause is defined), or a "normal" event or state is found, that is one which will occur frequently during normal operation of a plant. The process of building up the fault tree terminates when all event chains have been terminated with "normal" or "spontaneous events".

3.3.1 Fault tree analysis for software

The analogy between state transition functions for hardware components and predicate transformers can be utilised in building up fault trees for combined hardware and software systems. In building up the trees, some unwanted event is identified within the hardware and event chains are traced which can cause this event. When a "computer" component is reached, events at the output registers of the computer will be found. The "causes" of these are register manipulation statements within the software.

Chains of "events" within the software are then sought by tracing changes in program variables from statement to statement using a predicate transformer technique, until program inputs are found which are necessary for the particular event chain. The chains can then be extended once again to hardware, seeking the potential causes of the program input events found.

The mini-fault tree notation can be applied to individual program statements, allowing a uniform process of hardware/software fault tree construction. For each statement a set of mini-fault trees is generated according to the schemes shown in fig. 3.17. These are a modified form of weakest precondition predicate transformers used elsewhere in proving program correctness /Yeh77/.

The "events" in the program mini-fault trees are statements of the form:

"at time t, predicate P becomes true of the program variables"

There are corresponding fault trees for other program structures.

Note that the form of fault tree for IF and WHILE statements provides an OR branch for each direction of branching through the statement. This ensures that all paths through a program will be treated as different branches of the fault tree. This has the advantage of ensuring greater understandability, and of keeping individual predicates relatively simple. It has the disadvantage of producing very large trees in many cases. For this reason it has been found advisable to insist on quite severe structuring rules for programs to be used with this technique:- "Separate (possibly parallel) programs should be provided for each separate control or safety function within a computer system". This rule ensures at least that the program paths followed are relevant to the analyst's safety problem. An alternative formulation of the structuring criterion can be applied systematically:- "If there are two program outputs X and Y for which the values are functions of sets of inputs $I(X)$ and $I(Y)$, then if $I(X) \cap I(Y)$ is empty, programs producing outputs X and Y should be disjoint".

Various constructs for concurrent programs can be constructed in a similarly natural way. While the OR gate used in fault trees represents the alternative paths through a sequential program, an AND gate can represent parallel paths, in which processes must come together to create the conditions for an error.

104

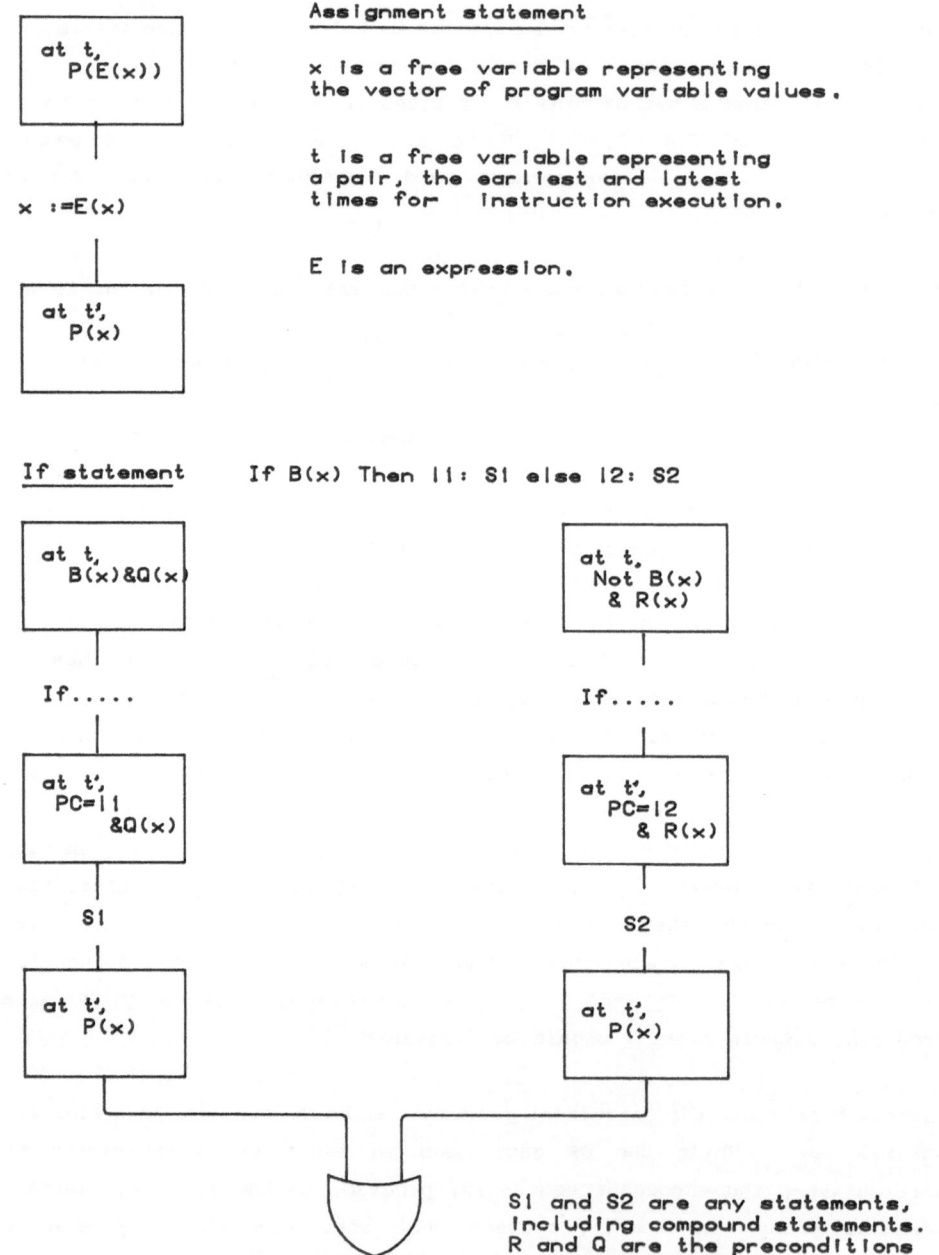

Fig 3.17   Mini-fault trees for basic program statements

WHILE statement

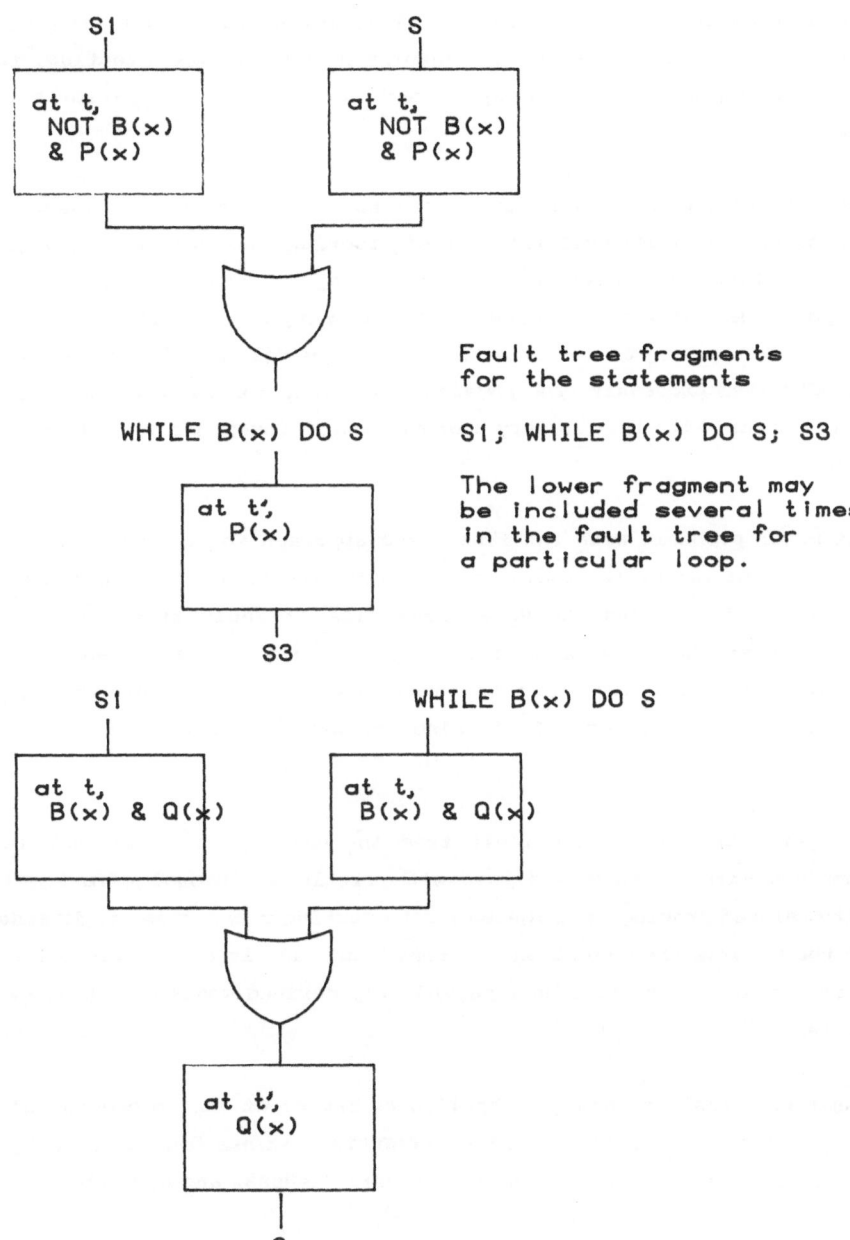

Fault tree fragments
for the statements

S1; WHILE B(x) DO S; S3

The lower fragment may
be included several times
in the fault tree for
a particular loop.

Fig. 3.17 Continued

3.3.2 Features of the approach

The problem of finding an unequivocal decision about which program outputs
are "correct", which limits the usefulness of path domain testing, is solved
with this approach by referring to the 'correct' or 'safe' performance of the
plant model.

Problems of specification errors are to a large extent avoided with this
approach. No formal specification of program requirements need be made, and
the "testing" is independent of the program specification.   The plant
component models used are drawn from a library of standard models which are
tested over a long series of analyses. The models are derived by means of a
standardised procedure from physical equations for the components /Bolo77/.
In other words the test is very thorough and is independent of the programming
process.

The major problems with the fault tree approach to software validation are
the need for inductive proofs for programs with loops (these must be provided
by the analyst), and the very large size of fault trees formed.   It is
doubtful whether any practical program could be validated as a whole.
Rather, it seems necessary to break down programs hierarchically, into
subroutines or modules. It is also not trivial to identify all dangerous
system outputs.

A major advantage of the fault tree analysis approach is that it can be
combined with hardware analysis with little additional effort.   Compared
with related proving techniques or path testing techniques, it is independent
of the program specification process. Instead, it has as its reference for
correctness of a program an independently derived model of the hardware of a
system.

Fault tree analysis has been applied by Taylor et al. to sequential control
programs for a distillation plant /TaJu82/. It has been applied by Leveson
et al. to satelite control system software /LeHa83/ and by Goldberg /Gold84/.

3.4   Review techniques

Review techniques aim at the analysis of different documents at different stages of the development life cycle, including development personel as well as independent teams. They can be regarded as human testing techniques in contrast to computer based testing techniques. The earliest used method probably was the desk checking, where the programmer himself took his program and ran through it by reading before testing it with the computer. The peer review technique is related to the desk checking. Both are rather informal methods. From these traditional manual methods some new methods were developed which are based on more formal procedures.

Two main methods will be described here; the inspection method /Faga76/ and the walk-through /AdBr82/ & /Myer79/. These can be distinguished from each other by the initiative team, an independent team, in the first case and the development team in the second case. Both techniques can be applied in the different phases of the development life cycle with slightly different emphasis.

These techniques will first be described separately in the following subsections. Then a comparison is made and some more information on the application of these methods and their support by tools is given.

3.4.1   Inspection method

In the inspection method the developer gives his product to a third party, which is doing the inspection. The inspection is made in a joint session, where the development team and the inspection team are going through the documents together. The documents are given to the participants prior to the meeting in order to allow a preparation of the session.

The design inspection, eg, includes a close look at the design documents, a check of their completeness and consistency and a comparison of the design with the requirements specification.

During the code inspection, a thorough review of the program code is undertaken: the inspection team checks the code for errors, in case of existing programming guidelines checks the observance of these rules, reviews the related documentation, and again compares the program with its specification.

Code inspection is sometimes also called code audit.

Although the inspection is done by a third party, the development team is also partially involved. Questions of the inspection team have to be answered, and additional information and documentation has to be provided.

3.4.2   Walk-through

In contrast to the inspection method the development team is still the active party during walk-through: in a meeting of the developer with a third party the developer explains his design or program code telling why he has chosen this design and why he programmed the problem in this particular way.

The other members of the walk-through meeting take a critical view to the presentation, can raise questions, and ask for additional information. As in the inspection the relevant documents are handed out to the participants prior to the meeting.

Walk-through is a kind of manual simulation of the program. Besides explaining the program the programmer chooses test data with which the program is executed. The resulting variable values and program states are manually written down on paper in order to keep track.

3.4.3   Comparison

Both techniques, walk-through and inspection, try to aid in the detection of errors or overlooks by applying the diversity approach.

In the inspection technique different people are looking at the problem and trying to find a solution. Although for the inspection there is already a solution present, the inspection team has to look at this solution rather critically, not believing everything at once, but questioning the correctness.

The walk-through is not quite that much a diversity approach. But still there is a high error detection capability due to two factors:

- during verbal explanation of a problem and its solution errors of different kinds are detected by the explainer himself, eg changes not completed, misunderstandings, missing cases.

- the listener applies a different thought scheme than the explainer and can detect misinterpretations or errors in the development.

The inspection method is more formalised and organised than the walk-through. Because in the walk-through the developer has control and actually only minor rules to apply, it is strongly influenced by· him. For the inspection detailed checklists exist and the moderator of the session has to follow strict rules conducting the meetings.

Since both techniques have a very similar behavior, there seems no reason to apply both of them in one project. Which one to use depends partly also on the people available. If there are people for review who have a good knowledge of the problem or system, and also of the applied techniques and languages for the solution, the use of the inspection technique seems more appropriate than the use of the walk-through.

In contrast if the available review team is aware of error areas, but not very firm in the problem and/or the languages, the walk-through technique should be applied. Here the reviewer is more in a passive role and can concentrate more on real problem areas instead of learning all about the environment.

Fagan /Faga76/ describes an experiment where inspections techniques and walk-throughs were used. Inspections were found to be superior to walk-throughs: 38% fewer errors were left in the inspected programs than in the programs where walk-throughs were applied.

3.4.4 Tools

The objective of the methods described here is the involvement of different people. The usage of tools is therefore only of secondary order. Nevertheless the use of tools is allowed and can be helpful. During the review process, analysis tools can do the information collection part of the work more accurately and systematically than people probably can do. But people still have to use the results of the tools and do the more important part themselves.

Useful information for the above mentioned techniques are

- program listing showing the nested structure of the statements
- control flow graph
- data flow graph
- definitions of the variables etc.
- i/o-interfaces (read and write statements)
- cross reference listing on module and system level
- module call hierarchy (system structure)
- module interfaces (parameters, global variables)

This information can be generated by pretty printers, compilers, analysis tools etc.

3.4.5   Effort and effectiveness

The effort necessary for these methods should not be underestimated.
Normally a review session should last for not longer than two hours.
Within this time period a program of about 300 statements can be
reviewed.   Additional time has to be allocated for the preparation of
the meeting.

But related to this, the error detection rate has to be considered.
Depending on the project, 30-80% of the errors detected during the
complete testing phase by different techniques were revealed by a
review technique like inspection or walk-through /Myer78/ & /Myer79/.

The actual time spent for detecting errors is often larger than would
have been during testing (not counting the computer time), but the
involved costs can be considered as being lower due to the following
reasons:

- Not only the error symptom, but also the error location is most
  often found directly. During computer based testing first only
  the wrong or missing output is recognised without hints to the
  location of the error. Debugging, although formally not part of
  the review process, is already partially done during the review
  session (but error correction has to take place separately).

- During testing one error at a time is detected, while in a review
  session a collection of errors is found.

- The probability of introducing new errors during the error
  removal process is lower since the stress of correcting the
  documents or programs is lower. No computer is waiting for the
  next test run.

Although it can not be guaranteed that a certain kind of errors will
be detected completely by applying the above mentioned techniques, the
detection of some errors is more probable than of other errors. The
following errors and problem areas are most likely to be detected
during inspection or walk-through:

- overlooked time constraints
- communication errors
- synchronisation errors and errors with resource competition
- deadlocks
- interrupt related errors
- errors regarding reentrancy
- incorrect history dependence.

Therefore the review techniques, in particular the inspection technique and the walk-through technique, should be used for early error detection during the development process. Their error detection capability compared with the necessary effort to use them should demonstrate the usefulness. But which of these techniques should be applied and to what extent has to be decided depending on the project.

3.5   Conclusions

Simple techniques for data and control flow analysis are well developed, and have reached the stage of industrial use. The main obstacles are ones of easy availability /Oste82/. They are valuable in removing some specific classes of programming error.

The SPECK type techniques for timing analysis of protection systems have been shown to work for systems of practical size. Their main limitation is the suitability of representation, which apparently restricts use to message passing and signal passing systems. Sharing of resources is not covered by the techniques. The main thrust of new work in this area is to develop better methods for stating performance specifications.

Petri net techniques can be used for analysis deadlock, termination, and some contention properties of programs. This will allow some kinds of errors to be detected, but does not provide a complete check even of specifically real time errors.

The main practical difficulty in applying Petri net techniques is the size of systems which can be treated. Computationally, this is limited at present to system with just a few process interactions. Results are especially needed for analytical treatment of Petri nets. These will presumably arise by restricting the class of structures which can arise in the nets, since several negative results are known for general nets.

Program proving is in its early stages as yet - most of the practical work has been done in USA - and costs and difficulty are high. Heuristic techniques for developing induction proofs for loops are promising, but require further work before they can be used conveniently.

One possibility which arose during the course of this study was of providing specific types of loop in programming language, each of which followed a specific axiomatic pattern, such as a FORALL statement for treating all elements of an array. Many practical problems could be solved with such languages, without introducing the problems associated with general WHILE statements.

At present, proving is limited to programs with a few hundred to a thousand lines of code.

Fault tree analysis is related closely to proving. The fault tree format helps in organising details of proofs, especially in real time systems. The advantage is in maintaining an overview. The heuristic of restricting the analysis to 'dangerous' computer outputs allows much larger systems to be treated in practice (in those cases where such a heuristic can be applied). Software fault tree analysis can be integrated with process plant fault tree analysis. As a result, the problems of providing a formal specification is avoided. It is replaced by a problem of plant modelling and plant hazard analysis.

Inspection is a necessary part of any program development - it is one of the most effective techniques of removing errors. There is need for documentation of the effectiveness of specific types of checks and inspection practice, and for investigating effectiveness in solving real time problems.

For very high reliability systems and safety systems, it has the drawback that it is unable to remove all errors - a maximum of 90% of errors has been found for the best techniques.

4 Systematic Testing

U. Voges and J. R. Taylor

This chapter deals with different techniques which can be applied for testing the final program in a systematic manner. Systematic does not relate to the combination of methods, but refers to each single method. It is mainly in contrast to probabilistic testing.

The common goal of these techniques is that the freedom from errors shall be demonstrated and that at least some feeling, maybe even figures, for the reliability of the program can be achieved.

The chapter will describe some methods which use information from within the program and some which are based only on external information. The different approaches for generating test data will be explained. Finally some comparison and evaluation of the described methods will be made.

4.1   Practical aspects of testing real time programs

Testing real time programs is an especially difficult task. Testing any program thoroughly requires a large number of input data combinations. If there are several programs operating in parallel, then the relative sequence of the inputs for each program normally is significant and should be tested.

Furthermore, unless some fairly precise conditions are fulfilled, as described below, not only the relative sequence, but also the precise timing of inputs can be significant. This occurs when synchronizing between various parts of a program is not carried out properly (design error or coding error). It also occurs when delays and clock timing pulses are used within the computer in order to synchronize with physical processes in peripheral equipment such as disc drives and tapes, or in the environment being controlled.

Real time software can be tested initially in the normal fashion, as sequential program software can. However this very quickly becomes inadequate if the real time aspects of the programs are to be tested. For multiterminal systems, in which the only inputs are from terminals, testing can be carried out using the actual terminals themselves and a 'script' to be followed by the testers, one at each terminal. When performing this kind of testing, instrumentation software which records incoming and outgoing messages is necessary. For test support, instruction execution registers or wrap around log registers in the computer are required. These can tell just what has been happening in the few machine cycles up to the point at which some failure occurs.

For most such systems, if extensive testing is performed, it is advisable to have equipment which can monitor and record signals on communication lines.

The system of using 'scripts' to be followed by a number of testers becomes cumbersome for large systems. The testers need to be in voice communication, and have a leader who controls the sequence. It is impossible in practice to control the timing of inputs in this way. The timing can be supervised only in a macroscopic way, but not in a microscopic way, e. g. machine instruction level or even finer.

For serious testing of large systems, a test generator/executor is needed which can provide inputs to the computer system to be tested. The needs are very similar to those for automatic test equipment (ATE) which is in use for hardware /BrFr76/. The ability to generate messages, communication protocols, and analogue signals are desirable. Also the ability to record both inputs and outputs.

Generation of test sequences to be used with such testing equipment is something of an art. Input sequences for single sequential programs can be generated straight-forwardly using the techniques described earlier.

Given a sequential program test, this might consist of inputs

1   OPEN VALVE A
2   READ PRESSURE P
3   CLOSE VALVE C

Given another program, another test might be

4   OPEN VALVE X
5   ADJUST REGULATOR 4

If the programs run in parallel and interact then a thorough test would involve the following sequences:

```
1 - 2 - 3 - 4 - 5
1 - 2 - 4 - 3 - 5
1 - 2 - 4 - 5 - 3
1 - 4 - 2 - 3 - 5
1 - 4 - 2 - 5 - 3
1 - 4 - 5 - 2 - 3
4 - 1 - 2 - 3 - 5
4 - 1 - 2 - 5 - 3
4 - 1 - 5 - 2 - 3
4 - 5 - 1 - 2 - 3
```

To test all such permutations of inputs is possible for such simple cases only. An algorithm to generate such test sequences is fairly simple. However the sheer volume of such tests prevents this approach being used in practice for large systems.

A heuristic method which limits the number of permutations tested is to examine the resources and interactions between programs activated. Permutations of just those inputs which activate interactions result in less voluminous test sets.

In general, the tests should be applied with varying time delays between inputs, particularly if programs use clock or delay statements. Design conditions can be applied which eliminate the need for varying timing during testing or at least minimize the necessary timing tests.

Van Horn /Horn68/ suggested three program design criteria for easy debugging and testing of real time software:

> IR   Input recordability
> IS   Input specifiability
> ARO   Asynchronous reproducibility of output.

The first two criteria are implicitly satisfied if the automatic test methods described above are used.

The last criterion, ARO, means that for any given set of input data, the same output is produced, irrespective of the speed of different processes in the system or the time intervals at which inputs are delivered.

While the ARO criterion is a good design goal, it cannot always be achieved for real-time systems. These may have to deliver signals within a given deadline, and may have to maintain time synchronisation with a physical process.

Even if the criterion is in principle achievable, it is doubtful whether any actual system, including its errors, will satisfy the criterion. Nevertheless, even partial achievement means that the task of testing is simplified.

In order to achieve the ARO requirement, parallel programs should work in terms of FORK and JOIN (or equivalent) primitives. They should communicate using SEND MESSAGE and RECEIVE MESSAGE primitives. The receivers, or servers for messages, should accept messages only from one sender or should serve senders in a round robin fashion. Sharing of data bases should be protected by interlocks or semaphores. If several resources are to be shared, the sequence of requesting should be fixed. The shared resources should preferably be memoryless. The actions performed by one task should not affect another task. For data bases, the area of information modified by one task should not be used by another task.

These conditions are far too restrictive for most real-time systems. They can be achieved in exceptional cases. An attempt should be made to achieve them as far as possible, if extensive testing is to be performed.

During testing the observance of the above stated restrictions and rules has to be checked. In addition analysis can support this checking.

Not just simple functional testing of this kind is required. The crash testing method described in section 4.3.2 is also a necessary aspect of testing. This relates also to interrupts and their consequences.

For systems which control analogue devices, even the use of automatic testing equipment is inadequate. Simulator equipment or online testing is necessary. Indeed, online testing will almost always be required. The criteria for thorough testing are the same as described above.

But additionally there is the problem of how to generate given inputs from a simulator at the start of a test sequence. Backwards cause analysis is generally necessary in the simulator model to find the required inputs.

A special case of interacting tasks is the use of interrupts. Certain sequences of code may be masked not-interruptable in order to guarantee the correct functioning. Analysis as well as tests have to be conducted to check the right operation.

Generally it can be stated that the most important thing for the
testing of real-time aspects is the assistance given by analysis, as
described in chapter 3. This should check the observance of design
rules in order to reduce the amount of testing or to make it even
possible to test. Petri nets techniques deserve special attention. This
relates to the combination of tasks and their interaction as well as to
such things as interrupts produced by process interfaces.

4.2   Glass box testing

Glass box testing, also called white box testing, is mainly used on
the module level: information from within a module is taken to choose
and develop test cases and test data and to control the execution of
the test runs.   Several different aspects of this glass box testing
will be discussed in the following sections.

Path testing involves the analysis of the different paths of a module
and a controlled execution of them.

Path domain testing is concerned with the input space and the
partitioning into correct subdomains.

The path predicates which are computed from the program code can be
compared with the program specification.

During mutation analysis, an error seeding technique is applied for
evaluation of the tests and additional error detection.

Symbolic execution, finally, is the execution of the program with
symbolic values and evaluation of the symbolic results.

4.2.1   Path testing

One of the methods used in glass box testing is path testing. Each module of a system is analysed and the corresponding control flow graph is constructed. From this graph the different paths through a module can be identified.

The goal of path testing is now to execute each path with a test case. For the generation and selection of the relevant test data the method of the weakest precondition can be used to calculate path predicates for each path.

The theory and application of the weakest precondition method is more closely described in section 3.2.2.

Inspection of the weakest precondition formula for an IF statement shows that it consists of two parts, corresponding to the two branches, THEN and ELSE. In a similar way the rule for a WHILE loop consists of many parts, one for zero traverses of a loop, one for one traverse of a loop, one for two traverses etc.

These rules can be used in a nested fashion in which each part of the preconditions, corresponding to a different path through a set of statements, is kept separate. If the rules are applied all the way starting at the end of a program and tracing back to the beginning, the result is a set of conditions, each one corresponding to a different path through the program. These conditions are called path predicates /Howd75, Huan75/. A simple example is given in figure 4.1.

Besides calculating the path predicates by use of the weakest precondition theory it can also be calculated by applying the symbolic execution technique. The result will more or less be the same. For the symbolic execution see section 4.2.5.

Each path predicate consists of a set of equations or inequalities. If these are solved, we have a set of test data which guarantees that all paths through a program will be tested. In this way, there will at least be a chance of detecting any error in the program.

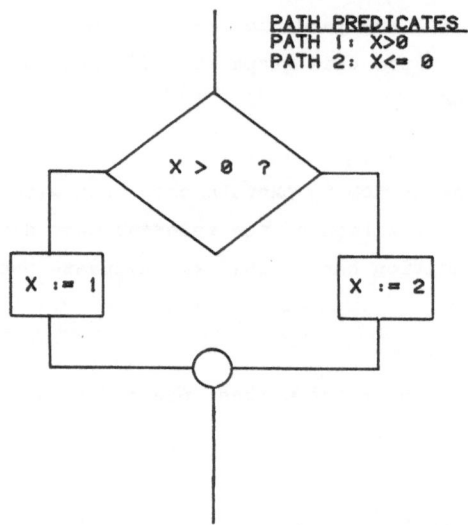

Figure 4.1: Path Predicates

In practice, the method can be used but requires a considerable degree of automation. The number of sets of test data may be enormous, for sequential control applications typically 2^{10} to 2^{50} sets. Criteria have been developed though for breaking such programs into independent units, so that the number of tests can be much reduced. Such testing can be kept within manageable proportions for control programs up to a few thousand statements in length.

The method will detect computation errors along a given program path, provided that one is not so unlucky that, for the given input values, the function computed along a given incorrect path is accidentally identical with the correct computation (see fig. 4.2). The probability of such coincidences can be reduced to very low levels by using not only one but several tests for each path predicate.

If a large number of tests is involved, it is very time consuming to

Intended function	Realised function	Test run
READ L	READ L	L=2
READ K	READ K	K=5
READ I	READ I	I=1
I=I+K	I=1+K	I=6
L=L*L	L=L+L	L=4
WRITE I	WRITE I	6
WRITE L	WRITE L	4

Figure 4.2: Insufficiency of a single test run

decide whether or not a result is correct. In particular if the program is large or complex some automatic method is required for judging whether outputs are correct, a so called oracle. Such judgements can be made by comparing output from two independently written programs, or by running tests with a simulator of the plant to be controlled.

The major weakness of path testing is that while the computation along a given program path may be correct, the correct path may not always be followed for a given set of input data. This problem is solved to some extent by the technique of dynamic analysis. Some more detail will be given in section 4.6.

Another problem with path testing is the feasibility of the paths. Not every path through a program is feasible: The IF-clause of an IF-statement can be contradicting the IF-clause of another later IF-statement, so the first IF-clause can only be executed in conjunction with the ELSE-clause of the second IF-statement.

The same is true not only for module internal control flow but also for the sequencing of tasks. Generally the sequence of tasks may be independent. But there can be coded certain restrictions which limit the free choice of sequence. This has to be evaluated and considered for testing.

The infeasible paths have to be eliminated from the set of executable paths and by that the number of test cases is reduced. But the detection of the infeasibility is not always trivial. The path predicates can become so complicated that the contradiction is not found very easily by inspection, and so far no automated tools exist which can reliably and efficiently assist this.

Test runs with test data according to path predicates or weakest preconditions are only showing the correctness of the weakest preconditions or path predicates. The correctness of the weakest preconditions and path predicates compared to the specifications has to be shown separately.

4.2.2 Path domain testing

The total set of possible input data combinations for a program is called its 'input space'. A program input space may be divided up into 'domains'. A path domain is a set of input data combinations such that, for each input data combination in the set, the program execution follows a specific path /WeOs80/. An example for a program which has two input variables is shown in Fig. 4.3.

The boundaries of the path domains are described by the path predicates. Points on the path domain boundaries can be found by solving the equations and inequalities of the path predicates.

By putting tests close to path domain boundaries, it is possible to check that the boundaries lie in the correct position to a close approximation. In general such surfaces are hypersurfaces in hyperspace. /WhCo80/ and /ClHa82/ have shown that if these surfaces are 'flat' (the equations describing them are linear) then a finite number of tests are sufficient to fix the position precisely, and to

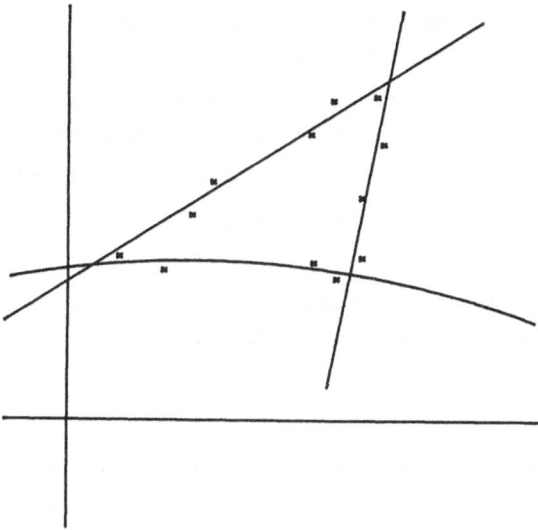

Figure 4.3: Path domains with test points on path domain boundary

reduce the probability of overlooking a path boundary error to a very low value.

There remains a problem with this technique. A program path may be missing entirely. This corresponds to a special case, for which the necessary program steps have been forgotten or overlooked. It is very unlikely that a missing path will be detected by this technique. The same is true for the afore mentioned path testing.

4.2.3   Path predicates and specifications

Bologna /Bolo78/ suggested that each path through a program corresponds to a particular case to be treated by the program. Thus there should be a correspondence between path predicates and elements of the formal program specification.

The suggestion turns out to hold quite well in practice, except for some instances in which several paths correspond to one case in the specification, typically in cases where the program involves loops. The correspondence depends to some extent on the level of language used in formulating the specification. Generally some logical manipulation of the formal specification is required so that it is transformed to disjunctive normal form, or case form.

A comparison can then reveal errors, either in the program input/output specification, or in the program itself. Note that the missing path problem is overcome in this way.

A practical use of this idea was made in developing the shutdown system of the Tapiro reactor in Italy. The formal specification was made independently of the program, in the form of a decision table. The comparison of path predicates and decision table, after transformation, revealed two specification errors and one program error /Bolo78/ (Fig. 4.4).

4.2.4   Mutation analysis

The method of mutation analysis /DeLi78/ starts out with an almost correct program. Into this program a number of changes (errors) is incorporated. This process is also called error seeding. Then the normal tests are executed and the results are compared to the results of the test runs with the unchanged version.

By the execution of the tests all the seeded errors should be detected. If they are not detected, additional test cases are necessary. The current experience is that the test cases will not only reveal the seeded errors but also some original errors.

This technique can be used to demonstrate the usefulness and completeness of the test case set. But the strength of this method heavily relies on the selection of the mutations (seeded errors). All classes of errors which can be made during software development have

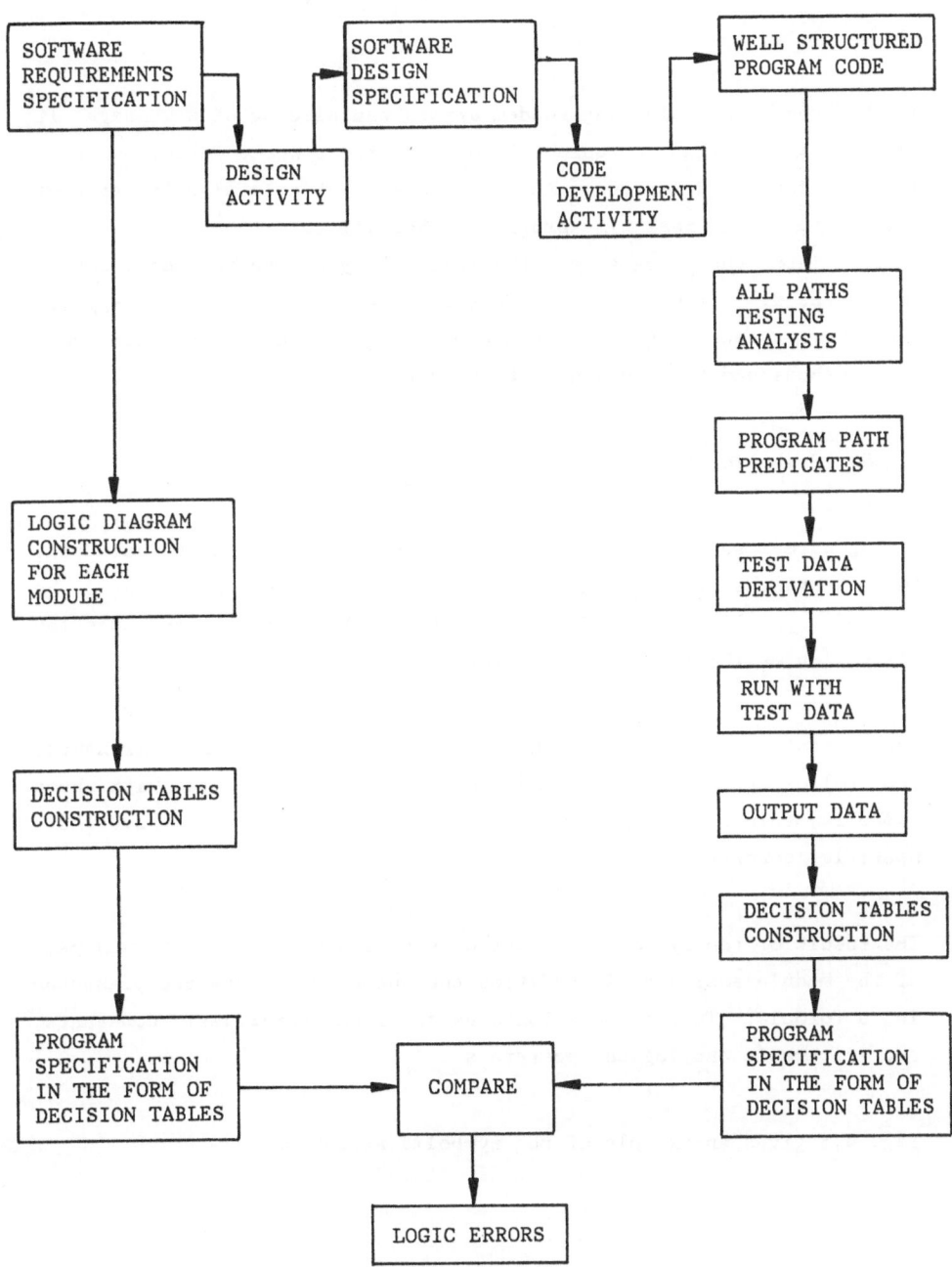

Figure 4.4: Code verification procedure for logic-oriented program
modules

to be covered by this technique.

On the other hand selecting seeded errors can also be of advantage. It can be shown that certain classes of errors whose detection seems unclear can be detected by the test cases. This is also the area of application for real-time programs. Special real-time errors can be seeded into the program and the reliability of the test sets can be demonstrated. If the seeded errors are detected by the applied methods, the coverage of test methods is good. Otherwise additional test methods and test runs have to be used.

4.2.5 Symbolic execution

During normal test of the program the code is executed with real data. In contrast the symbolic execution is a simulation of the execution by use of symbolic values for the input variables and subsequently for all variables /Clar76,Howd77,DaKi78/.

The execution starts with taking the input variables as their names. The following expressions and assignments are computed with these symbolic values. Only the constants which are used have their specific, concrete value.

The result of the symbolic execution is a path predicate for each path of the module analysed. In addition the output variables are presented in a formula. This formula contains the input variables, constants, and arithmetic and logical operators.

Fig. 4.5 gives an example of the symbolic execution.

4.2.6 Problems

Not all topics and constructions can be handled the same way with the

Program	Symbolic execution

```
Program                         Symbolic execution

READ A,B                        A=a, B=b
C = A - B                       C= a - b
IF C<0 THEN D = - C             if (a-b)<0   then D = - (a-b)

        ELSE D = 2 * C                    else D = 2 * (a-b)

C = D + C - B                   if (a-b)<0 then C = - (a-b) + (a-b) - b
                                                 = - b
                                   else C = 2 * (a-b) + (a-b) - b
                                          = 3 * a - 4 * b
WRITE C                         if (a-b)<0 then write -b
                                   else write (3 * a - 4 * b)
```

Figure 4.5: Symbolic execution

above mentioned techniques. Certain problems remain or require at least special treatment.

As already mentioned earlier, loops are the source for some problems. This concerns the loop of normal statements and even more the loop of execution of different tasks. This is true for loops with an unlimited iteration bound and internally calculated escape condition. Loops which iterate always a predefined and constant number of times, are not causing any major problems.

Arrays cause some difficulties during path predicate calculation and symbolic execution. If the index of the array is not a constant, or cannot be calculated from constants, its actual value is only known in symbolic form. Therefore it can be impossible to distinguish between the different elements of an array. The array elements used within expressions or calculations are unknown, and no specific value can be used. Simplification, which has to be used for path predicates as well as for symbolic executions, cannot be applied effectively if array indices are unknown.

The occurance of recursion results in similar problems as mentioned for loops. The depth of recursion is most often data dependent and therefore not fixed. Different depths of recursion result in different paths. In addition recursions have to be analysed and tested very carefully to show that they do not influence each other.

Path predicate calculation and symbolic execution are best done for single subroutines or modules only. If other modules are involved, eg calls to other modules, the evaluation of the path predicate and the symbolic execution is not completely possible unless this module has already been analysed and its results are available in symbolic form. Some new research seems to handle part of the problems concerning loops and functions /DaEr82/.

The dependence between the different modules should be minimal and clear to see, otherwise the calculation of the path predicate and the symbolic execution run into problems concerning the complexity and the number of paths which have to be considered.

As mentioned earlier the missing path problem is not easily solved. In particular, path predicate testing and symbolic execution show that the executed computations are correct, but they very seldom show that certain cases are not covered. This can only be solved by looking closely at the specification, doing specification analysis and generating tests from the application point of view. This will be described more detailed in section 4.5.

4.3   Black box testing

In contrast to glass box testing, black box testing makes no view into the module. The module is considered to be a black box. No structural information of the module is available, only the external interface description.

The testing of the module now can be conducted in two different ways,
by positive testing and by negative testing. Both are described in
more detail in the following.

4.3.1   Positive testing

During positive testing,   the tests are choosen according to the
specification. The functional specification of the module is taken and
test data are derived from there. Not only the most common input
values have to be used,   but also the input data with the low
probability of occuring during real operation.

Besides this selection of simple test cases, different combinations
also have to be used. The test has to be as complete as possible from
the functional specification point of view.

4.3.2   Negative testing

In contrast to positive testing, negative testing has to take into
consideration also the cases not specified. The goal is to show how
the program reacts to abnormal and even unspecified events. They can
be considered as tests for the robustness of the system. The crash
test and the unfriendly user test are parts of this testing.

The crash test tries to bring the system to a break down. Abnormal
situations are run. For a protocol system, which is printing warning
messages,   may be the occurrace of all alarm situations at once is
simulated in order to see whether the printer can deal with all
messages coming at once, or whether some get lost.

Concerning the timing aspect, different process situations have to be
simulated.   Not only the normal sequence of signals from the process,
but also abnormal sequences which are not probable in regular
situations shall be the input to the system. This includes the

generation of interrupts both in a high speed as well as in a stochastic sequence.

The unfriendly user test tries to simulate a user who is unaware of the correct use of the system and does not know the limitations of the system, or who is trying to break the system.

Both tests should not result in an unpredicted behavior of the system, but only messages should be produced or, in severe conditions, the system should come to a predefined stop or status. The robustness of the system and its error tolerance should cope with these attempts.

4.4 Hierarchic testing

The testing process can be conducted in different ways, eg top-down or bottom-up. Bottom-up testing again can be divided into several stages, module testing, integration testing, and system testing. In addition regression testing is important for the later development phases. These techniques will be described in the subsequent sections.

4.4.1 Top-down testing

Top-down testing is to be used during the early development phases of the system. If a high level description of the system or its upper levels exists, preferably in a compilable programming language, this can be executed. The lower level modules of the system are simulated by the use of stubs (dummy modules). As the development procedes the testing procedes, too. More and more stubs are replaced by their coded counterparts. Finally the complete system is tested.

4.4.2 Bottom-up testing

Bottom-up testing can start when the basic modules are coded. The first step is the module testing. Step by step the system is integrated until the complete system is tested.

4.4.2.1   Module testing

The basic modules are tested separately first. Basic coding errors should be detected by this method. For testing purposes, a test environment has to be provided, also called test harness. It consists of a test driver, which provides the module with the required input parameter values plus additional necessary interfaces.

Module testing should be as complete as possible. Other testing techniques like path testing have to be applied during the module testing. Especially the module test has to be done by the programmer himself, while the further testing can also be conducted by other persons.

4.4.2.2   Integration testing

After all the basic modules have been tested separately, integration testing starts. Some of the tested modules which communicate with each other are connected to a subsystem and tested. This is done for all subsystems.

Again a test environment is necessary because the final system environment cannot be used. The test case selection has to make sure that all the newly connected interfaces are tested sufficiently.

While during module testing the real-time aspect most often is to be neglected, it has to be taken into account during integration testing. Special test cases have to be constructed to check the correct coordination between the interconnected modules.

4.4.2.3   System testing

At the end of the integration process the complete system is interconnected. Now all the aspects which were not covered during the previous tests have to be considered.

Special attention has to be given to test cases concerning the timing of the system, capacity and throughput, synchronisation and global behaviour.

4.4.3 Comparison

The two techniques, top-down and bottom-up testing, serve different purposes: the former is more directed towards development concurrent testing, while the latter is more a post-coding effort. Due to this the resulting error detection is different. Both techniques require a hierarchical system structure in order to work efficiently.

Top-down testing results in good test coverage of the top level. Misbehaviour of the system can be detected and corrected before further code is written (which would have to be changed later, too). Top-down testing is therefore related to a simulation of the system from the system design.

Bottom-up testing detects the errors in the lower levels first. But major errors which relate also to wrong design and coding decisions are detected rather late during integration testing or system testing.

On the other hand both techniques have the advantage that the errors which are detected can be localised quite easily. Most often they are due to the newly integrated part, the lower parts in top-down testing, the higher modules in bottom-up testing.

A clean approach is not always possible or wanted. A mixed approach using top-down testing techniques where possible and bottom-up testing for specific parts is sometimes the most suitable. This mixed techniques is also called the sandwich techniques.

There are some advantages in applying both techniques in full. The system integration and the integration testing are easier if top-down testing was done. Information from this testing can be used during the bottom-up testing. The test case selection and also the test harness construction are simplified.

4.4.4 Regression testing

If corrections or changes are made to the code, a certain amount of retesting is necessary. Depending on the kind of change, this might be a complete new test or just a repetition of a previously conducted test series. The latter case is also called regression testing. The old test input data are given to the new version of the module or system - it is possible to apply this technique on all levels - and the new results are compared with the results of the previous test. If the results are identical, the probability that new errors were introduced is low.

Regression testing is necessary after each change of the program. The best support for this thechnique is a test environment which keepsthe test results and conducts the comparison automatically.

For real-time systems regression tests are most often not so easy, especially concerning the real-time aspects. Most tests are not repeatable due to timing restrictions, sequencing of events etc. This can result in some differences of the different executions which have to be taken into account for the comparison.

4.5 Test data

The test data generation consists of specifying and providing the test input data and of calculating the test output data. The techniques which have to be applied vary from method to method. Some of them will be explained in the following sections.

4.5.1   Test input data generation

The generation of the test input data for the module test is depending
on the test approach, black box testing or glass box testing. The
former uses outside information only, mainly the specification, while
the latter uses internal information.

For black box testing different specification documents from different
development phases can be used. The i/o-specification can be the
simplest form from which to extract the test data. In this
specification the inputs for which the module or the system should
work should be contained. The test data have to be within these
ranges.

Additional test data can be drawn from the global specification. There
the test data are selected from the environment.

Glass box testing includes the selection of test data according to the
module internal structure. The necessary information for the selection
process is drawn from static analysis of the module and also from the
path predicates and the weakest precondition calculations.

To guarantee a certain amount of diversity for the generation of test
data, different people have to be involved in the generation process.
In addition to this the time within the software development life
cycle when the test data are generated differs.

The specifier of the system is also to some degree concerned with the
test of the system. During the specification of the system, he has to
specifiy also a certain number of test cases. The information
contained within the test data specification may be used by the
implementer for the implementation of the system and also for the
test.

Independently, a test person has to take the specification and define test cases from the information contained in the specification. These test case specifications may not be used by the implementer for implementation purposes, but only by the tester for testing purposes.

From this it can be seen that not only test data for the actual development phase are specified but also for later phases. Especially during the final system test, test data which where specified during several other phases are used.

4.5.2 Test output data calculation and comparison

Not only the test input data, but also the related output data have to be specified. This can be done in several ways. Either there exists a precise specification of the output results, or there is a system model which takes the same input data as the original system and produces comparable results. Furthermore the validation of the test results after execution through comparison with the specification is possible.

This last case is the most time consuming process in general applications. The test input data are given to the system and the test output results are received. Then for each of the test runs a manual analysis of the results is conducted. This can be in the form of a manual simulation of the system. This procedure is not recommended at all. It seems only to be useful for small applications and limited number of test cases. Additionally it can be used for special test cases which require separate treatment for some reason.

If the test data are specified during the development process, especially during the specification phase, the input data and output data should be specified together. During testing the results can easily be compared with the corresponding specification.

Another way of controlling the test results is the use of a system model. Parallel to the development of the real system, a second system

138

is developed which does not have all the detail of the real system, but which includes the major functions of the system. This model can be programmed in a different language from the actual system and it can even run on a different computer in a different environment. For good utilisation, it is necessary to have some common interfaces between the real system and the system model. A possible configuration is shown in Fig. 4.6.

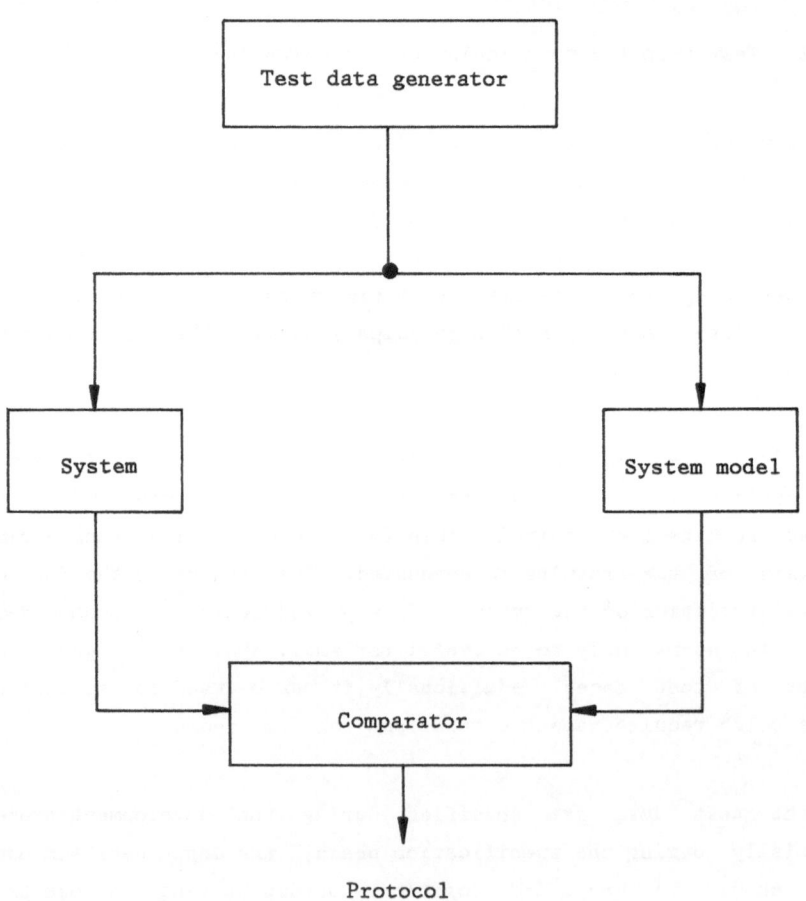

Figure 4.6: System test with system model

A different form of system model is a test oracle. This can be a
system model, but it can also be an even simpler thing, which is just
analysing the test results and judging on the correctness. If in the
early phases of system development a simulation model was used, this
can again be utilised for the system test as a test oracle.

Diverse implementations of the system can also be used as test oracles
or system models. They have the closest relation to the real system.
This is a reason why diverse implementation is sometimes favored: the
effort necessary during testing can be reduced quite remarkably if a
diverse implementation is present. The results of the diverse
implementations can be compared rather simple, not only during the
testing period, but even during later normal operation. This results
in an enlarged testing amount.

Watkins /Watk82/ gives also an example for testing software by an
output predictor and comparator which can be used for automatic
testing.

4.6   Test evaluation

The execution of the test cases has to be controlled to be sure that
the intended functions were executed. This can be done by controlling
the output of the test runs through comparison of the existing outputs
with the expected outputs. This has been described in the previous
section.

In addition the correct internal behavior of the system has to be
controlled. This can be achieved through the use of certain
instrumentation. The section on metrics will give some information on
this. The drawbacks of the instrumentation are a falsification of some
execution characteristics. This is explained in the section on the
effects of probes.

The documentation of the test runs is a very important matter. The important data should be kept in computer readable form. This is especially true for the test input and output data. For later regression tests, which are necessary after code modifications, the comparison of the new output results with the related old output results needs computer assistance.

All test runs have to be documented in a form that solves different purposes:

- the correct execution of the test runs and the completeness of the tests can be controlled by inspectors.

- later modifications require retesting. The repetition of the tests and the development of new test cases can be based on the old tests.

A list of software test documents, their purpose and contents together with an example can be found in /IEEE83/.

4.6.1 Metrics

For the systematic development of test cases it is important to know the achieved coverage. This coverage depends on the test object and the test objective. Different metrics can be used to control the test coverage /Mil177b/. Some of them will be described here.

Normally, complete or exhaustive testing is not possible. The number of different input data for a simple 16-bit input variable is already in the order of 10^4, for two such variables 10^8. As can be seen easily the different input data for systems with several input variables cannot all be tested by normal testing. The same is true for other test goals, like testing all executable paths of a program. Therefore subgoals have to be defined, and a structured approach is necessary. The use of test metrics shall guide this approach by telling the extent to which testing is required and finally achieved. Nevertheless it might even be impossible to define the test goal as a norm size, eg the total number of executable paths may be difficult to determine and sometimes has to be estimated /Mora78/.

In a first step the metrics can be divided into

- module oriented
- integration oriented
- system oriented

test metrics.

The module oriented test metrics take the internal structure of the program into account. There exists eg

m(s)	execution of all statements (c0)
m(a)	execution of all segments/arcs (c1)
m(i,n)	execution of each iteration n times
m(d)	execution of each data-dependent segment combination
m(p)	execution of all paths.

The coverage level of m(s)-testing is calculated as the ratio of the number of executed statements to the total number of statements ($0<=m(s)<=1$). The amount of coverage of testing is therefore indicated by these measures. To a large extent their use is supported by test tools which can do the appropriate instrumentation of the program and the evaluation of the test runs /Fair78,Huan78,Prob82/.

For the integration testing the test of the interfaces is most important. Therefore a class of integration or interface related test metrics can be defined:

i(i)	each i/o interface for each module used
i(s)	each output variable of a module is set in all possible assignments
i(r)	each input variable of a module is used in all possible reference points of the module.

These check the use of each input/output variable of each module and the kind of use as 'set' or 'referenced'.

On the system level the system structure as well as certain interface information is the basis for some test metrics:

s(m)	all modules called at least once
s(c)	all calls to modules exercised at least once
s(i)	all input variables to a module are set in all possible assignments
s(o)	all output variables of a module are used in all possible reference statements
s(s)	all different sequences of the modules.

Especially the last mentioned test metric is important for real-time software. The different modules of the system can be executed in various order. This sequencing can have an influence on the global execution of the system.

These metrics - or a selection of them - should be applied during the different stages of the testing process. They can add to each other, and information of the previous test phase can be utilised during later stages. The application of the test metrics heavily relies on the use of support tools. This topic will be covered in section 4.7.

4.6.2   Effects of probes

The control of the test run execution is not always possible without change of the original code. These additions to the code inlude

- assertions
- test output
- control flow trace
- data value trace.

The inclusion of these probes results in a change in the execution behaviour. This change of behaviour has to be controlled and examined, in case it leads to   a different result. Not all results of the test runs can therefore be used. Certain tests have to be repeated after removal of the probes.

Not only probes result in an unrealistic execution of the software. If
the tests are being made on a host machine, by emulation of the target
machine, or in some other simulated environment, the same is true. The
relevance of the test runs might be completely different than in the
final environment. Therefore a good analysis of the test environment
and its validity is necessary.

4.7 Use of tools

As already mentioned several times in the previous sections, the use
of tools is highly recommended for the different phases of the testing
process.

A list of different tools which not only support the test phase, but
partly cover also other parts of the software development cycle can be
found in /Houg82/. Only some of the tools and their characteristics
can be described in the following. Their main areas of application are
static analysis, dynamic analysis, and documentation.

One of the tools for analysing and testing Fortran programs is
RXVP80^{TM} /RXVP80, Deut82/. Fortran programs - from single subroutines
to complete systems - are statically analysed. The result of this
analysis is a number of reports which are not only useful for analysis
and testing purposes, but serve also as automatic generated
documentation, eg:
  - Check on the definition, initialisation and referencing of
    variables
  - check on definition and call of subroutines and functions
  - documentation of subroutine hierarchy (system structure)
  - subroutine internal control flow structure
  - documentation of the use of global common variables.

In addition, RXVP80 performs an instrumentation of the source code:
into the individual program segments (decision to decision paths)

144

probes are inserted. By executing this instrumented version of the
program the module oriented test coverage can be measured according to
m(a). Also information on s(m) and on variable values is available.
This part is called the dynamic analysis.

The SADAT test tool /VoGm80/ most of the features of RXVP80. In
addition to the static and dynamic analysis it is delivering some more
information for the testing. A test case generator develops a set of
paths which results in complete coverage of the program graph
(according to m(a)). Additionally the user can define program graphs
as starting sets for the test case generator. For these test cases
(paths through the program) the corresponding path predicates are
calculated by means of symbolic evaluation of the program. By
analysing the path predicates the tester can determine which paths are
feasible and which ones are not. For the feasible paths the test input
data can be calculated from the path predicate, which is a logical and
arithmetic expression.

Another test support system is TEVERE /TaBo77/ which was developed and
used for the validation of the TAPIRO safety system. TEVERE constructs
the path predicates and test data by application of the weakest
precondition rules. In contrast to the previous mentioned tools this
system is running in an interactive mode.

Of the here mentioned systems RXVP80^{TM} is the only commercially
available system with a good distribution. The other two tools are
more or less research tools.

Generally it can be stated that there exist different tools which
support the following:
  Structural analysis
  Symbolic execution
  Check on standards and guidelines
  Program statistics
  Interface checking
  Variable set/use checking

Test case evaluation

Test data generation

Test harness

Test evaluation

Execution trace information

Execution histogram

Time measurement

Weakest precondition calculation

Path predicate solver

This list can by no means be complete. No tool covers all the mentioned areas, most tools are language dependent and also machine dependent. For a selection of the right tool for the wanted application the NBS-report /Houg82/ can be of great help. It has to be taken into account that the different tools quite often serve several purposes, that is not only they assist the testing, but also give useful information for the debugging and the maintenance, not least through their automatically generated documentation.

4.8   Conclusion

In this chapter we have described several methods and techniques which are necessary and useful for the systematic testing of software. Some of them are stand-alone methods, but most of them are somehow related to each other or aid each other.

In order to do some testing, a certain amount of analysis is necessary to know what testing strategy is the best and how to select the test cases. In addition some errors cannot be detected by testing alone, but need some kind of proof. There are some constructive means to avoid deadlocks, but the use of these means has to be checked by analysis and proofs.

Generally testing cannot prove the error-freeness of the software, but only show the presence of errors. By systematic application of testing we feel that error-freeness can be demonstrated to a certain degree.

Some testing strategies have shown a good error-detection probability for certain kinds of errors. Nevertheless the theory of testing is still not so far advanced that a standard set of testing methods can be advised which is sufficiently thorough in all applications. Individual combinations are necessary to do the job. The overview in Fig. 4.7 gives a summary of the values of some of the different techniques mentioned.

Method	Errors probably detected	Errors not detected	Problems	Tools
path testing	-computation error along path	-missing path	-infeasible path -high number of paths	-dynamic analysis -path predicate evaluator
path domain testing	-domain boundary errors	-missing path	-test data selection	
path predicates and specification	-missing path -logic error	-execution errors	-comparability	
mutation analysis	-seeded error classes		-selection of seeded errors	
symbolic execution	-logic errors -algorithm errors	-execution errors		

Figure 4.7: Value of different techniques

5 Statistical Testing of Real Time Software

W.Ehrenberger

5.1 When to apply statistical testing techniques

In view of the difficulties with real-time software verification that were discussed in the earlier chapters of this book the reader might ask wether it can be easier, and therefore cheaper, to use probabilistic methods instead of systematic ones. As we will see later, however, it is normally quite costly to apply statistical testing for singular (i.e. not diverse) software system. This is mainly due to the large number of test runs that are required to achieve quantitative results which are acceptable for a system of any practical importance. This leads to the recommendation to use statistical tests only as a complement to systematic verification.

Only those software parts or those operating conditions of the software whose correctness or correct handling could not be proven by systematic means should be subject to statistical testing. The first step therefore is to determine which program part or operating conditions are not to be treated statistically.

If, however, the software system is diverse, i.e. if two independently developed subsystems solve the relevant problem, it can be cheaper to use statistical testing only. Systematic approaches can then be reduced to a minimum. This applies, if it is safety rather than availability that is most important. Statistical testing can also be beneficial in complementing operating experience already gained.

Apart from this, a random test may be executed without any quantitative reliability figure in mind. The test case number can then be small. But it is not this area of testing that we have in view during this chapter.

Since many peculiarities of real-time software are difficult to verify by systematic means, one may be inclined to reserve them for probabilistic treatment. The test then may even be restricted to real-time features. In general one test case of a real-time program will consist of a sequence of input conditions, by contrast to sequential software testing.

As we will see later during this chapter, it is normally helpful to have some knowledge about details of the tested object. This knowledge can be gained from analytical investigations and from appropriate documentation of the system to be verified. It can lead to a drastic reduction in the number of test cases necessary.

5.2   The statistical test aim

5.2.1 General

In contrast to systematic testing, statistical testing does not state that the tested object is correct or that it will work without any failure; the test result is always a probabilistic one, e.g.

>   an expected value
>   a risk
>   a probability.

Methods as suggested in this report normally also provide

>   confidence limits or levels of significance, or variances.

Typical test aims are to show that

- the probability of software failure is below a certain limit with a level of confidence of P %,
- the number of programming errors that still persist is expected to be below a certain value and the variance of that expectation has a certain value,
- the cost to be expected due to software failure is under a given value with a level of confidence of P%.

The test can refer to a whole program system, including a multi-task user program, an operating system, a library or data base and several mathematical standard routines. It can also be restricted to parts, e.g. the real-time parts. In real-time software, particular emphasis is on testing whether or not deadlocks occur

the sequence of outputs is correct

results or intermediate results occur in the right time interval.

5.2.2 Risk considerations

Recent discussions support the opinion that risk may evolve to one of the most important reliability features for the description of process control or commercial systems. The concept of risk forms a bridge between the probabilistic reliability aspects and the economic considerations of any system. Risk considerations can be used to derive probabilities, availabilities or safety goals that are to be met.

In the area of nuclear safety /Nure 82/ discusses some risk goals about nuclear reactors. See table 5.1

event	occurence frequency per reactor year
core melt	$1.\times 10^{-4}$
individual prompt fatality	$1.\times 10^{-6}$
individual delayed fatality	$5.\times 10^{-6}$

Table 5.1: Discussed safety goals from /Nure 82/

The risk is defined as

$$r = \sum_{a} H(a) \cdot X(a),$$

where H(a) is the frequency of the loss-causing event a during the relevant period of time, e.g. during life time or per mission.

X(a) is the loss caused by event a, e.g. in money. The sum is to be taken over all events. H(a) can be expressed as:

$$H(a) = \sum_i H(i) \cdot p(a/i) \cdot p(a/ai),$$

where H(i) is the frequency of the initiating event i that may lead to a loss causing event a.

p(a/i) is the probability that the considered system fails to react correctly on event i.

p(a/ai) is the probability that any alternative action which may have been installed provisionally fails simultaneously (such alternative action may be an operator interaction).

The events i include those that require discrete actions and those that require continous functioning over a certain period of time.
A method on how to proceed for risk evaluation is described in /IEEE 81/.

Example:
The operation of a plant faces three types of losses:
$X_1 = 10^6$ ECU, $X_2 = 10^5$ ECU, $X_3 = {}^4$ ECU. If no counteractions were taken these losses would occur with frequences $H_1 = 5$ per year, $H_2 = 1$ per year and $H_3 = 20$ per year. Loss X_1 can be caused by 5 types of initiating events, occuring with frequencies of $H_{11} = 1.5$, $H_{12} = 1$, $H_{13} = 1$, $H_{14} = 1$ and $H_{15} = 0.5$ per year respectively. X_2 can be caused by two types of events with frequencies of $H_{21} = 0.6$ and $H_{22} = 0.4$. X_3 has only one type of event. The aim of the computer installation is to reduce the probability of initiating events occuring. The associated probabilities are: $p(1/1) = 10^{-4}$, $p(1/2) = 10^{-4}$, $p(1/3) = 10^{-3}$, $p(1/4) = 10^{-3}$, $p(1/5) = 10^{-3}$, $p(2/1) = 10^{-3}$, $p(2/2) = 10^{-2}$. Alternative operator actions are estimated to fail simultaneously with a probability of 0.9 for H_{11} to H_{13}, 0.99 for H_{14} and H_{15}, 0.5 for H_{21} and 1 for H_{22} and H_3. The resulting new failure freqencies per year are:
$H_1 = 1.5 \cdot 10^{-4} \cdot 0.9 + 1 \cdot 10^{-4} \cdot 0.9 + 1 \cdot 10^{-3} \cdot 0.9 + 1 \cdot 10^{-3} \cdot 0.99$
$+ 0.5 \cdot 10^{-3} \cdot 0.99 = 0.00261$
$H_2 = 0.6 \cdot 10^{-3} \cdot 0.5 + 0.4 \cdot 10^{-2} \cdot 1 = 0.0043$.
$H_3 = 20$.
After installation of the computer systems the remaining risk is:
$r = 0.00261 \cdot 10^6 + 0.0043 \cdot 10^5 + 20 \cdot 10^4 = 203\ 040$ ECU.

5.3   Simple cases

5.3.1 The independency question

As already mentioned in section 5.1, the first problem is to isolate those functions and program parts that can be investigated independently from others. Even if such parts and their functions are so complicated that they can only be treated statistically, we gain through the separation effort in that we can specify in more detail how the test shall proceed. We also have a better chance to make a complete test by chance, as described under item 5.3.7.

At any particular time, the behaviour of a real-time system is dependent to some extent on its previous operational history. A fundamental question to be asked of any such system is: How long do these dependencies last? In particular, is there an inherent mechanism that brings the system back to a starting point or base line after a certain period of time or number of demands, regardless of intervening events or activity?

The verification that some dependencies are less than originally assumed may reduce the cases to be considered not only from

$$k \text{ to } k-1 \text{ or } k-2$$

but due to the structure being investigated, from

$$k! \text{ to } k-1 \text{ or } (k-2)!$$

So, detailed analyses of these dependencies may well pay off.

During this section, it is assumed that our analysis has led to the isolation of some quite simple features and that it provides a basis for deciding which test cases are independent from others. The formulae that will be derived are always based on the independency between the individual cases. Due to dependencies that last over several test runs, one test case may include a number of individual runs. So we can formulate prerequisite or assumption I:

> The sequence and number of test cases do not influence the result of a single test case (independency of test cases). (I)

152

Example:

Under certain circumstances, a realtime system uses 6 tasks in parallel. If no details are known, it is necessary to investigate the 6! = 720 possible sequences of running. If, however, it can be shown that one task works completely independent from the rest, only 5! = 120 sequences are to be investigated. If it is possible to prove that 2 tasks are independent both from the rest and from each other, only 4! = 24 sequences of task behaviour must be considered (see also 5.3.4).

5.3.2 Time windows

In real-time systems, specific reactions sometimes only occur during certain periods of time. Then it is important to hit that period, e.g. in order to trap an error or to show that a specific function is executed correctly.

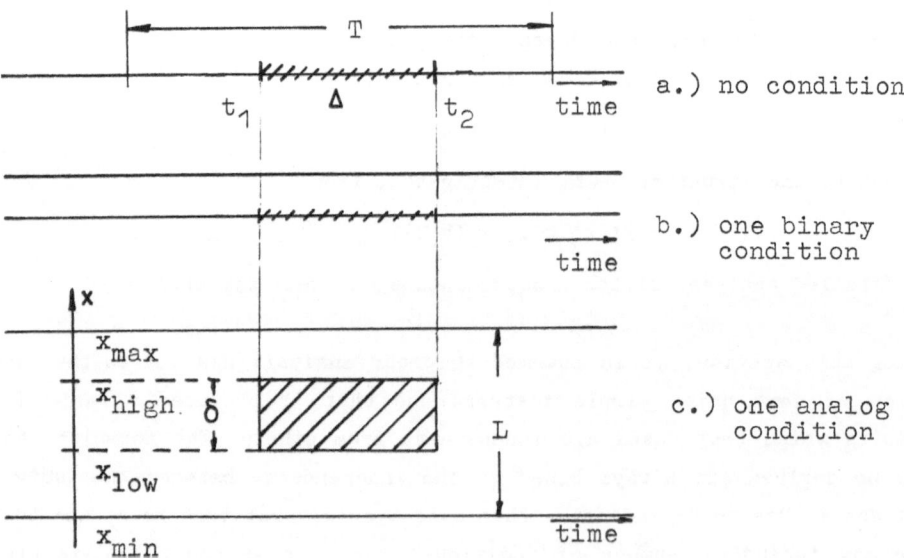

Fig. 5.1: Time windows without conditions and with conditions

If the window is not connected with any additional condition and if the test cases are distributed with equal probability over the interesting interval T, the probability of hitting it during one run is:

$$p_{w1} = \frac{\Delta}{T}$$

This is also the probability of finding a programming error that is connected with interval Δ. If we provide n test runs, p_w becomes:

$$p_{wn} = 1 - (1 - \frac{\Delta}{T})^n \qquad (5.1)$$

Proof: The probability of not hitting Δ during one run is:

$$1 - \frac{\Delta}{T}$$

The probability of not hitting Δ during n independent runs is:

$$(1 - \frac{\Delta}{T})^n$$

(5.1) is the complement of this $\langle$.

For evaluation of p_{w1} we assumed an equal probability of hitting any point of time in T. This is expressed in assumption II below, and will be deemed to hold for the remainder of this chapter, unless explicitly stated to the contrary.

> The probability of being selected is equal for all
> items of interest during all test cases (equal   (II)
> distribution of test cases).

We now come back to our time window and to figure 5.1. If conditions have to be met in order to find the window, which are not so well known from analysis that they can be circumvented during our test and if our test cases are equally distributed over this higher dimensional input space, we get for one binary condition:

$$p_{w1} = \frac{1}{2} \cdot \frac{\Delta}{T}$$

And with k binary conditions and n runs:

$$p_{wn} = 1 - (1 - \frac{\Delta}{2^k \cdot T})^n \qquad (5.2)$$

If we have similarly one or m analog conditions (see fig. 5.1), we get for one and n uns:

$$p_{w1} = \frac{\delta \cdot \Delta}{L \cdot T}$$

$$p_{wn} = 1 - (1 - (\prod_{i=1}^{m} \frac{\delta_i}{L_i}) \frac{\Delta}{T})^n \qquad (5.3)$$

Another version of the time window problem has to do with whether or not the output is provided in the correct time interval, or comes too late. This will be treated in another chapter.

5.3.3 Sequences of Tasks

If M tasks access one resource, we get M! possible access sequences. If some failure occurs during one and only one particular sequence, the probability to trap it with n independent test runs is:

$$p = 1 - (1 - \frac{1}{M!})^n, \qquad (5.4)$$

(if all sequences are executed with the same probability.)

We now look at several tasks with several resources.

N number of resources to be accessed

μ_{ij} number of accesses of resource number j during one run of task number i

ν_i number of runs of task number i

h number of accesses of all resources by all tasks.

$$h = \sum_{j=1}^{N} \sum_{i=1}^{M} \nu_i \mu_{ij} \qquad (5.5)$$

If all sequences are to be considered, h! possibilities exist.

The probability to check one of these possibilities during a random test
can be derived similarly to (5.1). As can easily be checked, it is quite
improbable to trap an error that causes a failure in connection with only
one specific sequence. Analysis must help to reduce the number of cases
that are to be investigated by random test.

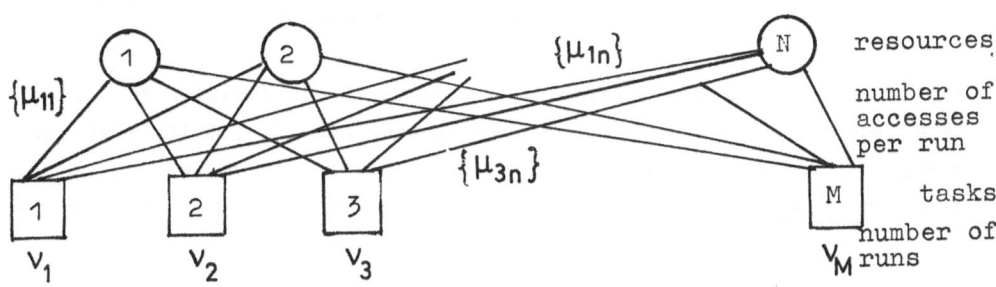

Fig. 5.2:   {N} resources are accessed by {M} tasks

5.3.4 Interrupts, priorities, reentrancy

Interrupts normally trigger tasks, if they are processed by the user
program. If several interrupts are feasible during one interesting time
interval, the sequence of such tasks may be a cause of failure. Interrupts
may also rearrange queues, in order to solve timing problems for some
tasks, and thereby produce deadlocks. Both the tasking problem and the
queuing problem can be treated from the combinatorial point of view similarly to the access question of sub-section 5.3.3.

Interrupts can also cause reentrancy problems with shared code, data items
or other resources. This is typically associated with the time window
problem already discussed.

5.3.5 Profiles of analog input signals

Sometimes in real-time systems not only actual values of signals are processed, but the shape of a signal is analysed and used as a basis for further decisions. The program builds up a history of its input. For our test design it is important to know how long that history can last. This must be found out analytically. For our further considerations ·in this subchapter we modify prerequisite I:

> The dependency of results of a test run from earlier
> input lasts only for a time interval of duration Δ.
> (Ia)

So, after Δ (I) is true again. It is reasonable to consider as a single test result not the result of a program run, but all results that occur during Δ. If Δ comprises $n\Delta$ program runs, and if the sequence of Z_1, $Z_2, \ldots, Z_{n\Delta}$, $Z_{n\Delta+1}, \ldots$ input states has been offered, the following sequences are to be considered as one test unit each

$$Z_1, Z_2, \ldots \qquad , Z_{n\Delta}$$
$$Z_2, Z_3, \ldots \qquad , Z_{n\Delta+1}$$
$$Z_3, Z_4, \ldots \qquad , Z_{n\Delta+2}$$
$$\ldots$$

If a single faulty intermediate result occurs during one of these sequences, that whole sequence is considered as being treated incorrectly.

Example:
A real time computer system samples its inputs every second. Every 10 seconds one set of outputs is provided to the subsequent control units. A history of one hour is kept. No effort was undertaken to analyse the relationship between the one hour history, the actual input and the output. The system is considered as a black box.
The 360 sets of output signals that are provided hourly are to be considered as the output of one test case. The first test case comprises time 0 to 1 hour, the second 0+10 sec. to 1 hour + 10 sec., the third 0 + 20 sec. to 1 hour + 20 sec. etc.

If a program system comprises several interdependent functions, where each has different periods of dependency Δ_1, Δ_2,...Δ_k, we have to take the smallest common multiple of all, Δ_{common}, as our basis.

In order to provide the required input conditions at the appropriate points of time, one will normally need automatic assistance: e.g. a computer controlled test mock-up.

5.3.6 Testing of time constraints

If time constraints are to be tested during a large number of runs, automatic assistance is again required. Inputs have to be presented at exact instances and output has to be checked at distinct points of time. This is particularly difficult if several time intervals must be controlled simultaneously. Analysis must normally be used to find out which input conditions can really be critical and what must be supervised.

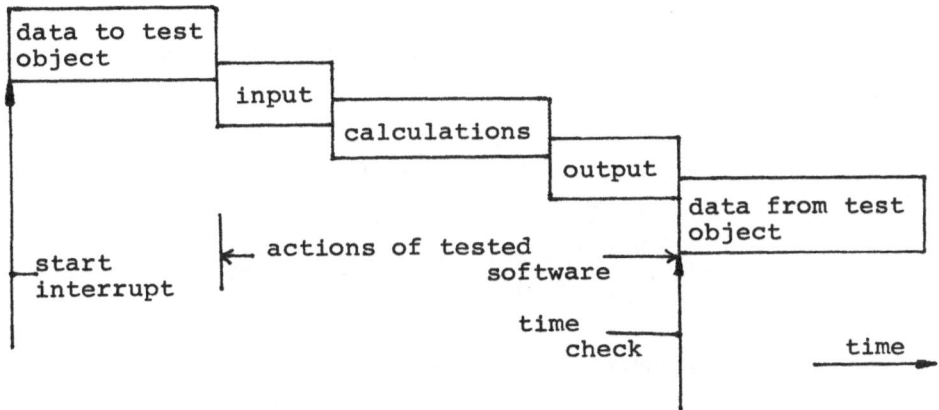

Fig. 5.3:   Time control of a test

If the allowable reaction times are specified in advance, the test result will be that the test object meets its requirements or it does not. If such a detailed specification does not exist, it can be reasonable to measure the reaction times of the individual test cases. This will lead to a distribution. The distribution may be used later to determine whether the system worked acceptably.

5.3.7 Probability of exhaustive testing

In order to investigate under what conditions it is feasible to test a
real-time program completely by chance, we need an estimate of the total
number of program properties. This estimate cannot be found by statistical
means. Either analysis must be used or it must be derived from the specification. From this estimate, we can drive another conditional estimate of
the number of test cases necessary to test the program completely.

This leads to assumption III.

> The program system can be tested exhaustively by N
> test cases.   (III)

Let n stand for the number of test cases that are performed on {N} at
random. The probability p_d to test one distinct but arbitrary case out of
the {N} is:

$$p_d = 1 - (1 - \frac{1}{N})^n \qquad (5.6)$$

The derivation of this formula is similar to (5.1). The test is done with
replacement.

If n > N, we achieve a complete test of all {N} cases with probability p_c.

$$p_c = 1 + \sum_{j=1}^{N-1} (-1)^j \binom{N}{j} \cdot (\frac{N-j}{N})^n \qquad (5.7)$$

For the proof see appendix.

Normally we will not be able to hit exactly one from the {N} cases during
one random test case. Then n has to be modified. If more than one of the
"relevant" cases is included in one random case, a larger number can be
taken; if less than one, a smaller number. The first case can occur if the
test provides a heavy load on the test object. The second will apply, if
{N} is not well known.

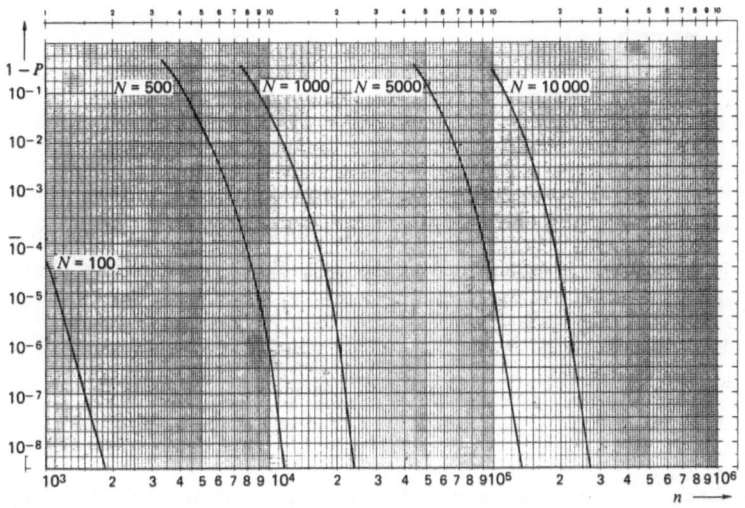

Fig. 5.4:   Graphical representation of (5.7): probability of having
              something left untested as a function of the necessary test
              runs N and the executed test runs n.

Example:

A real time program system has 5000 program properties, such that 5000
single test runs would be required in order to test it completely, if the
cases were known and if only one property could be tested during one run.
During one use of that system, several of its properties are normally
addressed. The frequency of addressing varies considerably betwenn two
properties. It is assumed that during each independent system use one of
the seldomly used properties is addressed at random. The system has been
installed at 100 sites. At each site two independent uses are performed
per day on the average. Independent means that the respective demands are
sufficiently different from each other. After 500 working days at each of
the sites, 100 000 independent runs have been performed. Figure 5.4 shows
that the probability of having one of the seldomly addressed program
properties left untested is 10^{-5}.

160

5.4   Reliability growth models

Reliability growth models are used to derive reliability figures from the debugging process of a software product. The encountered failures and the removed errors are recorded and conclusions are drawn from these observations on the failure rate still to be expected or on the number of errors still persisting. Such models belong to the oldest software reliability prediction methods that were investigated. See e.g. /Shoo 71, DiHe 72, Shoo 73/.

All the models that came to the knowledge of the authors of this report ignore the program structure. Figure 5.5 shows a typical debugging process.

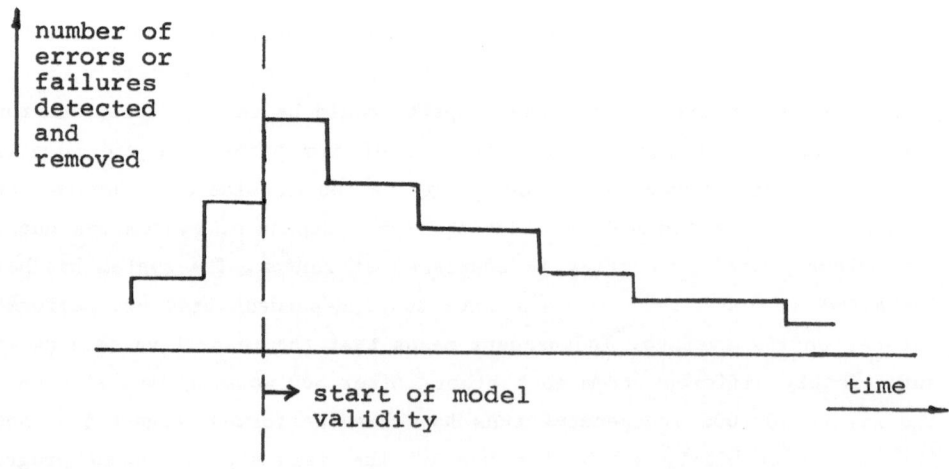

Fig. 5.5:   Typical error removal curve during a debugging process

We do not intend to treat all the different proposed models here in detail. Such models have been developed by many authors.

The models of Jelinski and Moranda /JeMo72/ and Schick and Wolverton /ScWo73/ aroused wide international interest. Other theoretical models have been published by Littlewood and Verall /LiVe73/, Hallendal, Hedin and Östrand /HaHe75/ and Anderson, Peiram and Strandberg /AnPe76/. This last reference also includes a debugging example which shows some agreement with their model. Further debugging experiences have been reported by Akiyama /Akiy 71/, Coutinho /Cout73/ and Shooman and Ruston /ShRu77/. More recently, new models have been developed and used, including /GuOt82/.

Using such models may, however, be accompanied with difficulties. Such difficulties concern the type of errors or failures that should be considered, the necessary knowledge about program package use or its internals, the fact that the models fail whenever no errors or failures are reported and that the model assumptions require a certain uniformity in finding errors.

The models described in the literature are quite useful for large programs whose reliability requirements are not too high. They enable one to guess the number of errors still remaining in the program after a certain time of debugging, and the time which is still necessary to reach a certain level of "cleanliness", using data collected during the debugging process.

On the other hand, some real time programs must be extremely error free. The requirements on the level of cleanliness which must be demonstrated are very high. None of the above mentioned models is able to show MTBFs which are large enough or failure probabilities per demand which are small enough for systems with high reliability requirements, e.g. safety systems.

5.5   Testing large systems

5.5.1 General

As in sections 5.3 and 5.4 we assume here that we are testing a large system of real-time programs that is already completely developed and regarded as error-free by the developers. Three cases will be distinguished:

- testing for a certain freedom from errors
- testing to verify a certain failure probability
- testing to show that the risk involved with the use of a program is below a certain limit.

The main emphasis will be on the last point.

5.5.2 Testing for freedom from errors

The results stated in section 5.3 were based on some knowledge on the internal structure of the program and on the fact that the distinct program properties to be tested were a finite and well known number. We now ask what we can get if the number of program properties is so large as to be considered practically infinite.

We assume that the individual test runs are independent from each other, that each possible program error can be found from each run with equal probability and that during each run the probability to find an error is equal for each error. (Assumptions I and II.)

The probability to have m erroneous program properties among n different tested program properties then is p(n,m), according to /EhPl 78a/, where

$$p(n,m) = \binom{n}{m} p_o^m (1-p_o)^{n-m} \qquad (5.8)$$

p_o is the probability that one distinct but arbitrary program property is faulty. (5.8) represents the binominal distribution. This distribution decays to the normal distribution, if p_o is relatively large, and to the Poisson distribution, if p_o is relatively small (See /HeGa 72/). In our case we can use the Poisson distribution

$$p(\lambda,m) = \frac{\lambda^m}{m!} e^{-\lambda} \qquad (5.9)$$

where $\lambda = np_o$.

When putting some requirements on the level of confidence P of our test result p_o, we gain values for λ which are for example:

$$P = 99 \text{ \%, } \lambda \overset{\sim}{=} 4,6 \qquad\qquad (5.10)$$
$$P = 95 \text{ \%, } \lambda \overset{\sim}{=} 3$$

From this we can derive the necessary number n_t of distinct program properties to be tested in order to show that p_o is below a limit $\tilde{p}_o$. If during n_t test runs no failure occurs we have:

$$n_t = \frac{4,6}{\tilde{p}_o} \text{ for P = 99 \%}$$

$$\qquad\qquad (5.11)$$

$$n_t = \frac{3}{\tilde{p}_o} \text{ for P = 95 \%}$$

If a failure occurs during n_t test runs, the testing process must be stopped and restarted after error correction. Should some program parts exist which are error free, this can be taken into consideration. If the portion a of a program, $0<a<1$, is error free, the probability that an arbitrary program property contains errors is smaller than $\tilde{p}_a$, where

$$\tilde{p}_a = (1-a)\tilde{p}_o \qquad\qquad (5.12)$$

Approaches using other distributions lead to similar results. For fuller details, the reader is referred to reference /BoEh79/.

Taking into account that some programs must be error free with a probability of $1-10^{-4}$ to $1-10^{-7}$, depending on the application, the number of program properties to be tested according to (5.11) is very high. In most cases, automatic test equipment will be indispensible and even then, there will be many cases where it is impossible to perform the number of program runs needed. An associated problem is to verify that different test runs also test different programs properties, that is to derive the actual n_t from the number and kinds of test runs performed.

The kind of thinking of this subsection is, however, applicable if the portion a in (5.12) is large enough. This must be shown by systematic investigations rather than statistical ones. So a statistical test following these considerations can be used as a complement to a systematic proof or test.

Example:

A large real-time system was submitted to systematic verification. Here by 40% of the code could be verified, 60% however, proved to be so complex that statistical methods should be tried. Based on the foregoing systematic analysis results 300 program properties were randomly selected and tested exhaustively. No error was found. This means: An arbitrary program property from the randomly tested set is faulty with a probability of $\leq 10^{-2}$ with a confidence level of 95%. An arbitrary program property of the whole system is faulty with a probability $\leq 6 \cdot 10^{-3}$ with a confidence level of $\geq$ 95%.

5.5.3 Testing for failure during operation

In paragraphs 5.3 and 5.5.2 , we considered the question of getting some knowledge on a program itself. This was in contrast to paragraph 5.4 where the program behaviour was the aim of our interest. Here we come back to this second kind of approach. We try to give a statement on the survival probability during real operation if we have no knowledge of the internal structure of the program. However, it is easier to derive the complement of this quantity, the failure probability.

We again assume the independence of individual test cases. Additionally, we suppose that each input data combination is tested with the same probability as during on line operation. According to ref. /EhPl78a/ we come to similar results as in the previous section. If m stands for the number of observed failures, n for the number of test cases performed and p_o represents the probability of a faulty case, (5.8) and (5.9) then give the relevant failure distributions. The number of necessary test cases n_t is given by (5.11). The difference is that n_t stands for the number of necessary runs as mentioned and not for the number of program properties to be tested. So, if no faulty case occurs:

$$n_t = \frac{4 \cdot 6}{\tilde{p}_o} \text{ for } P = 99 \text{ \%}$$

$$(5.13)$$

$$n_t = \frac{3}{\tilde{p}_o} \text{ for } P = 95 \text{ \%},$$

where $\tilde{p}_o$ is an upper limit for the failure probability per run p_o. Large numbers of test cases may be necessary, as described in the last section.

Example:

A large real time system has been used in 10 installations. In total 10^7 demands have been successfully treated by that system. No failure has occured during that period. The probability that the next demand to that system will be treated incorrectly is below $4.6 \cdot 10^{-7}$ with a level of confidence of 99% and below $3 \cdot 10^{-7}$ with a level of confidence of 95%.

5.5.4   Testing with respect to risk

5.5.4.1 Preliminary remarks

Due to the importance of risk considerations, this goes into more detail than do the two previous ones. The test described here belongs to a kind of testing called "partition testing" where the input data domain is decomposed into subsets and random sampling is appropriately performed over these subsets. Structural and path testing are examples of partition testing.

In testing with respect to risk, the input data domain is decomposed into strata according to the loss profile, and the random sampling is performed according to stratified sampling /HeGa 72/. The aims of the test procedure are to determine

- an upper (e.g. 95 %) confidence bound for the risk
- the smallest number of test cases to be performed in order to verify some specified figure r_o to be the upper confidence limit for the risk.

5.5.4.2 Notations, definitions and assumptions

We follow the considerations of /Krzy 82/. Let the input data domain for the program to be tested be decomposed into subsets, called strata as follows.

Let L_1, L_2,...L_K be all possible amounts of loss which can result from the consequences of possible program failures. The stratum h is defined as the set of all input data which, in case of a program failure, lead to the loss L_h, h = 1,2,...,K. In this way the entire input data space is decomposed into K disjoint and exhaustive strata.

Let π_h be the probability of stratum h, i.e. the probability that an input data point from this stratum will be selected for execution during real operation.

We assume that K; L_1,...,L_K; π_1,...,π_K are known. Corresponding to the operational demand profile L_1,...L_K, π_1,...π_K can be called te operational risk profile. Let ρ_h be defined by

$$\rho_h = \frac{L_h \pi_h}{\sum\limits_{i=1}^{K} L_i \pi_i} \qquad (h = 1,\ldots,K)$$

ρ_h is a known constant, because L_h and π_h are known. It is called the importance of stratum h, since it can be interpreted as the proportion that stratum h contributes to the expected loss under the condition of program failure.

Let p_h be the probability of program failure in stratum h during real operation, i.e.

p_h = probability of program failure when the input data are sampled from stratum h, (h = 1,...,K)

Each p_h is a constant, but it is unknown. Let L be the loss caused by a program failure in one program run during real operation. L is a discrete random variable and can only take the values $0, L_1, \ldots, L_K$.

The risk r of the program to be tested is defined as the expected value EL of the random variable L, i.e.: r = EL.

$$r = EL = \sum_{h=1}^{K} L_h \pi_h p_h \qquad (5.14)$$

The risk r of the software must be treated as an unknown constant, because the probabilities $p_1, \ldots, p_K$ are not known.

5.5.4.3 The test procedure

Let H be a discrete random variable defined over the set $1, \ldots, K$ with $p(H=h) = \rho_h, (h=1, \ldots, K)$, i.e. H is a random variable which selects the stratum h with probability ρ_h.

The test is now performed in two steps:

a) A stratum is selected at random according to the distribution of H, i.e. stratum h is selected with probability ρ_h. This means sampling according to importance.

b) One test case from the previously selected stratum is executed. The input data for this test case are selected at random from this stratum according to the (conditional) distribution in real operation.

This is repeated n times. The faulty program runs are recorded. k faulty runs are assumed.

5.5.4.4 Confidence statements for the risk

Having performed the described test procedure, we can make the following statements:

(1) The upper confidence bound $\hat{r}_{0.95}$ for the software risk r at the level of confidence of 95 % is given by:

$$\hat{r}_{0.95} = (\sum_{h=1}^{K} L_h \pi_h) \frac{(k+1) F_{0.95}(2(k+1), 2(n-k))}{(n-k) + (k+1) F_{0.95}(2(k+1), 2(n-k))} \qquad (5.15)$$

$F_{0.95}$ $(\ldots,\ldots)$ = 95 % quantile of the F-distribution with
2(k+1), 2(n-k) degrees of freedom

(2) For the important special case k=0, i.e. no failures observed and for large n, e.g. n≧100, the upper 95 %-confidence bound for the risk is given by

$$\hat{r}_{0.95} = (\sum_{h=1}^{K} L_h \pi_h) \; (1 - \sqrt[n]{0.05}) \; \sim \; (\sum_{h=1}^{K} L_h \pi_h) \cdot \frac{3}{n} \qquad (5.16)$$

(3) If it is known a priori that no malfunction will be observed during the entire test, i.e. that k will be zero, one can obtain the total number n of program runs that are necessary to verify some specified figure $\tilde{r}$ to be the upper 95 % confidence limit for the risk. n is given by:

$$n = \frac{\ln 0.05}{\ln (1 - \tilde{r}/\sum_{h=1}^{K} L_h \pi_h)} \; \sim \; \frac{3}{\tilde{r}} \sum_{h=1}^{K} L_h \pi_h \qquad (5.17)$$

The second equation holds, if $\tilde{r} \ll \sum_{h=1}^{K} L_h \cdot \pi_h$.

Example:

The allowable loss that is connected with the system to be investigated is 10^5 ECU per year. The system has 5 modes of operation, each connected to losses according to the following table. The last column gives the probability of selection for each mode of operation during one demand.

mode	loss/ECU	π
1	10^7	0,2
2	10^6	0,3
3	10^5	0,2
4	10^4	0,1
5	10^3	0,2

The systems gets 10^4 demands per year.

The allowable loss for one demand is 10 ECU. The number of necessary test runs is

$$n = \frac{3}{10} \ (0,2\cdot10^7 + 0,3\cdot10^6 + 0,2\cdot10^5 + 0,1\cdot10^4 + 0,2\cdot10^3) =$$
$$= 3\cdot10^{-1} \ (0,23212\cdot10^7) \approx 7\cdot10^5$$

(π can also be gained from the operating experience).

5.5.4.5 Distribution of messages

The above derivations have been made without any specific relationship to real time. This was done to keep them as simple as possible. In real time systems, however, not only the static conditions must be met, but also the time conditions, if the assumptions of the derivations shall be valid. They have to be adjusted to real operation. This concerns the timing of interrupts, message arrivals, message durations, including the delays and possibly associated transmission errors. New time conditions can lead to establish new strata for them, thus increasing K in the above formulae. The same usually applies for new sequences of demands. The whole considerations are no longer to be based on the static input data space only, but on that space with addition of the time as another dimension. Random variables of the test procedure change to sequences of one mission and vice versa. A stratum may be a particular type of mission or accident and the set {K} of strata stands for the set of all possible missions from which the test cases must be selected according to the discussed strategy.

5.5.4.6 Concluding remarks

a) Taking $L_1 = ... = L_K = 1$, we obtain the statistical software test with respect to failure probability.

b) Taking K=1 and L_1=1 we obtain the black box test with respect to failure probability.

c) The number N_h of test cases for each stratum $h=1,\ldots,K$ is a random variable. The joint distribution of $N_1,\ldots,N_K$ is a poynomial distribution with parameters $n,\rho_1,\ldots,\rho_K$. The expected value $E(N_h)$ of test cases for stratum h is therefore given by

$$E(N_h) = \rho_h \cdot n = \frac{L_h \cdot \pi_h}{\sum\limits_{i=1}^{K} L_i \pi_i} \cdot n \qquad (5.18)$$

d) The confidence statements on software risk presented here make use of the results of statistical test cases only. No earlier deterministic tests or other verification attempts are taken into account.

5.5.5   Criticism

The methods that have been discussed under chapter 5.5 qualify in principle to show that test objects meet high reliability requirements. However, to execute a test procedure that meets all the assumptions and all the necessary prerequisits will in general be very costly. High costs are also caused by the necessary large number of test runs and the evaluation of the correctness of the results. Therefore, it is reasonable to look for other means of providing reliable software. Such means will be discussed in the next section, where we treat diverse software structures.

5.6   Testing of diverse systems

5.6.1 Diversity versus singularity

Testing of complex real time systems can cost a lot of effort if the number of tests is high enough that meaningful reliability figures can be derived. The search for system structures that require a smaller number of test runs leads to diverse arrangements. Diverse systems contain several independently developed real time software packages that solve the same problem. Their results are compared before any output is made. In this connection only systems with "simple" diversity are considered, i.e. systems with only two diverse subsystems. See figure 5.6.

If the comparison of results leads to no discrepancy of the independent computation outputs, one of the output areas is transmitted. If discrepancies are recognised, a warning is issued. From this follows that the first merit of diverse systems is to be expected in safety related applications. As we will see later, however, this is not the only one.

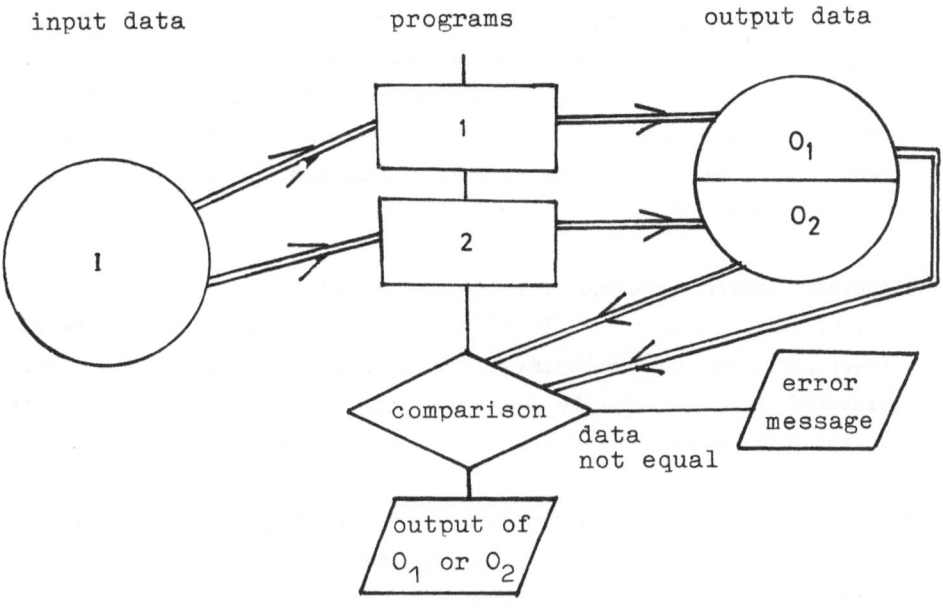

Fig. 5.6:   Structure of a diverse program system

The obvious drawback of diverse systems is the high cost of two-fold independent development. Another is the requirement of two-fold independent program maintenance. This means: The fixed cost associated with the software system will be doubled. Obviously, the savings during the verification phase must be considerable in order to come to overall economic solutions.

To be able to give a quantitative statement about this, we need assumptions on the relationship of test cost and development cost. This is done best by means of examples. Following the considerations in /Ehre83/, four scenarios are considered:

a) A relatively simple system requires two man years of development effort. It is estimated that one additional man year will be needed to get the system commissioned and keep it working during its life time. The total non verification related effort is therefore 3 man years, roughly 500 working hours. Considering the simplicity of the function solved by the system it is assumed that during one hour, 10 test cases can be prepared, executed and evaluated. During three years 50 000 test runs can be made according to this assumption. This can be considered as optimistic.

b) Another system requires for design, development and maintenance an estimated 6 man years of effort. We assume that we can make more than 3 tests per hour, corresponding to the higher complexity of the functions executed and the thereby involved larger amount of time per test. During 6 man years 30 000 test runs can be executed.

c) A more complex real time system needs in total 10 man years for design, development and maintenance. During that period 3 750 tests could be made, corresponding to less than 2 per day.

d) A large complex system needs in total 20 man years effort for design etc. During that period 1 000 tests could be made, corresponding to one test in four days.

Using (5.13) one can now draw curves for each of the four systems, which show the dependency of the demonstrated failure probability per demand from the provided effort. Figure 5.7.

They start from point 1, corresponding to the simple development effort that had already been invested for the singular system before the statistical test was to start.

5.6.2 Test effort in diverse systems

In order to come to quantitative estimates about the necessary effort for
the test of two diverse programs, we make another assumption:

With respect to each demand to the real time system,
each of the diverse programs fails independently from   (IV)
the other program with probability p_1.

This assumption is a very idealistic one. It will never fully apply for
any real system, but it gives a good starting point for calculations. This
is all we need here, because we want to show only the principal rela-
tionships. If (IV) is not valid, the formulae become much more complex.

Due to the assumption of independency we can immediately derive the probability p_c of common failure of <u>both</u> programs with respect to one demand.

$$p_c = p_1^2 \qquad (5.19)$$

The probability of failure of one <u>or</u> the other of these programs is p_d. It
is the probability for the use of the error exit of the structure of
Fig. 5.6.

$$p_d = p_1 + p_1 - p_1^2 \approx 2 \cdot p_1 \qquad (5.20)$$

If the system has safety functions to fulfil, it will be designed such
that p_c characterises its safety and p_d characterises its availability.

p_d has the same confidence level as p_1. The confidence level of p_c is
smaller, because the relative uncertaintis add. Apart from this aspect,
the same formulae can be used in principle as for the singular system.
They give results for p_1, and (5.19) and (5.20) transfer the results to
our diverse system. The outcome is depicted in fig. 5.7 for the important
case that no failure occurs. The curves start from point 2 of the abs-
cissa, because the initial development effort was twice as high as for
singular systems. As can be seen, the failure probabilities for common
failures (safety) quickly get smaller than the failure probabilities for
singular systems. As it was to be expected, the availability is mitigated
by our diverse system. This is because we always prevent output if disagreement between the two diverse parts exists, as shown in Fig. 5.6.

174

We now look at a particularity of diverse systems. A diverse system
provides another advantage over a singular one: The possibility to test
the two subsystems against each other. Once the necessary test mock-up is
finished, a very high number of test runs is feasible, without too much
additional effort. The check of the correctness of the results does not
need manual interaction, but can use the system inherent comparison. The
majority of expectable failures will be in one of the subsystems only and
therefore self reporting. Only a small minority is to be expected to be
common to both, according to (5.19).

The effort to design such an automated test can be considerable. It may
not only require the installation of a random number generator for providing input data, but perhaps a partial simulation of the environment of
the real time software. In Fig. 5.7 another unit of effort was assumed for
the preparation of this test. Then it was assumed that 250 000 test runs
would be equivalent to the development effort for the singular system. The
number of test runs no longer depends on the system complexity because it
can be executed during nights and over week-ends, without any permanent
human observation. As can be seen from the figure, this type of test can
become the cheapest one if safety and availability requirements get high.

Example:
The four scenarios from section 5.6.1 are considered again. It is required
that the failure probability per demand remains below 10^{-3} as far as
availability is concerned and below 10^{-4}, with respect to safety. From
Fig. 5.7 ohne can conclude: For system a and b the singular solution is
the cheapest one, for system c and d diverse solutions are cheaper. The
availability requirements for both systems requires so much testing that
the two systems should be tested against each other.

175

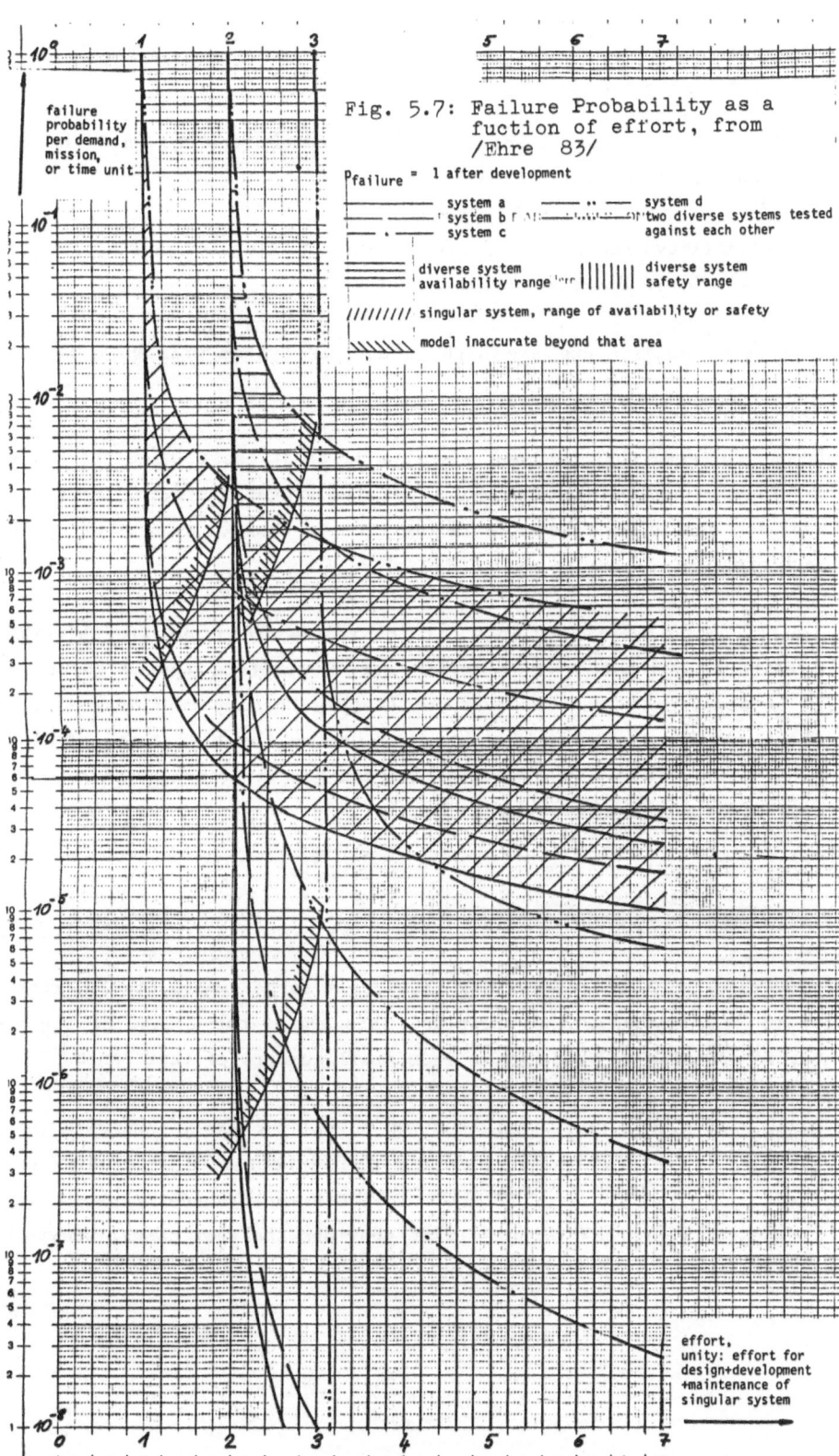

Fig. 5.7: Failure Probability as a
fuction of effort, from
/Ehre 83/

5.6.3 Criticism

Form the earlier considerations and in particular from fig. 5.7 the following recommendations can be given:

- If reliability requirements are modest, a singular system is more economic, than a diverse system.

- If safety requirements are high, a diverse system will be cheaper in general.

- If one foresees that the test effort will be at least twice the design, development and maintenance effort of the singular system, the diverse approach should be taken, including test of the two subsystems against each other.

Diversity can be beneficial only, if the system functions are so complex that neither systematic verification nor a complete test according to (5.7) is promising. This, however, will apply to many real time systems. Last but not least we should point out: Due to the high cost associated with diversity, it may be reasonable to design only complex parts diversely and leave simple ones singular.

5.7   Problems with large tests

In many cases statistical testing requires a large number of test runs in order to lead to meaningful results. This poses the following requirements, in addition to those known from small numbers of test runs:

- Since real time software behaviour is normally closely connected to its hardware, the total computer system should be tested, including hardware, software and external devices. The computer under test should be connected to another computer that provides the test cases, steers the timing and monitors the output.

- The hardware of the test mock-up should be suitably reliable. If e.g. several 100 000 test runs are to be executed, it is not tolerable to be confronted with failures of the test equipment during each 10 000 cases. Because such a test must go on during night time and during week ends, even few hardware failures can block a lot and can make many retries necessary.

- Test control must include a random number generator with a suitably long repetition period.

- Test control must be able to simulate real environment. In particular the actual time conditions must be simulated. This poses hard constraints on both hardware and software of the test mock-up. Every input condition to the tested object and every result or intermediate result should be able to be recorded, if possible with the associated time conditions. Protocols themselves, however, should be restricted to significant cases, e.g., if the reaction of the tested object differs from the expected one.

5.8   Conclusions

Statistical methods for performance verification and validation of real time systems are important as complement to systematic methods. They are useful if the system to be investigated is so complex that no systematic method can verify complete freedom from errors for the system as a whole. Statistical methods immediately lead to reliability figures. Some sub-methods regard the test object as a black box. Their drawback is the necessity to know details abaout the intended system use, in particular about the timing involved and the kind and sequence of demands to be expected. Other submethods ignore the system but need instead some detailed knowledge about the internals of the real-time system to be verified of validated.

Statistics are useful if operating experience shall be considered. The mathematics involved allows one to quantify the future performance to be expected of a system if its history is well known. For many applications it will be sufficient to use equations (5.11) or (5.13) as rules of thumb. The other considerations of this chapter, however, become important if more detailed results are required.

Due to the large number of test cases required, statistical testing is normally quite experience if it is the only method to be used. Therefore it is recommended that systematic verification methods be tried prior to any statistical attempts if no operating experience exists. If systematic efforts do not lead to ratisfactory results, the considerations of section 5.3.7 about exhaustive testing should be applied provided the system to be considered is not too large. The rest of the methods of chapter 5 refer to large systems.

6 Simulation and System Validation

S. Bologna, W. J. Quirk and J. R. Taylor

A simulator can be defined as any device which calculates, emulates or predicts the behaviour of another device, or some aspect of the behaviour of the world. Simulators can be implemented using either analogue or digital computers. In the field of real-time system validation, they are used to:

- simulate the real world to provide inputs to the system
- simulate the real world for evaluating the outputs from the system
- simulate the system itself to evaluate its acceptability.

All three of these are important. Simulation offers a bridge between a real-time system considered in isolation during its development and its final real world environment. Furthermore, both sides of this bridge are especially relevant to real-time systems. It has been estimated that more than 50% of errors in a typical project are due to specification problems /Endr75/. Simulating the real world concentrates the mind on precisely what aspects of the world are of concern to the control system, while simulation of the system itself, especially at an early stage, enables its functional adequacy and acceptability to be established before costly design and implementation stages are undertaken. It should also not be forgotten that time itself is of the essence in real-time systems and no amount of individual module testing can validate the temporal performance of the complete system. Only the real world or, more likely, an accurate model of the real world can provide realistic input test data for the final stages of system validation.

The following sections enlarge on the detailed applications of simulation techniques. Though at present the cost of simulation can be high, the increasing complexity and responsibility of control systems is making this technique correspondingly more important, see, for example, the safety application of a Pressurised Water Reactor simulator described

180

in /LaBe82/. One can also predict that continuing advances in electronics should provide more powerful and cheaper simulation hardware in the future, thus extending the range of systems for which real-time simulation is feasible. In any case, the example shows how a large amount of system validation can be achieved without extraordinary expense or difficulty.

6.1 Simulation of plant as a testing aid

As discussed in the previous two chapters, testing real-time systems is difficult because of:

- the large volume of test data
- the critical dependence on timing and sequencing of test inputs
- the impossibility (sometimes) of using the real world for testing.

Testing, in general, involves assessing the system performance with respect to a specification of what the system should do. This means that testing is highly dependent on having a good specification. However, a good specification for programming is not the same as a good one for testing, and this leads to problems because:

- a specification says what the program should do from a constructional point of view, and not from a testing point of view.

- specifications rarely say what a program should not do.

- the specification is a source of common mode errors if used for both program construction and testing.

- testing does not validate the specification but rather verifies that the design meets the specification by concentrating on the internal structure of the program.

Thus testing is more effective in the individual verification steps rather than for overall system validation.

It is possible to go one step further back using a simulator and test with respect to a model of the real world. This is more effective as a validation technique because it checks both the specification and the system in terms of the real requirements of the system. It is the nearest one can get to real life use. Needless to say, system validation is a very late phase in the software production cycle to detect requirement specification inadequacies. The techniques discussed in section 6.2 are much more valuable in this respect. None-the-less, it is never too late to detect a fault which could lead to a dangerous incident.

6.1.1 Simulation and diversity

Against a random test generator and to a lesser extent against a system-structure-influenced test generator, a simulator can be a slow way of generating test data. However for validation, a simulator has a great advantage in that while both the system specification and the simulator may be incorrect because of difficulties in understanding the real world, they are not usually both based on the same development personnel or environment. Consequently, any inconsistencies are less likely to coincide and testing with respect to a simulator may, in suitable circumstances, offer enhanced reliability expectations analogous to the use of diverse design and implementation techniques. It is especially noteworthy that the requirements specifications for the simulator and control system are likely to be separately derived. This is often not the case for diverse implementations of the control system, where the specification can be a worrying potential source of common mode errors. In this respect, simulation may offer a greater degree of confidence than diversity of the system itself.

This independence between control system program and plant simulator is enhanced by the fact that simulators can often be constructed from standardised modules and can, to a large extent, be validated independently from any specific application. There are, in fact, several languages such as DSL77 /Hall78/ and CSMP /Swis78/ which are designed specifically to allow plant to be described in control-theory terms. These are then automatically translated into the system equations necessary for a continuous simulation. In fact, DSL77 is a non-procedural language and

the necessary procedure is synthesised from the control expressions. No
doubt with the recent advances in 'expert' systems, such translations
into procedural form could be made redundant. The direct use of a
control-theoretic model again adds to the effective diversity of control
system and plant simulator. In such cases, there are only two possible
sources of modelling error:

- mistaking the structure of the plant
- mis-estimating one or more parameters of the plant.

The former is unlikely to go unnoticed although the latter can be source
of error common to both control program and simulator. However,
calibration is a routine, well understood process and the different
parameters can often be estimated in isolation before the full generality
of the simulator exercises their interrelations.

The same observations apply to using a simulator as a test performance
analyser. In this case, data should be fed into the system under test
for which the real plant response is known. Any deviations from this
response indicate a problem either with the simulator or with the system
under test. The more accurate the simulator is, particularly with respect
to its response in real time, the more rigorous is the effective testing
of the system.

One can even complete the loop. For if a complete plant simulator is
available, then the input simulator and the output simulator become the
same. A full plant simulator can actually provide on-line diversity.
Comparison of the plant state with the simulator prediction will indicate
anomalies if they occur. Further, if the simulator states are limited
to those known to be safe, then this comparison becomes a safety monitor
for the control system.

A variant of this technique, combining simulation, disturbance analysis
and control, was proposed in /Jana79/. The system in this case was a
power distribution network and a hybrid simulator was to be 'patched'
on-line by a digital disturbance classifier computer. One or more
simulations could then be run to evaluate different possible control

responses. It is clear that very fast simulation time compared to system response time is necessary for this approach to be viable (the reference proposed a simulated time 100 times faster than real time).

Full plant simulators were the subject of a previous detailed report /SRS81/ and the large number of references contained therein show just how much interest there is in this field. This interest is very significant. Test harnesses tend to be ad hoc software developments, often constructed in a hurry and themselves prone to error. But simulators for the real plant may already exist, either as engineering or design aids (such as transient performance or stress prediction) or as training aids. Both types, but particularly the latter, can offer valuable assistance in the overall validation of a control or safety system. It is also worth underlining that the interface between the system and the operators may be just as critical as any interface to the plant. Consequently, this interface also requires detailed validation from both functional and ergonomic viewpoints.

6.1.2 Effectiveness of simulation as a validation technique

The general structure of a validation simulator is shown in figure 6.1. However, it should not be thought that such simulators trivialise real-time system validation. Accurate simulation can be very expensive and real-time simulation even more so. Precision simulators for large process plant can take many man-years to construct. For this reason, the use of simulation techniques must be carefully considered in relation to other validation techniques. It should also be stressed that the comparison of the actual simulator behaviour with its real world prediction needs to be automated if any reasonable degree of confidence is to be established, both because of the number of cases to be compared and the accuracy of the comparison. But again, a suitable comparator may already be available from the simulator commissioning. Whenever this comparison reveals a discrepency, there is still the problem of determining whether it is the system under evaluation or the simulator itself which is at fault.

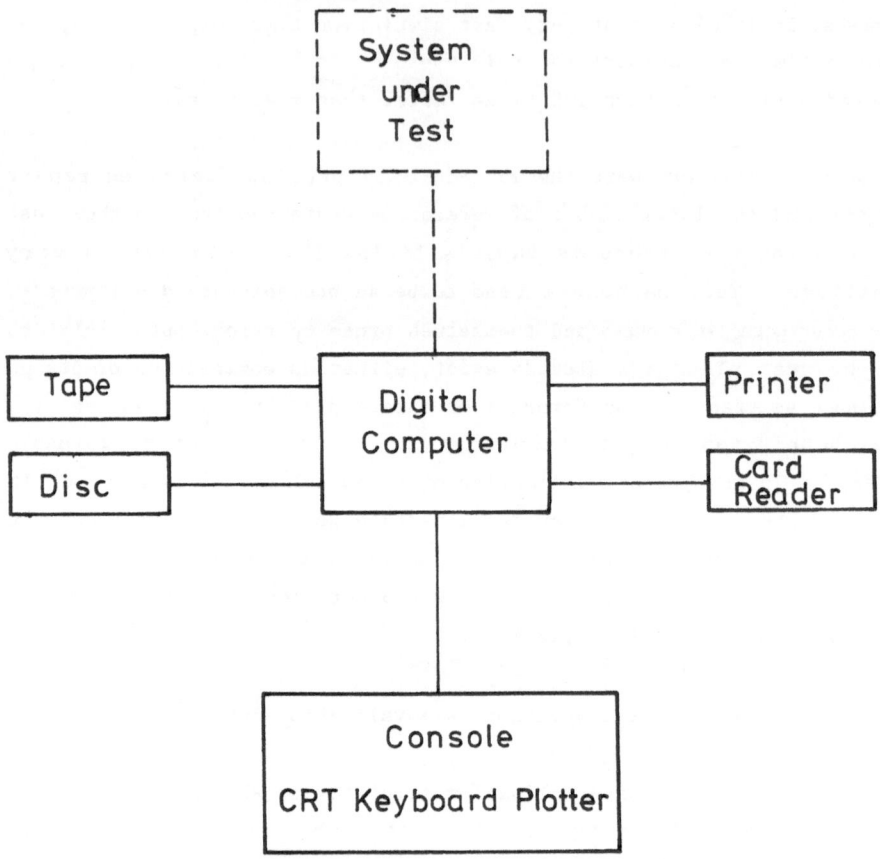

Fig. 6.1 General configuration for a Real-Time Engineering Simulator.

It is most important that any such problem revealed by this procedure is carefully analysed before a correction is applied: one must not correct the real world to fit the error. However it is often the case that this identification involves much work in analysing the plant or computer requirements specification. Some indication of correct model behaviour can be gained by implementing checks on simple criteria within the simulator. Such criteria can include absolute limits on quantities being calculated and checks on suitable conservation laws. However, such simple criteria are rarely sufficient: there is often a band between the correct behaviour and the limits set by the criteria within which performance may be unacceptable but which goes undetected. Similarly, the error may only be detectable by analysing correlations between a number of the model variables. This whole area is still relatively unstudied, though some results were reported in /KhHo78/ and more recently in /Lind82/.

It is not uncommon, particularly for simulations of continuous systems, to find that the simulation is not in real time but in scaled time - usually slower than real time. This comes about because of the complexity of the equations which model the real world and have to be solved at very frequent intervals. Simulators may still be of use in such circumstances provided that the time apparent to the system being validated can be similarly scaled. This may be possible by suitable changes to the clocks of the system processors. Clearly, however, the confidence gained in such circumstances is less than that corresponding to a similar test of an unaltered real system, and any alterations must be kept to an absolute minimum. Any software changes would more-or-less invalidate the procedure. It should also be noticed that in a few cases, more especially with analogue simulators, the simulator may run more rapidly than real time. In such cases, it may be possible either to slow the simulator to match the speed of the system being validated or, alternatively, to speed up the system and take advantage of the ability to carry out more tests.

6.1.3 Continuous system simulation construction

As already mentioned, constructing a simulator is a difficult, expensive
and time-consuming problem in real-time software development - the very
subject of this report. It should not be undertaken lightly. Indeed, it
is a little surprising that it is only fairly recently that the software
problems of constructing simulators (as distinct from the numeric
problems) have been recognised /Shep83/. A typical development experience
is reported in /Cham78/. The model - a training simulator for a nuclear
reactor - involved a stiff system of about 400 differential equations.
Even using one of the most successful solution methods /Gear71/, numerous
simplifications had to be made in order to achieve anything near real-time
performance. A recent survey of such simplification techniques is
/InRe83/. It is also worth noting that the advent of cheap multiple
micro-computers is widening the field where real-time simulation is
possible /Pime83/. For completeness, a brief description of the necessary
steps is included here. The effort required and the pay-off expected
should be carefully compared with those for other validation procedures
before embarking on this route of system validation.

For general continuous systems such as process plant, mechanical and
medical systems, the simulator modelling involves determining a suitable
set of differential equations for the behaviour of the relevant variables.
These equations are generally mass and energy balance equations, equations
relating physical parameters such as temperature and pressure, and
equations describing the performance of components such as pumps and
valves. The detailed steps involved in this are as follows:

- The system must be divided into a set of compartments. Each compartment
is a volume of physical space with nominally uniform contents. For
example, a pressure vessel might be regarded as a compartment.

- The interconnections between compartments which allow mass or energy
flow must be identified.

- For each compartment, mass and energy balance equations must be
established. If there are several substances or phases within a
compartment, there must be separate equations for each one.

- For each compartment, equations for each relevant physical parameter must be determined. Again if there are multiple phases in a compartment, then further equations governing the relationship between the phases may be necessary. If such inter-phase effects are ignored, the model is referred to as a pseudo-equilibrium model.

- Similar equations must be established to describe the parameter dependence between connected compartments.

- The third class of equations describing equipment performance must be established.

- The complete model must be quantified - ie. specific volumes, flow rates, pump speeds etc. taken from observations or specifications.

- Any discontinuities, such as safety valve openings, must be noted and the model suitably adapted to cope with these effects.

- All these equations should be put into a uniform format, with consistent meaning and scaling of variables.

- Finally, the equations must be solved, either by suitable digital numeric techniques or by appropriate design of analogue computers.

Note that sophisticated numerical techniques may be needed for accuracy, speed and stability of the solution. This is especially so when the system of equations turns out to be stiff (ie. the time constants of the system vary rather widely) and there is only a limited amount of information currently published. The most successful methods are described in /Curt79/ and /ShGe79/, and the most serious work on achieving real-time performance is reported in /Gear77/. These aspects are dealt with more comprehensively in appendix 3 of /SRS81/ and also in /NDES77/.

It should be clear from the foregoing that the validation of a simulator is itself a challenging undertaking. The use of a simulator in system validation can, on its own, only lead to a confidence in the system of the same magnitude as the confidence in the accuracy of the simulator itself. Like testing techniques, the use of a simulator only detects anomalies; no anomalies detected does not prove that the system under investigation is error-free. For safety-related systems, much caution is needed and a simulator should have been extensively used per se before it is accepted as part of the overall validation procedure. Appendix 5 of /SRS81/ goes into more detail concerning the Verification and Validation of the simulator itself.

6.1.4 Discrete system simulation construction

For another class of systems, including the major group of safety-related traffic control systems, discrete modelling is possible. In such cases, the system state (eg. position, number and status of vehicles) is represented by a vector of tokens, and the way these tokens change is described by finite state transition functions. In general, these models are easier to validate. Limiting-case behaviour (eg. no traffic, steady state, heavy overdemand) together with token conservation can often be used to establish the correctness of the transition functions. This comes about because the real limiting case behaviour is accurately known and there are usually no mechanistic changes in the simulation for the intermediate cases. If these functions are described in tabular form, the program interpreting these tables is also usually simple and relatively easy to check.

There are a number of possible implementation routes for such simulators. Some standard systems, such as GPSS (/Gord77/, /Gord78/, /MuSt79/), exist. However there can be problems interfacing such simulators with the computer system to be tested and consequently more specialised implementation techniques are usually employed. Typically these use state transition tables, as described above, which are either interpreted or translated into a compilable language. The actual states are maintained by a controlling program which determines the state transition routines to apply on the basis of the current state and the input event sequence. The problem state can be evaluated by the control program at either fixed or variable time intervals. Some overall performance benefits may be achieved by using variable steps, but for real-time systems, a fixed time step is more appropriate because of its inherent behavioural constancy.

Just as for continuous system simulators, the model underlying the simulation must be carefully validated. Furthermore, the time step chosen for the simulation must provide suitably realistic temporal response. Finally, not only must the individual outputs from the simulator represent the real world correctly, but the statistical distribution of the outputs must also be accurate. This is particularly important for overload testing which can be highly sensitive to changes in distribution.

6.1.5 Example of the use of simulation in real-time system validation

The computerised real-time protection system for the TAPIRO fast research reactor (/BoAg79a/ & /BoAg79b/) at the Casaccia Center, ENEA, Rome provides a good example of the use of simulation for system validation. This system, based on a ULP-12 (16 bit) minicomputer, is installed in parallel with conventional hard-wired protection equipment and was tested by simulating all the expected input signals to the protection system as derived from the system specification. The detailed hardware configuration of this particular example is shown in figure 6.2.

The simulator hardware used is a hybrid computer similar to the EAI Pacer 700. It consists of an EAI Pacer 100 (16 bit, 32K core) digital computer closely coupled to an EAI 781 analogue unit. The Pacer 100 generates the logical signals to the protection system directly via an i/o interface (a PLAYCARD), and the analogue signals indirectly by controlling the EAI 781 unit. The PLAYCARD also allows the hybrid to control the protection system computer and to read its outputs, as shown in the figure.

The testing cycle can be divided conceptually into four steps:

- production of input test cases
- execution of system runs
- results analysis
- documentation.

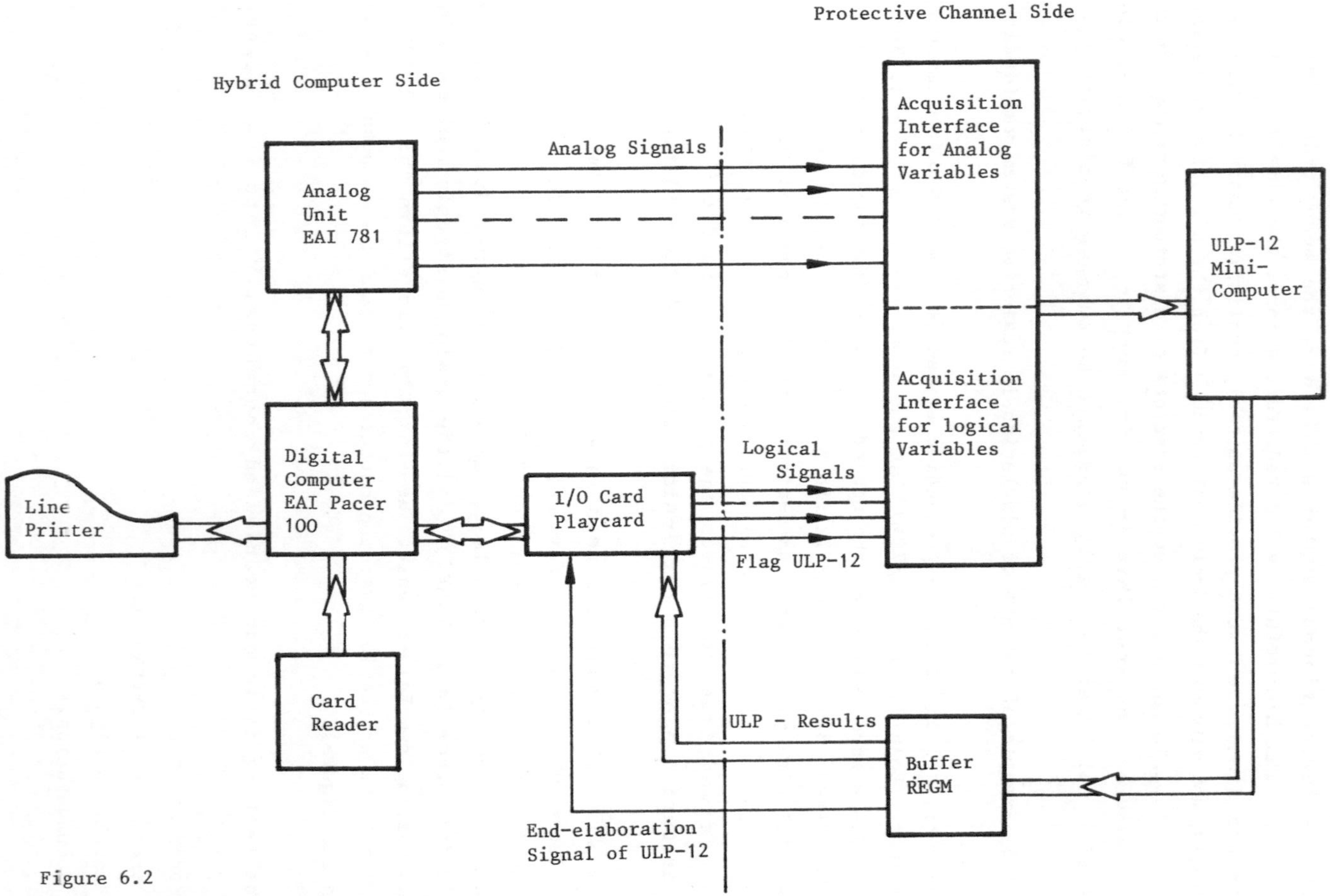

Protective Channel Side

Hybrid Computer Side

ULP-12 Mini-Computer

Acquisition Interface for Analog Variables

Acquisition Interface for logical Variables

Buffer REGM

Analog Signals

Logical Signals

Flag ULP-12

ULP – Results

I/O Card Playcard

End-elaboration Signal of ULP-12

Analog Unit EAI 781

Digital Computer EAI Pacer 100

Card Reader

Line Prirter

Figure 6.2
Detailed Hardware used in the Example Simulation

Data for the first step was obtained from previous results. The individual modules had already been tested with respect to both functionality and structure. The data for each module was amalgamated (by use of another computer) so that a complete path test set was produced for the whole software system. The number of tests in this test set is equal to the maximum of the number of paths in each individual module. The set was further augmented to provide the necessary complete functional tests as well. Each test case and its associated expected outcome was stored on cards which were directly readable by the simulator hybrid computer.

To execute each test, the simulator read the test data, set and checked the analogue and logical signals required, and then enabled the execution of the protection algorithm through the use of the ULP-12 Flag. At the end of each cycle of the protection algorithm, the Pacer 100 read the results back from the ULP-12. It also noted the time delay between each cycle initiation and completion. After a predetermined number of cycles, the simulator stopped the protection computer and proceeded to the third step.

In this step, the Pacer 100 compared the various results from the protection system (safety actions and alarms) with the expected outcomes for each test case. It also checked that the results had been provided within the time allowed (in this case, 100 msec). Finally, each test case and its outcome was printed.

This complete validation procedure is shown in figure 6.3. Using this method, the following aspects have been verified:

 - the functional adequacy of the protection algorithm, as implemented in independent modules.

 - time independency for those modules which implement combinatorial functions.

 - time adequacy as specified for the execution of the protection algorithm.

 - satisfactory compilation and linkage editing of the software.

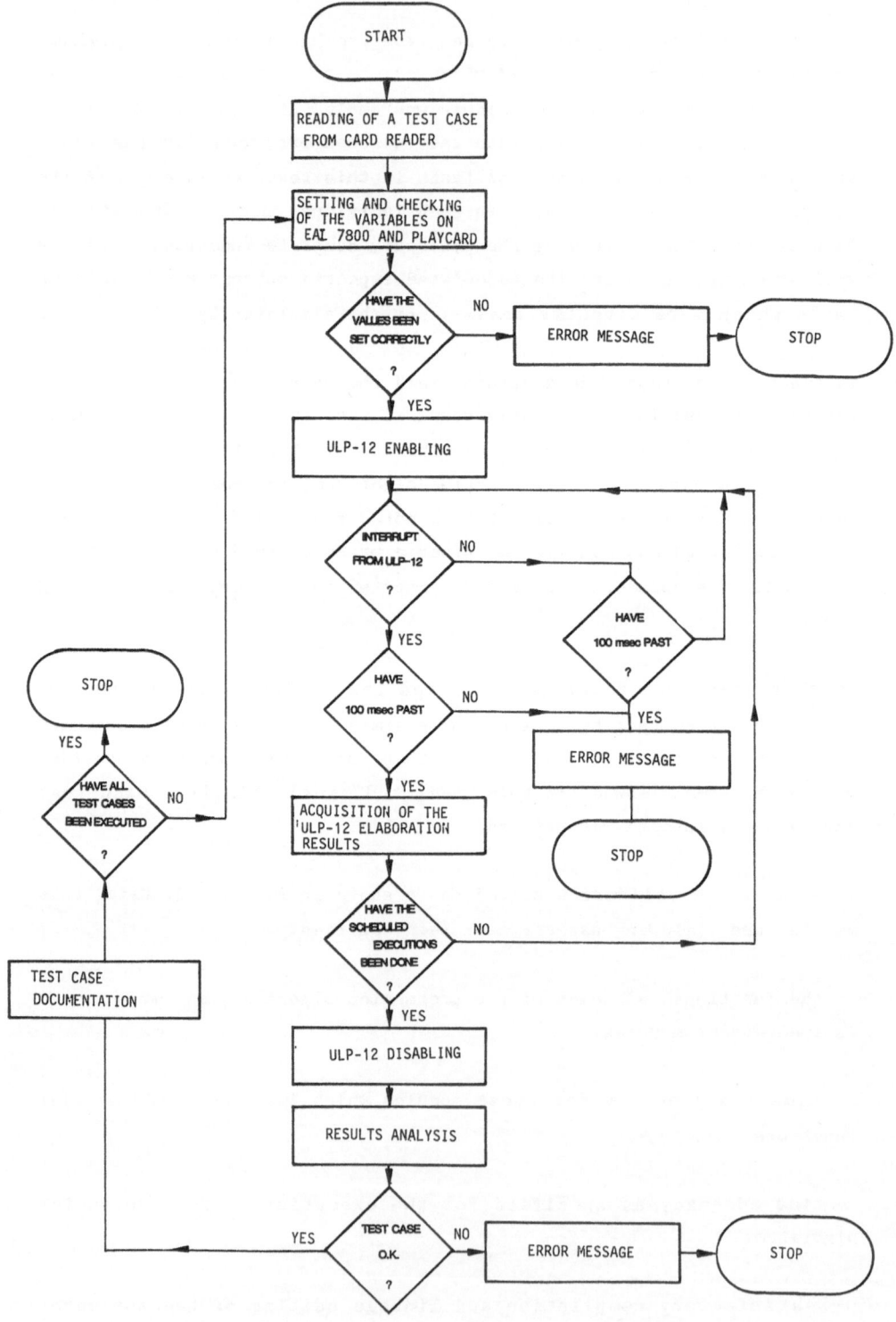

Fig. 6.3 Flow chart of system testing on the hybrid computer side.

- correct behaviour and addressing of the (assembler language) input-output routines.

- adequacy of the hardware in fulfilling its requirements for the protection system.

Notice that all these have been shown with a relatively simple and cheap simulator. The alternative of constructing a complete plant model able to simulate all the input signals to the protection system, in transient as well as static conditions, would have involved not only more complicated modelling but also the latest hardware technology and interactive CRT-based display consoles. This would have been much more expensive. Furthermore, as the objective in this case was to validate the system integration rather than the specification, the extra expense was unnecessary and even the test cases which the simulator was required to generate had already been established during earlier verification steps.

6.2 Simulation of the system itself

As described in the introduction, it is not just the performance targets of real-time systems which have to be achieved. Both functionality and interfacing details are equally important characteristics of such systems. Because development of these systems can be both costly and lengthy, it is important the 'right' system is developed from the start. One - and possibly the only - way to test the specification in these respects is to build a system which accurately reflects such aspects of the specification and then validate that system: in other words, simulate the system required. The field of robotics has already made much use simulation in this manner /Loza83/, /Meye81/, /Soro80/ & /HeDo79/. Clearly, this technique is only viable if the simulation can be made significantly cheaper or easier than constructing the final system. Consequently, automated procedures such as the SPECK simulator described in chapter 3.5 are invaluable. Particular aspects of this area of system validation are described in the following two subsections.

6.2.1 System functionality and interfaces

These two areas of the system are closely related and have to do with the completeness and unambiguity of the requirements specification. There seems to be no hope of any formal analysis detecting a completely missing requirement in a specification which is itself otherwise consistent and apparently complete. Thus it is only by demonstrating the specified requirements back to the customer or final user that will give some chance of bringing such missing requirements to light. Therefore, it can be very desireable that a simulation of the system functionality be carried out early in the system development phase. It is worth noting that actual real time performance is not an aspect of interest in this area (which is just as well since that cannot be simulated except by the final system which must achieve it!). In particular, computing power is not a key issue. Furthermore for interface simulation, functional accuracy is also not necessary so that relatively simple software can be used. However, it is clear that to be a useful tool in system validation, the simulation must run fast enough to cover a reasonable number of event scenarios or a reasonably long simulated time for the system operation.

There are a number of possible routes to achieve this system animation. With a suitable data-flow-based specification held in machine readable form, the control flow necessary to support the desired data flow can be derived. Thus all that is necessary (in principle) is to provide code for each data transformation process specified. This can be done by allowing special comment-like descriptions within the specification which contain (or allow the derivation of) the necessary code by the simulator but are ignored by any specification analysis. The code could be either procedural or non-procedural, and its execution can be by way of separate tasks per process (the current SPECK implementation), subroutine call to resident libraries or interpretation. The first and third alternatives are relatively simple to implement (with suitable operating system support) but produce rather slow running simulations. The second is faster running but more complex to implement completely automatically and offers less protection against faults in the software provided for the simulation. The first also offers the possibility of running on multi-processor configurations.

If the system to be simulated is structured in a top-down manner, then it is possible to simulate some or all of the system at a relatively crude high level until an 'interesting' event occurs. Then the high level component can be replaced by its next lower level expansion allowing the event to be followed in greater detail. This gives a useful way of improving the time performance of the simulation when it is known in advance that a proportion of the simulated events are not of interest.

The inputs to and outputs from such a simulation can be handled in a number of ways. Input data can be generated dynamically during the simulation (eg. real operator responses) or be taken from previously produced files of data (eg. recordings of real plant sensor data). The outputs likewise can be recorded for off-line comparison and analysis, displayed directly or even interfaced to real actuators. If a full plant simulator is available, the loop may be closed as described in 6.1.1.

There are two possible meanings for functional testing. The first concerns testing the system via its interfaces to the plant to determine that no relevant physical parameters have been completely forgotten. As already explained, such missing requirements are impossible to detect analytically and may only come to light before going live as a result of simulation. Here again, accurate and detailed algorithmic simulation of the system internals is not required. All that is necessary is that the various cause-effect or response paths through the system are highlighted. Alternatively, there may be a real concern over the detailed behaviour of some particular aspect of the system internal function. In this case, a simulation can provide a test-bed for software, offering an environment close, if not exactly similar, to its real operating environment. Of course, if the host simulator hardware is different from the final target system hardware, further problems may be introduced by cross compilation (especially due to optimising attempts by the compiler). Against this, the simulation should be carried out at the design level and the design environment should be hardware independent. Assuming this to be the case, the transfer from host to target should be invisible at the module level and assuming that the module is not reentrant (or does not use real time explicitly), the lack of real-time accuracy in the simulation will be of no consequence.

6.2.2 System performance simulation

It is important to differentiate between two different classes of system
performance requirements. There will be certain performance aspects
which have to be achieved in all circumstances. As such, the system must
be designed to meet these demands and the demonstration of that successful
design will probably be by analysis rather than by testing. For example,
freedom from deadlock will generally be shown by application of relevant
net theory, not by exercising of the system itself. For this part of the
overall system validation, therefore, the scope for simulation is rather
limited. It would generally only be applied if it were possible to carry
out an exhaustive test of all the system states.

However, there is a second class of requirements based on statistical
measures of system performance. For some classes of real-time system
(for example, systems specifically dedicated to safety monitoring), all
the performance objectives are hard and must be proved. But other classes
of system (for example message switching systems) may have to be designed
to achieve a statistical performance because of the excessive cost of
providing guaranteed performance in all possible circumstances. For
example, a telephone exchange is unlikely to be able to support
simultaneously a call between every pair of telephones connected to it.
Both the design to achieve a statistical performance and its demonstration
can be difficult. This is because the resource handling and queuing
theory are not amenable to analytic solution. Consequently, approximations
have to be used in the design – hopefully conservative approximations –
and these have to be verified.

Simulation can be used both to derive the necessary design constraints
and to verify the design meets its requirements. Again it is only a
model of the real system which is simulated: in this case a model of the
resource handling by the system in response to external demands. If the
resources include such items as processor and memory together with their
utilization, then the overall time response of the system can be obtained.
A simple but typical example might be to estimate the optimum size of
fast cache memory on a processor. This clearly depends on the expected
amount of branching within the code being executed in response to a

particular demand profile. Another example might be determining the speed of communication lines between processors to cope with the likely traffic. In this model, the actual system functionality is unimportant and again, real-time performance is not required of the simulator, only a performance adequate to achieve sufficient confidence in the statistics gathered.

Some progress has been made in automating this sizing problem. The DSIGNR system /PaSt82/ supports the top-down design of real-time systems and helps to produce both instruction rate estimates and throughput requirements, but the system does still need some manual intervention. It proceeds by taking a pseudocode description of the system, successively refining this and producing IFTRAN control skeletons for the system together with embedded monitoring calls to count the execution frequency of each code block. The actual code for each block is inserted manually and, to turn the execution frequency into a time, block instruction counts must also be manually generated. Several classes of instruction, corresponding broadly to different execution speeds, are separately tabulated by the simulator, so that the total execution time can be calculated automatically. The method is acknowledged still to be tedious, but if library modules with known performances are used, then the refining process may be stopped correspondingly earlier.

In fact, this sort of performance aspect is becomming more important as local area networks become incorporated into plant control systems. It is not only expensive to lay end-to-end lines between processors, sensors and actuators, but the large number of lines may have other undesireable implications. Incorrect installation and maintenance procedures, over-power dissipation in cable trunking and lowered vessel integrity due to the number of penetrations can all cause safety problems. However, to be acceptable as an alternative, such networks must have well-founded and assessed performance (as well as guaranteed delivery and error correction or recovery).

Simulation systems, such as SMARTIES /DiKo82/, have been produced to simulate computer networks with multi-level protocols. Most of the protocol standards which have been proposed are multi-level and the performance of such networks is still not well predicted by analytic techniques. These simulators model the protocol levels within the system architecture and allow the evaluation of different designs of protocols, including the allocation of protocol function to level and efficiency in normal and error situations.

6.2.3 System design simulation

Simulation of the results of one of the stages of the development cycle can offer an important verification method. As has already been mentioned in chapter 2, increasing interest is being shown in executable requirements specifications and rapid prototyping /RPW82/, /Goma82/. The specification must be expressed in a language which is both application oriented and be machine processable. A small number of essentially experimental systems are currently being developed: see the work of Davis (on RPS), Goguen (on OBJ) and others in /RPW82/. Similarly, the use of logic programming languages such as LISP /McAb62/, /WiHo81/ and PROLOG /ClMe81/ is becoming increasingly common for developing such specifications.

The use of simulation need not stop at the specification stage, however. There are often areas of the design which can be more effectively verified by simulation before the implementation phase proceeds. If the design has been expressed in a suitable form (such as a PDL), then some form of symbolic execution may be possible. Automating such execution is a form of system simulation /Balz81b/. Alternatively, finite state models of systems, such as petri nets or protocol transition diagrams, may be activated so as to simulate behaviour in some or even all possible cases /RaEs80/.

6.2.4 System error simulation

Most real-time systems have to be able to carry on working satisfactorily despite partial failures - both transient and permanent - within themselves. But just as it may not be feasible to supply all possible plant input signals to the system from real plant, so too it may not be desireable or possible to produce the full range of such partial failures to which the system is supposed to be immune. To this end, simulation of the system itself with such failures included in the simulation provides a powerful method of verifying the design of these error recovery procedures. As mentioned in chapter 2, failures in error recovery can contribute very significantly to observed system unreliability /Toy78/ and it is thus very important that error recovery code is very fully exercised.

The types of error usually dealt with in these circumstances are failure of a functional unit within the system and data corruption. Both can be simulated with a data-flow model of the system. The technique has been used in hardware design for some time, with the effect of gate failures on digital systems being simulated. The normal faults in such cases are limited to 'stuck-at' gates. With general software systems, the class of expected faults may be larger, necessitating correspondingly more simulation runs.

Ideally, simulators for use in this area should have 'physically correct structure'. That is, each component module of the simulator should represent directly the physics of a corresponding component of the plant. Furthermore, the model should reflect accurately the possible two way flows of mass and energy, as well as allowing for the 'two way causality' demonstated by disturbances spreading bidirectionally down pipes or wires. By being so constructed, the simulator can treat a wide range of transients accurately, including those not envisaged in the test specification. Such general simulator models tend to be very large compared with rather more specific ones and tend to be expensive in computer time also (although not necessarily in analyst time). However, the results can be very valuable.

6.2.5 Simulation and operator interfaces

Although the operator interface can be viewed as being no different in principle to any other system interface, it is worthy of special mention. In many real-time systems, the operators carry a heavy responsibility for the economic running of the plant and in some cases they also carry a safety responsibility. Unlike the interfaces to other physical systems, the interface to the operators is rather flexible, matching the flexibility of the human mind. Furthermore, it is not just the content of the information displayed which is important: it is becomming more and more evident that both the form of the presentation and the ergonomics of the necessary responses are important. The Three Mile Island accident has stimulated work recently in this area /Belt83/. Because the science or engineering of ergonomics is still relatively young, there are as yet few areas where there is complete agreement on standards. Consequently, operator interfaces still tend to be one-off developments.

This operator interface has to be validated in two quite separate ways. First of all, it must display information correctly to the operator and react correctly to command inputs. This is just part of the normal system validation procedure. Secondly, it must be functionally acceptable to the operators so that their task is assisted and not hampered by the form of the display or the procedures necessary to interact with it. In particular, the display must not overwhelm the operator with information. This latter aspect can only be assessed by having operators and the system together and it is here that system simulation can be of assistance. If the proposed interface is simulated early in the system production phase, then any shortcomings in this area can be corrected before too much effort has been expended. It goes without saying that for such an assessment to be of greatest value, the simulation must proceed in reasonably precise real time.

6.2.6 Simulation throughout system development

Although the advantage of having a functional simulator available at an early stage has been stressed in the foregoing discussion, the simulator may be used throughout the construction phase. In particular, if the design of the simulator is logically similar to the real system design, an attribute already identified above as being highly desireable, then parts of the simulator may be replaced with parts of the real system as these become available. These parts may be hardware as well as software. Thus the system integration phase can start earlier. This is a technical advantage in that incompatibilities, particularly at subsystem interfaces, are detected early. It can also have economic advantages. Normally, integration testing cannot begin until all the system is available. As some parts will be completed before others, personnel involved with those parts may have to wait for others. With a suitable simulator, the testing can be carried out in parallel with other developments.

6.3 Conclusion

Despite the relative brevity of this chapter, simulators can be important in real-time system validation. When the process plant to be controlled is too dangerous to be used for testing the system, or the plant is not yet in existance, a simulator provides the only means of checking the system in terms of its real world requirement rather than as a computer system on its own. In other cases, and especially where a simulator for the plant already exists, thorough testing with this simulator may obviate the necessity to use diverse methods for the system itself. Finally, simulation of particular aspects of the system itself, and particularly its interfaces, can be a highly effective way of demonstrating gross system behaviour at a very early stage of its development and thus generate confidence in the suitability of its general functionality and its interfaces. Although these are not specifically real-time aspects of the system performance, they are aspects which take on a more critical importance in real-time systems than for other classes of off-line system.

7 Conclusion

W.D.Ehrenberger

7.1 Review of the problem

In addition to the critiques of the individual techniques of real-time
software verification and validation in the previous chapters, some
general views about their applicability and their future importance seem
to be in order. This chapter therefore will emphasise some of the aspects
already mentioned and try to build some sort of a roof over the other
chapters.

In general the area of real-time software will grow in the future, as
will all fields of digital computing and digital computer applications.
The area of verification and validation of that sort of software will
gain even more importance, because of the risks involved with on-line
computer applications. Since the technical processes that are being
controlled by real-time software and the organisational areas that are
involved get more and more powerful and complex, the harm that can be
done to individuals or to society due to failures of that software is
ever increasing. Since costs go up in many technical areas and are
continuously climbing in particular in all areas where human labour is
involved, more and more responsibility will naturally be allocated to
real-time computing systems that are, in principle at least, capable of
solving extremely complex tasks in an extremely reliable manner. Such
systems have the advantage over human labour done at any technical plant
that their strategies can be thoroughly considered and planned by experts
who do not have to work under the constraints imposed on site. Once such
a computing system does function correctly, one can be sure that its
software will always work as it should, as long as it is not changed.
The responsibility of correct function is to a considerable degree
associated with verifying and validating that function. This again can
be done by experts who, at least in principle, do not have to work under
the same time pressures as do, for example, plant operators. Software
itself does not suffer from deficiencies and shortcomings to the same

degree as do functions implemented in mechanical, electrical or electronic equipment. It is just the intrinsic complexity of the function that must be mastered.

7.2 The methods reported

In the life cycle chapter of this report, methods were described which help to keep the real-time software as simple as possible and to make sure from the very beginning that the problem to be solved is well understood and realistically attacked. The individual steps are described, in particular the intermediate verification stages which help to get a product being both error free to a certain degree and easy to validate at the end of its development. The desirability of uniform approaches is emphasised, the benefit of combining different techniques is described and the related management actions are mentioned. The last few years have not brought many new aspects in this area. At present it is important to use already well-proven methods effectively and to convince project participants about their advantages over unstructured ways of working or unstructured products.

In the chapter about structural analysis and proving techniques, the individual analytical methods presently available have been reviewed. Although schemes exist which give insight into the complex behaviour of real-time systems, the problem of proving and understanding is not solved in general. The available methods slightly enlarge the natural human perception but they are not suitable to solve the problem of complete understanding of complex system behaviour. Even if they can be automated, as can some of the means described, the factor of enlargement remains modest. The techniques described are nevertheless important for kernels or for other small but crucial system parts.

At present the area of tools with analysis and proving capabilities is rapidly developing. This in fact seems to be the most promising area that is covered by this report. The ultimate limits of such systems can hardly be estimated today. In the future, more powerful computers may help to overcome difficulties during the analysis due to combinatorial complexity. Integration of such tools with specification tools and translators can help to detect problems early in the software development stages.

In contrast to the tool supported methods, manual methods were described. They will probably not attract more attention in the future because they have achieved a certain maturity and their use normally requires much human effort. Probably code inspection, code reviews and walk throughs will maintain the importance they enjoy today, because of their remarkable effectiveness. Manual program proving, however, will possibly never gain more than academic interest.

Perhaps future development will automate one or other of the currently manual techniques. Some possibilities seem to exist with simulation of structures derived from program code, such as Petri nets or Fault Trees.

Instead of simulating a representation of a program however, one can also execute the program itself. The chapter about systematic testing describes the relevant methods. They are to be employed after analysis, based on the analysis results. Complete testing is feasible in simple cases but high cost prohibits exhaustive testing in more complex cases. The future, here too, may be with the use of automatic aids that generate data on the basis of analysis results, execute program parts and store the results of their execution. At present several metrics are being developed for characterisation of degrees of completeness of such tests. Here again, the field for progress is still open.

With respect to both testing and proving, the question of the functional requirements specification is very important: only explicitly stated requirements can be verified. No means exist to find programming errors or execution failures whose underlying requirements are not known.

The statistical methods that were discussed take an alternative approach to the systematic ones: a more global view of the real-time software system is taken in order to avoid the problem of combinatorial complexity. At least in some of the approaches presented, the internal structure of the validation object can be reflected and tests can be made according only to the functions required and the importance they have. For very complex systems this overall view of the test object is quite important. Unfortunately the effort connected with the required high number of test cases, the provision of test data and, in particular, the evaluation of the results is very high. It may even exceed the development cost for the system. Then it becomes economic to consider diverse software, solving the same problem in two independently developed subsystems. This is particularly worth considering if an automatic test can be made, where the two diverse parts can be tested against each other. However, this is recommended only if they are regarded as nearly error free already.

Other methods complement these global views of the test object. They take advantage of some knowledge of the internal program structure, the sequences of tasks and the timing requirements. Here, however, the same applies as for systematic means: in program systems of any notable complexity the combinatorial explosion is prohibitive for their use. On the other hand they offer some potential for a combination of systematic and probabilistic approaches. This area remains a very interesting one where much theoretical effort still seems to be necessary.

7.3 Hints for practical use

The reader may ask how he should approach any practical verification and validation problem of real-time software. This depends on the state of the project. Three stages in the system life cycle can be distinguished where V&V exercises may take place: during system development, at the end of development and after some use in the field.

7.3.1 V&V during system development stage

The person who is responsible for reliable or safe system operation or licensing should carefully monitor the development process as described generally in chapter 2 and particularly in section 2.3. He should enforce the proven guidelines which already exist for system development, should encourage the production of proper documentation and should foster the use of appropriate tools from the requirements specification onwards. Care should be taken over appropriate reviews, walk throughs or inspections after each individual development step, as described in section 3.4.

The growing importance and availability of formal methods should not be overlooked. The use of such techniques often helps V&V activities, as described in sections 2.2 and 2.3. Likewise, the use of an integrated support environment throughout as much of the system life cycle as possible can be beneficial in many ways (section 2.4). In particular, it can promote concise and timely documentation.

7.3.2 V&V activities after the coding stage

The first debugging will certainly be done by the software manufacturer. The use of reliability growth models (section 5.4) is commonly restricted to system integration testing, and not to the earlier stages of module testing. Never-the-less, both module testing and integration testing should make the most use of those automatic tools described in section 4.7 which provide details about control and data flow, interruptability and the use of shared resources.

Once the system is considered reasonably error free, formal verification methods described in chapter 3 should be used. If the reliability requirements are very high, then program proving may be applied to some parts of the system. One should also try to analyse the complete system in order to find an exhaustive set of test cases. This usually involves manual analysis and takes in some of the concepts behind program proving. Where exhaustive testing is infeasible, then at least some stated test coverage measure (chapter 4) should be achieved. For some applications, this V&V effort will be sufficient. One will tolerate finding any remaining errors in the field.

For safety related applications, this will not be sufficient. It may be necessary to provide a specific test mock-up ant to simulate the environment of the real-time system in order to provide realistic test cases. This is described in chapter 6. Simulation will be necessary in particular for handling time constraints and sequences of demands. Analysis results should be used to indicate where these simulation techniques can be used to best effect and not merely produce an excess of test data. It may be possible to achieve exhaustive testing by simulation.

Again, this will be seen as sufficient V&V effort in some cases. In others, especially where exhaustive testing or complete verification of some parts of the system have not been achieved, a statistical assessment may be required. A consideration of risk factors will determine the reliability goals to be verified (section 5.2.2). Sections 5.3 and 5.5 give the criteria for selecting and executing the necessary test cases. For safety related parts, a preliminary analysis may well reveal that the necessary test effort would be extremely high. In this case, one might consider diversification of these parts, as discussed in section 5.6, or the use of a simulator, as discussed in section 6.1.1.

7.3.3 V&V of systems with operating experience available

The amount of operating experience available must first be assessed: a first feel can be obtained from the rule of thumb given in formula (5.13). The next step is to evaluate the reliability requirements for the new system to be installed and, once these are known, the detailed requirements for statistical verification can be established according to the equ. (5.15) through (5.18). In some cases the operating experience alone may be sufficient. More likely, supplementary tests will be required. For certain parts of the new system, with little operating experience and a heavy burden of responsibility, systematic verification, as described in the previous paragraphs, may be needed.

This form of reliability assessment is complicated when the systems in the field were themselves subject to modification. In this case, the whole operating experience cannot be considered in a uniform manner. Rather, it has to be treated as new since the last change and only experience since that time should be considered. Where the modified parts and their functions can be clearly separated from the unmodified parts, then the longer experience from the unmodified parts may be considered valid.

7.4 Final remark

Generally the area of real-time software verification and validation still contains a lot of unsolved problems, whose clarification would be very beneficial to informatics and industry. On the other hand, the field is mature enough to allow solutions that have not been feasible during the era of hardwired control equipment.

References

/Abba81/   G. Abbate "Requirements Specifications of a PWR Protection System". International Conference on the Use of Computer Aids in Systems Development, London, 25-26 June 1981.

/Abri80/   J.R. Abrial "The Specification Language Z: Syntax and Semantics". April 1980.

/ACM78/   Proc Software Quality and Assurance Workshop. ACM SIGSOFT Software Engineering Notes, Vol 3 No 5, November 1978.

/AdBr82/   W.R. Adrion, M.A. Branstad, J.C. Cherniavsky "Validation, Verification and Testing of Computer Software". ACM Computing Surveys, Vol 14 No 2, 1982.

/AGAR82/   Software for Avionics. AGARD Conference Proceedings No 330, The Hague-Kijkduin Netherlands, 6-10 September 1982.

/Akiy71/   F. Akiyama "An Example of Software System Debugging". IFIP Congress, Ljubljana, 1971.

/Alfo77/   M.W. Alford "A Requirements Engineering Methodology for Real-Time Processing Requirements". IEEE Trans Software Engineering, Vol SE-3 No 1, January 1977.

/AlGa83/   A.J. Albrecht, J.E. Gaffney Jr "Software Function, Source Lines of Code and Development Effort Prediction: A Software Science Validation". IEEE Trans Software Engineering, Vol SE-9 No 6, November 1983.

/Alle76/   F.E. Allen "A Program Data Flow Analysis Procedure". Comm ACM, Vol 19 No 3, March 1976.

/AnPe76/   H. Anderson, L. Peiram, K. Strandberg "A Study of Software Reliability". 8th International Teletraffic Congress, Melbourne, 1976.

/Apt81/   K.R. Apt "Ten Years of Hoare's Logic: A Survey". ACM Trans on Programming Languages, Vol 3 No 4, October 1981.

210

/ASDM81/   ADA-based System Development Methodology Study Report. Department
           of Industry, London, 1981.

/AyCo82/   J.M. Ayache, J.P. Courtiat, M. Diaz "REBUS, A Fault-Tolerant
           Distributed System for Industrial Real-Time Control". IEEE Trans
           Computers, Vol C-31 No 7, July 1982.

/AzBe80/   P. Azema, B. Berthoumieu, P. Decitre "The Design and Validation by
           Petri Nets of a Mechanism for the Invocation of Remote Servers".
           Proc IFIP World Conference, Melbourne, 1980.

/BaGa83/   R.H.T. Bates, K.L. Garden, T.M. Peters "Overview of Computerized
           Tomography with Emphasis on Future Directions". Proc IEEE, Vol 71
           No 3, March 1983.

/BaGo79/   R. Balzer, N.M. Goldman "Principles of good Software Specification
           and their Implications for Specification Languages". Proc Specification
           of Reliable Software, Boston Massachusetts, IEEE Cat No 79CH1401-9C, 1979.

/BaJa78/   W.A. Babich, M. Jazayeri "The Method of Attributes for Data Flow
           Analysis. Part I: Exhaustive Analysis & Part II: Demand Analysis".
           Acta Informatica, Vol 10 No 3, 1978.

/Balz81a/ H. Balzert "Methoden, Sprachen und Werkzeuge zur Definition,
           Dokumentation und Analyse von Anforderungen an Software-Produkte".
           Informatik-Spektrum, Vol 4, 1981.

/Balz81b/ R. Balzer "Design Specification Validation". Univ S Cal Information
           Sciences Institute Report RADC-TR-81-102, 1981.

/BaPe84/   V.R. Basili, B.T. Perricone "Software Errors and Complexity: an
           empirical investigation". Comm ACM, Vol 27 No 1, January 1984.

/BaWe80/   V.R. Basili, D.M. Weiss "Evaluation of the A-7 Requirements Document
           by Analysis of Change Data". MRL Report 8445, December 1980.

/BaYe75/   S.K. Basu, R.T. Yeh "Strong Verification of Programs". IEEE Trans
           Software Engineering, Vol SE-1 No 3, 1975.

/Bled74/ W.W. Bledsoe "The SUP-INF method in Presberger arithmetic". Memo
          ATP-18, Math Dept, Univ of Texas at Austin, Tex, December 1974.

/Belt83/ L. Beltracchi "Iconic Displays, Rankine Cycles and Human Factors for
          Control Rooms of Nuclear Power Plants". IEEE Trans Nuclear Science,
          Vol NS-30 No 3, June 1983.

/BoAg79a/ S. Bologna, E. de Agostino et al. "An Experience in Design and
          Validation of Software for a Reactor Protection System". IFAC
          Workshop SAFECOMP '79, Stuttgart, 16-18 May 1979.

/BoAg79b/ S. Bologna, E. de Agostino et al. "A Computerized Protection System
          for a Fast Research Reactor". IEEE 1979 Symposium on Nuclear Power
          Systems, San Francisco, 17-19 October 1979. Proceedings published
          in IEEE Trans Nuclear Science, Vol NS-27 No 1, February 1980.

/Boch82/ G.V. Bochmann "Hardware Specification with Temporal Logic: An
          Example". IEEE Trans Computers, Vol C-31 No 3, March 1982.

/BoEh79/ S. Bologna, W. Ehrenberger "Applicability of statistical software
          reliability models for reactor safety software verification". CNEN
          Report RT/ING(79)1, 1979.

/Boeh78/ B. Boehm et al. "Characteristics of Software Quality". TRW Series
          of Software Technology, North-Holland, 1978.

/BoGr84/ B.W. Boehm, T.E. Gray, T. Seewaldt "Prototyping Versus Specifying:
          A Multiproject Experiment". IEEE Trans Software Engineering, Vol SE-10
          No 3, May 1984.

/Bolo78/ S. Bologna et al. "Deriving test data from specifications". CNEN
          Report RT/ING(78)3, 1978.

/Bolo82/ S. Bologna "The Problem of Requirements Specification and PSL/PSA,
          a facility for storing and analysing requirements on a computer".
          AICA Congress, Padova, 6-8 October 1982.

/Bolo83/ S. Bologna "The use of PSL/PSA as a Formal Language for Reliable
          Requirements Specification". ISDO 1983 Europe Project Review Meeting,
          Pisa, 30 May-1 June 1983.

212

/BrFr76/   M.A. Breuer, A.D. Friedman "Diagnosis and Reliable Design of Digital
           Systems". Computer Science Press Inc, Woodland Hills, Cal, 1976.

/Bros77/   J. Brosch "Hybridrechnertest von zeitverzögerten Reaktorschutzmaßnahmen".
           Diplomarbeit am Lehrstuhl für Reaktordynamik und Reaktorsicherheit
           der TU-München, 1977.

/BrSi82/   W.L. Bryan, S.G. Siegel, G.L. Whiteleather "Auditing throughout the
           Software Life Cycle - A Primer". IEEE Computer, Vol 15 No 3,
           March 1982.

/CaEs78/   I.M. Campos, G. Estrin "SARA Aided Design of Software for Concurrent
           Systems". AFIPS Conference 1978, AFIPS Press, Montvale NJ, 1978.

/CaGo75/   S.H. Caine, E.K. Gordon "PDL - A Tool for Software Design". NCC Proc,
           Vol 44, 1975.

/Cham78/   T. Chambers "Some numerical techniques for use in a large digital
           simulator". UKSC conference on computer simulations, Chester UK, 1978.

/Chez79/   B. Chezalviel "Une outil graphique interactif pour la vérification
           des systèmes à évolution parallèle décrits par les reseaux de Petri
           (OGIVE)". Thesis, Université P. Sabatier, Tolouse, December 1979.

/Chin80/   Chin-Kuei Cho "An Introduction to Software Quality Control". J.
           Wiley & Sons, New York, 1980.

/ChNe80/   S. Chenut, J.M. Nerson, M. Demuynck, B. Meyer "Le Système ZAIDE,
           Conception générale, l'analyseur". EDF Department Methodes et Moyens
           de L'informatique, 1980.

/ChYe83/   B.-S. Chen, R.T. Yeh "Formal Specification and Verification of
           Distributed Systems". IEEE Trans Software Engineering, Vol SE-9
           No 6, November 1983.

/Clar76/   L.A. Clarke "A System to Generate Test Data and Symbolically Execute
           Programs". IEEE Trans Software Engineering, Vol SE-2 No 3, 1976.

/ClEm81/   K.L. Clark, M.H. van Emden "Consequence Verification of Flowcharts".
           IEEE Trans Software Engineering, Vol SE-7 No 1, January 1981.

/ClHa82/ L.A. Clarke, J. Hassell, D.J. Richardson "A Close Look at Domain Testing". IEEE Trans Software Engineering, Vol SE-8 No 4, 1982.

/ClHo72/ M. Clint, C.A.R. Hoare "Program Proving: Jumps and Functions". Acta Informatica, Vol 1 No 3, 1972 .

/ClMe81/ W.F. Clocksin, C.S. Mellish "Programming in PROLOG". Springer-Verlag, 1981.

/COD76/ Concise Oxford Dictionary (Sixth edition). Oxford University Press, 1976.

/Cohe81/ B. Cohen "Further Thoughts on the Contractual Model of Product Development", in: "System Design Seminar". STL, 1981.

/Cohe82/ B. Cohen "Justification of formal methods for system specification". Software & Microsystems, Vol 1 No 5, August 1982.

/CONT79/ CONTEXT User´s Guide. System Designers Limited, UK, November 1979.

/Cout73/ J.de S. Coutinho "Software Reliability Growth". IEEE Symposium on Computer Software Reliability, IEEE Cat No CHO741-9-CSR, 1973.

/CrFu78/ A.H. Cribbens, M.J. Furniss, H.A. Ryland "An Experimental Application of Microprocessors to Railway Signalling". Electronics & Power, March 1978.

/Curt79/ A.R. Curtis "The FACSIMILE numerical integrator for stiff initial value problems". HARWELL Report AERE-R 9352, April 1979.

/DaEr82/ R.B. Dannenberg, G.W. Ernst "Formal Program Verification using Symbolic Execution". IEEE Trans Software Engineering, Vol SE-8 No 1, 1982.

/DaIs80/ G. Dahll, G. Isaksson, J. Lahti "The use of a formal language for the specification of computer programmes". OECD Halden Project, Tech Report HPR 266, May 1980.

/DaKi78/ J.A. Darringer, J.C. King "Application of Symbolic Execution to Program Testing". IEEE Computer, Vol 11 No 4, 1978.

214

/DaLa78/ G. Dahll, J. Lahti "Investigation of Methods for Production and Verification of Safety Related Computer Programmes". Halden Internal Tech Report HIR-95, December 1978.

/DaLa79/ G. Dahll, J. Lahti "An investigation of methods for production and verification of highly reliable software". IFAC Workshop SAFECOMP '79, Stuttgart, 16-18 May 1979.

/DeLi78/ R.A. DeMillo, R.J. Lipton, F.G. Sayward "Hints on Test Data Selection: Help for the practicing Programmer". IEEE Computer, Vol 11 No 4, 1978.

/DeMa78/ T. DeMarco "Structured Analysis and System Specification". Yourdon Inc, New York, 1978.

/Deut82/ M.S. Deutsch "Software Validation and Verification - Realistic Project Approaches". Prentice-Hall Inc, Englewood Cliffs NJ, 1982.

/DiHe72/ J.C. Dickson, J.L. Hesse, A.C. Kuentz, M.L. Shooman "Quantitative Analysis of Software Reliability". Proc Annual Reliability and Maintainability Symposium, San Francisco, 1972.

/Dijk75/ E.W. Dijkstra "Guarded Commands, Nondeterminacy and Formal Derivation of Programs". Comm ACM, Vol 18 No 8, August 1975.

/Dijk76/ E.W. Dijkstra "A Discipline of Programming". Prentice-Hall Inc, Englewood Cliffs NJ, 1976.

/DiKo82/ M. Didic, P. Kohlhepp, R. Oberle "Performance analysis of a distributed real-time system". Real-Time Systems Symposium, Los Angeles, 7-9 December 1982.

/DoSt78/ H.R. Downs, E.A. Straker, C.E. Fenner, J. Penland, T.E. Albert "Software Verification and Validation Plan". Science Application Inc, TVP-001 SAI-78-RP-54-SV, 1978.

/EhPl78a/ W. Ehrenberger, K. Plögert "Einsatz statistischer Methoden zur Gewinnung von Zuverlässigkeitskenngrößen von Prozeßrechner-Programmen". Bericht des Projekts "Prozeßlenkung mit DV-Anlagen" beim Kernforschungszentrum Karlsruhe No 151, 1978.

/EhPl78b/ W. Ehrenberger, K. Plögert "Statistical Verification of Reactor Protection Software". International Symposium on Nuclear Power Plant Control, Cannes, 24-28 April 1978.

/EhPu79/ W. Ehrenberger, P. Puhr-Westerheide "Analytical Software Verification". AGARD Conference on Avionics Reliability, its Techniques and Related Disciplines, Ankara, 9-13 April 1979.

/Ehre76/ W. Ehrenberger, et al. "Programanalysis - A Method for the Verification of Software for the Control of a Nuclear Reactor". 2nd International Conference on Software Engineering, San Francisco, 13-15 October 1976.

/Ehre83/ W. Ehrenberger "Safety, availability and cost questions about diversity". 4th IFAC/IFIP/IFORS International Conference on Control in Transportation Systems, Baden-Baden, April 1983.

/Endr75/ A. Endres "An analysis of errors and their causes in system programs". IEEE Trans Software Engineering, Vol SE-1 No 2, 1975.

/EWIC81a/ Guidelines for the Documentation of Safety Related Computer Systems. EWICS TC7, Documentation Subgroup, in "Real-Time Data News". Nos 2,3,4 1981 & No 6 1982. Also EWICS TC7 WP 350, August 1984.

/EWIC81b/ Development of Safety Related Software. EWICS TC7 WP 268, October 1981.

/EWIC83/ Guidelines for Verification and Validation of Safety Related Software, EWICS TC7 WP 333, May 1983.

/EWIC84/ Techniques for Verification and Validation of Safety Related Software, EWICS TC7 WP 400, October 1984.

/Faga76/ M.E. Fagan "Design and code inspection to reduce errors in program development". IBM System Journal, Vol 15 No 3, 1976.

/Fair78/ R.E. Fairley "Tutorial: Static Analysis and Dynamic Testing of Computer Software". IEEE Computer, Vol 11 No 4, 1978.

/FIPS76/ Guidelines for Documentation of Computer Programs and Automated Data Systems. FIPS PUB 38, USDOC/NBS, February 1976.

/Floy67/   R.W. Floyd "Assigning meaning to programs", in: "Aspects of Computer
           Science". Proc Am Math Soc Symposia in applied mathematics,
           vol 19, 1967.

/FoOs76/   L.D. Fosdick, L.J. Osterweil "Data Flow Analysis in Software
           Reliability". ACM Computing Surveys, Vol 8 No 3, 1976.

/Garm81/   J.R. Garman "The bug heard round the world". ACM SIGSOFT Software
           Engineering Notes, Vol 6 No 5, 1981.

/Gear71/   C.W. Gear "DIFSUB for solution of ordinary differential equations".
           Comm ACM - Algorithms, Vol 14, 1971.

/Gear77/   C.W. Gear "Simulation: Conflicts between real-time and software".
           Mathematical Software III, Academic Press, 1977.

/GeLa79/   H.J. Genrich, K. Lautenbach, P.S. Thiagarajan "Elements of General
           Net Theory", in: W. Brauer (Ed.) "Net Theory and Applications".
           Lecture Notes in Computer Science, Vol 84, Springer-Verlag, 1980.

/Gerh80/   S. Gerhart et al "An Overview of AFFIRM: a Specification and
           Verification System". Proc IFIP Congress, Australia, October 1980.

/GiCh72/   P. Gilbert, W.J. Chandler "Interference between Communicating
           Parallel Processes". Comm ACM, Vol 15 No 6, June 1972.

/Gilb83/   R.S. Gilbert "Digital Computers in CANDU Safety Systems, Part II:
           Implementation and Experience". IEEE Trans Nuclear Science, Vol NS-30
           No 3, June 1983.

/Glad82/   G.R. Gladden "Stop the Life Cycle, I want to get off". ACM SIGSOFT
           Software Engineering Notes, Vol 7 No 2, April 1982.

/Glas79/   R.L. Glass "Software Reliability Guidebook". Prentice-Hall Inc,
           Englewood Cliffs NJ, 1979.

/GmVo79/   L. Gmeiner, U. Voges "Software Diversity in Reactor Protection
           Systems: An Experiment". IFAC Workshop SAFECOMP '79, Stuttgart,
           16-18 May 1979.

/GoCo79/   D.I. Good, R.M. Cohen, J. Keeton-Williams "Principles of proving Concurrent Programs in GYPSY". University of Texas at Austin Tech Report ICSCA-CMP-15, 1979 & "Proc 6th ACM Symp Principles of Programming Languages". ACM SIGPLAN Notices, 1979.

/Goel81/   A. Goel "Hardware/Software Systems: Operational Performance Models". IEEE Trans Reliability, Vol TR-30 No 3, 1981.

/GoGe75/   J.B. Goodenough, S.L. Gerhardt "Towards a theory of test data selection". IEEE Trans Software Engineering, Vol SE-1 No 2, 1975.

/GoEn78/   S.G. Godoy, G.J. Engels "Sneak Circuit and Software Sneak Analysis". Journal of Aircraft, Vol 15, August 1978.

/Gold84/   J. Goldberg "The Problem of Confidence in Fault-Tolerant Computer Design". Informatik-Fachberichte 78: Architektur und Betrieb von Rechensystemen, 8. GI-NTG-Fachtagung, Karlsruhe, 26-28 March 1984, Springer-Verlag, Berlin, 1984.

/Goma82/   H. Gomaa "The Impact of Rapid Prototyping on Specifying User Requirements". ACM SIGSOFT Software Engineering Notes, Vol 8 No 2, April 1982.

/Good82/   D.I. Good "The Proof of a Distributed System in GYPSY". University of Texas at Austin Tech Report ICSCA-CMP-30, 1982.

/Gord77/   G. Gordon "Systems Simulation" (Second Edition). Prentice-Hall Inc, Englewood Cliffs NJ, 1977.

/Gord78/   G. Gordon "The development of the General Purpose Simulation System (GPSS)". ACM SIGPLAN Notices, Vol 13, 1978.

/Gour83/   J.S. Gourlay "A Mathematical Framework for the Investigation of Testing". IEEE Trans Software Engineering, Vol SE-9 No 6, November 1983.

/GoWi79/   N. Goldman, D. Wile "A Database Foundation for Process Specifications". Information Sciences Institute, 1979.

/GuHo78/ J.V. Guttag, J.J Horning "The algebraic specification of abstract data types". Acta Informatica, Vol 10, 1978.

/GuOt82/ M. Gubitz, K.O. Ott "Quantifying Software Reliability by a Probabilistic Model". Reliability Engineering, 1982.

/Hack72/ M. Hack "Analysis of production Schemata by Petri Nets". Master's thesis, Dept of Electrical Engineering, MIT Cambridge, Mass, February 1972.

/HaHe75/ G. Hallendal, A. Hedin, A. Östrand "A Model for Software Reliability Prediction for Control Computers". The Royal Institute of Technology, Stockholm, Report TRITA TTS-7502, 1975.

/Hall78/ S.P. Hallam "Towards a portable simulation language DSL77". UKSC conference on computer simulation, Chester UK, 1978.

/Hals77/ M.H. Halstead "Elements of Software Science". Elsevier Press, New York, 1977.

/HaMa82/ W. Harison, K. Magel R. Kluczny, A. DeKock "Applying Software Complexity Metrics to Program Maintenance". IEEE Computer, Vol 15 No 9, September 1982.

/Have68/ J.W. Havender "Avoiding Deadlock in Multi-Tasking Systems". IBM System J, Vol 2 No 7, 1968.

/Hayn79/ G.A. Haynes "Program Verification Applicability to Contemporary Distributed Computer Systems: a cas study". Texas Instruments, 1979.

/HeDo79/ W.B. Heginbotham, M. Dooner, K. Case "Robot Applicaton Simulation". Industrial Robot, June 1979.

/HeGa68/ J. Heinhold, K.W. Gaede "Ingenieurstatistik", Oldenbourg Verlag, München, 1972.

/HeKa78/ K.L. Heninger, J.W. Kallander, J.E. Shore, D. Parnas "Software Requirements for the A-7E Aircraft". NRL Memorandum Report 3876, November 1978.

/HeMc83/ C.L. Heitmeyer, J.D. McClean "Abstract Requirements Specification: A New Approach and its Application". IEEE Trans Software Engineering, Vol SE-9 No 5, September 1983.

/HeMe80/ B. Heilbronn, B. Meyer, A. Poujol "A Study in Formal Specification and its Application to the SPIN Nuclear Reactor Protection System". EDF Department Methodes et Moyens de l´Informatique, HI/3519-01, 1980.

/Hoar69/ C.A.R. Hoare "An axiomatic basis for computer programming". Comm ACM, Vol 12 No 10, October 1968.

/Hoar72/ C.A.R. Hoare "Proof of Correctness of Data Representations". Acta Informatica, Vol 1 No 4, 1972.

/Hoar78/ C.A.R. Hoare "Communicating Sequential Processes". Comm ACM, Vol 21 No 8, August 1978.

/Horn68/ E.C. van Horn "Three criteria for designing computer systems to facilitate debugging". Comm ACM, Vol 11 No 5, 1968.

/HoTa77/ E. Hollo, J.R. Taylor "Experience with Algorithms for Automatic Failure Analysis", in: J.B. Fussell, G.R. Burdick (Eds.) "Nuclear Systems Reliability Engineering and Risk Assessment". SIAM, 1977.

/Houg82/ R.C. Houghton "Software Development Tools". National Bureau of Standards Special Publication 500-88, 1982.

/Howd75/ W.E. Howden "Methodology for the Generation of Program Test Data". IEEE Trans Computers, Vol C-24 No 5, May 1975.

/Howd77/ W.E. Howden "Symbolic Testing and the DISSECT Symbolic Evaluation System". IEEE Trans Software Engineering, Vol SE-3 No 4, 1977.

/Howd82/ W.E. Howden "Life-Cycle Software Validation". IEEE Computer, Vol 15 No 2, February 1982.

/HoWi73/ C.A.R. Hoare, N. Wirth "An Axiomatic Definition of the Programming Language PASCAL". Acta Informatica, Vol 2 No 4, 1973.

/Huan75/ J.C. Huang "An Approach to Program Testing". ACM Computing Surveys, Vol 7 No 3, September 1975.

/Huan78/ J.C. Huang "Program Instrumentation and Software Testing". IEEE Computer, Vol 11 No 4, April 1978.

/IEC81/ Software for Computers in the Safety Systems of Nuclear Power Stations. IEC Subcommittee 45A/WG-A3(WG Experts)5, August 1981.

/IEEE81a/ Standard for Software Quality Assurance Plans. IEEE Std 730-1981.

/IEEE81b/ A method for determining requirements for instrumentation, control and electrical systems and equipment important for safety. IEEE Trial use guide, 1981.

/IEEE83/ Standard for Software Test Documentation. IEEE Computer Society, Software Engineering Standards Subcommittee, Std 829-1983.

/InRe83/ G. Innis, E. Rexstad "Simulation Model Simplification Techniques". Simulation, Vol 41 No 1, July 1983.

/ISDOS/ Problem Statement Language (PSL), Introduction and User´s Manual. ISDOS Ref 7742-0143-0.

/Jack75/ M.A. Jackson "Principles of Program Design". Academic Press, New York, 1975.

/Jack82/ M.A. Jackson "Jackson System Design (JSD)". Michael Jackson Systems Limited, London, 1982.

/Jana79/ K. Janac "Control of large power systems based on situation recognition and high speed simulation". IEEE Trans Power Apparatus and Systems, Vol PAS-98 No 3, 1979.

/JeMo72/ F. Jelinski, P.B. Moranda "Software Reliability Research", in: W. Freiberger (Ed.) "1971 Conference on Statistical Methods for the Evaluation of Computer System Performance". Academic Press, 1972.

/Kell76/ R.M. Keller "Formal Verification of Parallel Programs". Comm ACM, Vol 19 No 7, July 1976.

/Kemb82/   N.F. Kember "An Introduction to Computer Applications in Medicine".
           Edward Arnold, London, 1982.

/KhHo78/   N.A. Kheir, W.M. Holmes "On Validating Models of Missile Systems".
           Simulation, Vol 30 No 4, April 1978.

/Kodr78/   U.R. Kodres "Analysis of Real-Time Systems by Data Flowgraphs". IEEE
           Trans Software Engineering, Vol Se-4 No 3, May 1987.

/Kosa73/   S. Kosarajn "Limitations of Dijkstra's Semaphore Primitives and
           Petri Nets". Operating Systems Review, Vol 7 No 4, October 1973.

/Krzy82/   B. Krzykacz "Ein risiko-orientiertes statistisches Software-Testverfahren".
           PEARL-Rundschau No 2, July 1982.

/LaBe82/   J.M. Lanore, P. Bernard, J. Romeyer, D. Herbey, C. Bonnet,
           P. Quilichine "Conception of a PWR Simulator as a Tool for Safety
           Analysis", in: "Proc International Meeting on Thermal Nuclear Reactor
           Safety". Chicago, 29 August-2 September, 1982.

/LaSc74/   K. Lautenbach, H.A. Schmid "Use of Petri Nets for Proving Correctness
           of Concurrent Process Systems". IFIP 1974, North Holland, 1974.

/LeHa83/   N.G. Leveson, P.R. Harvey "Analyzing Software Safety". IEEE Trans
           Software Engineering, Vol SE-9 No 5, September 1983.

/Lind82/   M. Lind "Multilevel Flow Modelling of Process Plant for Diagnosis
           and Control". International meeting on Thermal Nuclear Reactor
           Safety, Chicago, 1982.

/LiVe73/   B. Littlewood, J.L. Verall "A Baysian Reliability Growth Model for
           Computer Software". IEEE Symposium on Computer Software Reliability,
           IEEE Cat No CH0741-9-CSR, 1973.

/Lond77/   R.L. London "Perspectives on Program Verification", in: R.T. Yeh
           (Ed.) "Current Trends in Programming Methodology: Vol II".
           Prentice-Hall Inc, Englewood Cliffs NJ, 1977.

/Loza83/   T. Lozano-Perez "Robot Programming". Proc IEEE, Vol 71 No 7,
           July 1983.

/Lude81/ J. Ludewig "Specification of a Specification Language". IFAC/IFIP Workshop on Real-Time Programming, Kyoto Japan, 1981.

/Lude83/ J. Ludewig "ESPRESO - A System for Process Control Software Specification. IEEE Trans Software Engineering, Vol SE-9 No 4, July 1983.

/MASC80/ The Official Handbook of MASCOT (Final Draft). MASCOT Suppliers Association, September 1980.

/McAb62/ J. McCarthy, P.W. Abrahams, D.J. Edwards, T.P. Hart, M.I. Levin "LISP 1.5 Programmer´s Manual". MIT Press, Cambridge Mass, 1962.

/McCa60/ J. McCarthy "Recursive Functions of Symbolic Expressions and their Computaton by Machine, Part I". Comm ACM, Vol 3 No 4, April 1960.

/McCa63/ J. McCarthy "A Basis for a Mathematical Theory of Computation", in: P. Braffort, D. Hirshberg (Eds.) "Computing Programming and Formal Systems". North Holland, Amsterdam, 1963.

/McJa82/ D.D. McCracken, M.A. Jackson "Life-Cycle Concept Considered Harmful". ACM SIGSOFT Software Engineering Notes, Vol 7 No 2, April 1982.

/McPa67/ J. McCarthy, J.A. Painter "Correctness of a Compiler for Arithmetic Expressions", in: J.T. Schwartz (Ed.) "Mathematical Aspects of Computer Science". Providence R.I., American Math Soc, 1967.

/Mer82/ E. Le Mer "OVIDE: a Software Package for Verifying and Validating Petri Nets". Proc 3rd IFAC/IFIP meeting on Software for Computer Control, Madrid, October 1982.

/Meye81/ J.M. Meyer "An emulation system for programmable sensory robots". IBM J Res Devel, Vol 25 No 6, November 1981.

/Miko74/ A. Mikolajczuk "Three years Experience with Computer-Assisted Patient Monitoring". Medinfo, 1974.

/Mill76/ J.K. Millen "Security Kernel Validation in Practice". Comm ACM, Vol 19 No 5, May 1976.

/Mil177a/ E. Miller "Program Testing Techniques Notebook". Software Research Associates, San Francisco, 1977.

/Mil177b/ E. Miller "Program Testing: Art meets Theory". IEEE Computer, Vol 10 No 7, 1977.

/Mil179a/ E. Miller "Tutorial: Automated Tools for Software Engineering". IEEE Cat No EHO 150-3, 1979.

/Mil179b/ J.K. Millen "Operating System Security Verification". MITRE Corp Tech Report M79-223, September 1979.

/MILS74/ Software Quality Assurance Program Requirements. MIL - S - 52779 (AD), April 1974.

/Mol182/ M.K. Molloy "Performance Analysis Using Stochastic Petri Nets". IEEE Trans Computers, Vol C-31 No 9, 1982.

/Mora78/ P.B. Moranda "Limits to Program Testing with Random Number Inputs". COMPSAC´78, Chicago, November 1978.

/MuOk83/ J.D. Musa, K. Okumoto "Software Reliability Models: Concepts, Classification, Comparison and Practice", in: J.K. Skwirzynski (Ed.) "Proc ASI on Electronic Systems Effectiveness and Life Cycle Costing". Springer-Verlag, 1983.

/Muss80/ D.R. Musser "Abstract Data Type Specification in the AFFIRM System". IEEE Trans Software Engineering, Vol SE-6 No 1, January 1980.

/MuSt79/ H. Musielak, M. Stossel "Comparison of Simulation Languages". Elektron Rechenanlagen, Vol 21, 1979.

/Myer78/ G.J. Myers "A controlled experiment in program testing and code walkthroughs/inspections". Comm ACM, Vol 21 No 9, 1978.

/Myer79/ G.J. Myers "The Art of Software Testing". John Wiley & Sons, New York, 1979.

/NDES77/ Numerical methods for Differential Equations and Simulation: Proc IMACS(AICA) Int Symp on Simulation Software and Numerical Methods for Differential Equations, A.W. Bennett, R. Vichnevetsky (Eds.).

Virginia Polytechnic Institute and State University, Blacksburg VA, 9-11 March 1977, North Holland, 1978.

/NeHa83/ R.A. Nelson, L.M. Haibt, P.B. Sheridan "Casting Petri Nets into Programs". IEEE Trans Software Engineering, Vol SE-9 No 5, September 1983.

/Neum56/ J. von Neumann "Probabilistic logic and synthesis of reliable organisms from unreliable components", in: C.E. Shannon, J. McCarthy (Eds.) "Automata Studies". Annals of Mathematical Studies Vol 34, Princeton University Press, NJ, 1956.

/Niel71/ D.S. Nielsen "The Cause-Consequence Method as a Basis for Quantitative Accident Analysis". Riso National Laboratory Report Riso-M-1374, 1971.

/Niel82/ F. Nielson "A Denotational Framework for Data Flow Analysis". Acta Informatica, Vol 18 No 3, 1982.

/NURE82/ Safety goals for nuclear power plant. US Nuclear Regulatory Commission, February 1982.

/ODon82/ M.J. O´Donnell "A Critique of the Foundations of Hoare Style Programming Logics". Comm ACM, Vol 25 No 12, December 1982.

/OIL82/ Electronics in Oil - Proceedings of Technical Program, Earls Court London UK, 12-14 October 1982. Published by Cahners Exposition Group SA, Guildford Surrey UK, 1982

/OsFo76/ L.J. Osterweil, L.D. Fosdick "DAVE - A validation, error detection and documentation system for FORTRAN Programs". Software Practice and Experience, Vol 6 No 4, July 1976.

/Oste83/ L.J. Osterweil "Toolpack - An Experimental Software Development Environment Research Project". IEEE Trans Software Engineering, Vol SE-9 No 6, November 1983.

/OwGr76a/ S. Owicki, D. Gries "An Axiomatic Proof Technique for Parallel Programs I". Acta Informatica, Vol 6 No 4, 1976.

225

/OwGr76b/ S. Owicki, D. Gries "Verifying Properties of Parallel Programs: an Axiomatic Approach". Comm ACM, Vol 19 No 5, 1976.

/PaHe80/ R.A. Parker, K.L. Heninger, D.L. Parnas, J.E. Shore "Abstract Interface Specifications for the A-7E Device Interface Module". NRL Memorandum Report 4385, November 1980.

/Pall81/ N.J. Palladino "Nuclear Regulatory Reform". US Nuclear Regulatory Commission News Release, NUREG/BR-0032, Vol 7 No 45, 8 December 1981.

/Palm82/ D.F. Palmer "Requirements Engineering for Modular Computer Systems", in: S.P. & S.I. Kartashev (Eds.) "Designing and Programming Modern Computers and Systems". Prentice-Hall Inc, Englewood Cliffs NJ, 1982.

/Parn75/ D. Parnas "On a Solution to the Cigarette Smokers Problem". Comm ACM, Vol 18 No 3, March 1975.

/PaSt82/ D.F. Palmer, R.L. Stone "Real-Time System Design, Sizing and Simulation using DSIGNR". Proc Real-Time Systems Symposium, IEEE Cat No 82CH1812-7, 7-9 December 1982.

/PENV81/ NBS Workshop on Programming Environments. ACM SIGSOFT Software Engineering Notes, Vol 6 No 4, August 1981.

/Pete81/ J.L. Peterson "Petri Net Theory and the Modelling of Systems". Prentice-Hall Inc, Englewood Cliffs NJ, 1981.

/Petr62/ C.A. Petri "Kommunikation mit Automaten". PhD Dissertation University of Bonn 1962. (Translation: C.F. Greene "Communication with Automata". Supplement I to Tech Report RADC-TR-65-337 Vol 1, RADC Griffiss AFB, NY 1966.)

/Pime83/ J.R. Pimentel "Real-Time Simulation using Multiple Micro-Computers". Simulation, Vol 41 No 2, August 1983.

/Pres29/ M. Presburger "Uber die Vollstandigkeit eines genissen Systems der Arithmetic ganzer Zahlen". In: "Welchem die Addition als Einzige Operation hervortritt", Sprawozdanie z I Kongresu Matematykow Krajow Slowcanskich Warszawa, Poland, 1929.

/Prob82/ R.L. Probert "Optimal Insertion of Software Probes in Well-Delimited Programs". IEEE Trans Software Engineering, Vol SE-8 No 1, 1978.

/QuGi77/ W.J. Quirk, R. Gilbert "The formal specification of the requirements of complex real-time systems". HARWELL Report AERE-R 8602, 1977.

/Quir78/ W.J. Quirk "The automatic analysis of formal real-time system specifications". HARWELL Report AERE-R 9046, 1978.

/Quir80/ W.J. Quirk "Relational Analysis". EWICS TC7 WP 217, 1980.

/Quir83/ W.J. Quirk "Recent Developments in the SPECK Specification System". HARWELL Report CSS.146, 1983.

/RaAt83/ H.R. Ramsey, M.E. Atwood, J.R. Van Doren "Flowcharts Versus Program Design Languages: An Experimental Comparison". Comm ACM, Vol 26 No 6, June 1983.

/RaBa81/ C.V. Ramamoorthy, F.B. Bastani, G.H. Chin, Y.R. Mok, K. Suzuki "Application of a Methodology for the Development and Validation of Reliable Process Control Software". IEEE Trans Software Engineering, Vol SE-7 No 6, November 1981.

/RADC79/ Quantitative Software Models. RADC/ISISI Data and Analysis Center for Software, Research Review SRR-1, Griffiss AFB NY, 1979.

/RaEs80/ R. Razouk, G. Estrin "Modeling and Verification of communication protocols in SARA: The X.21 Interface". IEEE Trans Comp, Vol C-29 No 12, December 1980.

/RaKe83/ K. Ramamritham, R.M. Keller "Specification of Synchronizing Processes". IEEE Trans Software Engineering, Vol SE-9 No 6, November 1983.

/Ramc74/ C. Ramchandani "Analysis of Asynchronous Concurrent Systems by Timed Petri Nets". PhD Thesis, MIT Cambridge, Mass, 1974.

/Rank73/ J.P. Rankin "Sneak-Circuit Analysis". IEEE Trans Nuclear Science, Vol NS-14 No 5, September 1973.

/Reyn79/   J.C. Reynolds "Reasoning About Arrays". Comm ACM, Vol 22 No 5,
           May 1979.

/RoRo77/   R. Robinson, D. Roubine "SPECIAL: a SPECIfication and Assertion
           Language". Stanford Research Institute Tech Report CSL 146, 1977.

/RPW82/   ACM SIGSOFT Rapid Prototyping Workshop, Columbia MD, 19-21 April 1982.
           Published in ACM SIGSOFT Software Engineering Notes, Vol 7 No 5,
           December 1982.

/RXVP80/   RXVP80 User's Manual. General Research Corporation, Santa
           Barbara, 1980.

/SADT76/   An Introduction to SADT. SofTech Technical Report 9022-78R,
           November 1976.

/ScMe83/   R.L. Schwartz, P.M. Melliar-Smith, F.H. Vogt "An Interval Logic for
           Higher-Level Temporal Reasoning: Language Definition and Examples".
           SRI Tech Report CSL-138, February 1983.

/ScWo73/   G.J. Schick, R.W. Wolverton "Assessment of Software Reliability".
           Proc Operations Research, Physica-Verlag, Würzburg-Wien, 1973.

/ScWo78/   G.J. Schick, R.W. Wolverton "An Analysis of Competing Software
           Reliability Models". IEEE Trans Software Engineering, Vol SE-4 No 2,
           March 1978.

/SEAT82/   Software Engineering Automated Tools Index. Software Research
           Associates, San Francisco, 1982.

/Shep83/   S. Sheppard "Applying Software Engineering to Simulation". Simulation,
           Vol 40 No 1, January 1983.

/ShGe79/   L.F. Shampine, C.W. Gear "A user's view of solving stiff ordinary
           differential equations". SIAM Review, Vol 21 No 1, 1979.

/Shoo71/   M.L. Shooman "Probabilistic Models for Software Reliability
           Predictions" in: W. Freiberger (Ed.) "1971 Conference on Statistical
           Methods for the Evaluation of Computer System Performance". Academic
           Press, 1972.

/Shoo73/ M.L. Shooman "Operational Testing and Software Reliability during Program Development". IEEE Symposium on Computer Software Reliability, IEEE Cat No CHO741-9-CSR, 1973.

/Shos77/ R.E. Shostak "On the SUP-INF Method for Proving Presberger Formulas". JACM, Vol 24 No 4, October 1977.

/ShRu77/ M.L. Shooman, H. Ruston "Summary of Technical Progress, Software Modelling Studies". Polytechnic Institute of New York Report RDAC-TR-76-465, January, 1977.

/Sidl78/ R.F. Sidley "Sneak Circuit Analysis of Nuclear Power Systems", in: "Proc Topical Meeting on Thermal Reactor Safety". Sun Valley Idaho, July 31-August 4, 1977.

/Sifa79/ J. Sifakis "Performance evaluation of systems using nets", in: W. Brauer (Ed.) "Net Theory and Applications". Lecture Notes in Computer Science, Vol 84, Springer-Verlag, 1980.

/Soro80/ B.I. Soroka "Debugging Robot Programs with a Simulator". Proc SME CADCAM-8, Dearborn MI, November 1980.

/SRS81/   Final Report on Phase III of the Study Contract: Feasibility of a Generalised Simulation System. System Reliability Service, UKAEA, SRS/ASG/1227, February 1981.

/STARS83/ The DoD STARS Program. IEEE Computer, Vol 16 No 11, November 1983.

/Ster79/ B.J. Sterner "A Geographical Model for Computerized Interlocking and Dispatching". AIT Symp on Railway Cybernetics, Madrid May 1979.

/StFe78/ E.A. Straker, C.E. Fenner, J. Penland, T.R. Albert "A Methodology for the Validation of Real-Time Software used in Nuclear Plant Safety Applications". Science Applications Inc, SAI-78-517-L5, 1978.

/StTh83/ E.A. Straker, N.C. Thomas "Verification and Validation as an Integral Part of the Development of Digital Systems for Nuclear Applications". Nuclear Safety, Vol 24 No 3, May-June 1983.

/SuJe80/ N. Suzuki, D. Jefferson "Verification Decidability of Presburger Array Programs". JACM, Vol 27 No 1, January 1980.

/SuTh82/ C.A. Sunshine, D.H. Thompson, R.W. Erickson, S.L. Gerhart, D. Schwabe "Specification and Verification of Communication Protocols in AFFIRM using State Transition Models". IEEE Trans Software Engineering, Vol SE-8 No 5, September 1982.

/Swis78/ G.M. Swisher "Simulation of a non-linear control system for a multi-inertia plant", in: G.S. Fishman (Ed.) "Principles of discrete event simulation". John Wiley & Sons, New York, 1978.

/TaBo77/ J.R. Taylor, S. Bologna "Validation of Safety Related Software". IAEA/NPPCI Conference on Software Reliability for Computerised Control and Safety Systems in Nuclear Power Plants, Pittsburgh, 20-22 July 1977.

/TaJu82/ J.R. Taylor, M. Justesen, O. Hansen, S. Kjürsgaard "Risk Analysis for a Distillation Plant". Riso National Laboratory Report M 2319, 1982.

/TaOs80/ R.N. Taylor, L.J. Osterweil "Anomaly Detection in Concurrent Software by Static Data Flow Analysis". IEEE Trans Software Engineering, Vol SE-6 No 5, November 1980.

/Tayl74/ J.R. Taylor "Proving Correctness for a Real-Time Operating System". IFAC-IFIP Workshop on Real-Time Programming, Budapest, March 1974.

/Tayl75/ J.R. Taylor "Sequential Effects in Failure Mode Analysis", in: Barlow, Fussel, Singapurwalla (Eds.) "Reliability and Fault tree Analysis". SIAM, 1975.

/Tayl79/ J.R. Taylor "A background to Risk Analysis". Vols 1 to 4, Riso National Laboratory, 1979.

/Tayl82/ J.R. Taylor "Recommendations for the Safety Validation of Safety Related Software". EWICS TC7 WP 260, April 1982.

/Tayl83/ J.R. Taylor "An Algorithm for Fault Tree Construction". IEEE Trans Reliability (to appear), 1983.

/TeHe77/   D. Teichroew, E.A. Hershey "PSL/PSA: A Computer-Aided Technique for Structured Documentation and Analysis of Information Processing Systems". IEEE Trans Software Engineering, Vol SE-3 No 1, 1977.

/Thom81/   N.C. Thomas "Incorporating Software into Nuclear Power Plant System Design". IEEE Trans Nuclear Science, Vol NS-28 No 1, February 1981.

/ThRe80/   N.C. Thomas, H.L. Reeves "Experience from Quality Assurance in Nuclear Power Plant Protection System Software Validation". IEEE Trans Nuclear Science, Vol NS-27 No 1, February 1980.

/Toy78/   W.N. Toy "Fault-Tolerant Design of Local ESS Processors". Proc IEEE, Vol 66 No 10, October 1978.

/Trau81/   H. Trauboth "PCSL-A Language for Describing Real-Time Software Systems". International Conference on the use of computer aids in systems development, London, 25-26 June 1981.

/Voge76/   U. Voges "Aspects of Design, Test and Validation of the Software for a Computerized Reactor Protection System". 2nd International Conference on Software Engineering, San Francisco, 13-15 October 1976.

/VoGm80/   U. Voges, L. Gmeiner, A. von Mayrhauser "SADAT - An Automated Testing Tool". IEEE Trans Software Engineering, Vol SE-6 No 3, May 1980.

/Watk82/   M.L. Watkins "A Technique for Testing Command and Control Software". Comm ACM, Vol 25 No 4, April 1982.

/WeOs80/   E.J. Weyuker, T.J. Ostrand "Theories of Program Testing amd the Application of Revealing Subdomains". IEEE Trans Software Engineering, Vol SE-6 No 3, May 1980.

/WhCo80/   L.J. White, E.I. Cohen "A domain strategy for computer program testing". IEEE Trans Software Engineering, Vol SE-6 No 3, May 1980.

/WiHo81/   P.H. Winston, B.K.P Horn "LISP". Addison Wesley, 1981.

/YaCh80/   S.S. Yau, F.-C. Chen "An Approach to Concurrent Control Flow Checking". IEEE Trans Software Engineering, Vol SE-6 No 2, March 1980.

/YaGr81/   S.S. Yau, P.C. Grabow "A Model for Representing Programs using
            Hierarchical Graphs". IEEE Trans Software Engineering, Vol SE-7
            No 6, November 1981.

/Yeh77/   R.T. Yeh "Verification of Programs by Predicate Transformation", in:
            R.T. Yeh (Ed.) "Current Trends in Programming Methodology: Vol II".
            Prentice-Hall Inc, Englewood Cliffs NJ, 1977.

/YoCo79/   E. Yourdon, L.L. Constantine "Structured Design: Fundamentals of
            Computer Program and Systems Design". Prentice-Hall Inc, Englewood
            Cliffs NJ, 1979.

/YoGi80/   M. Yoely, A. Ginzburg "Control Nets for Parallel Processing".
            Proc 1980 IFIP Congress, North Holland, 1980.

/Zave82/   P. Zave "An Operational Approach to Requirements Specification for
            Embedded Systems". IEEE Trans Software Engineering, Vol SE-8 No 3,
            May 1982.

/Zave84/   P. Zave "The Operational versus the Conventional Approach to Software
            Development". Comm ACM, Vol 27 No 2, February 1984.

Appendix

I   PROOF OF (5.7)

The proof has been made by K. Okroy. It has been published in [EhPl 78a].

I.1   Number of n-tuples in a set of N elements (n>N), which
        contain all elements

$d,i,j,k,l,n,m,r,s,N \in \mathbb{N}$. A is a set, containing N elements. $n > N$. The number of n-tuples that can be composed from A and which contain all elements of A is to be evaluated.

$f_n(N)$ is evaluated from the difference of the number of all n-tuples of A and the number of n-tuples that do not contain all elements of A.

By means of induction over N one can prove that the number of all k-tuples in A is N^n. The number of n-tuples of A that do not contain all elements of A is the sum of all n-tuples of A in which exactly $1,2,\ldots i,\ldots N-1$ distinct elements of A are contained.

The number of n-tuples that contain exactly one element is $\binom{N}{1} \cdot f_n(1)$, because:
There are N subsets of 1 element in A, called $A_j^{(1)}$ ($1 \leq j \leq N$). If $T_j^{(1)}$ denotes the set of n-tuples of $A_j^{(1)}$ that contains all elements of $A_j^{(1)}$, we get: $f_n^{(1)} = |T_j^{(1)}| = 1$ and $T_r^{(1)} \cap T_s^{(1)} = \emptyset$, ($1 \leq (r,s) \leq N$), ($r \neq s$).

The number of n-tuples of A that contain exactly i elements of A is $\binom{N}{i} \cdot f_n(i)$, because:
The number of subsets of $A_j^{(i)}$ that contain i elements ($1 \leq j \leq \binom{N}{i}$) is $\binom{N}{i}$. If $T_j^{(i)}$ denotes the set of k-tuples of $A_j^{(i)}$ that contain all elements of $A_j^{(i)}$, we get: $f_n^{(i)} = |T_j^{(i)}|$ and $T_r^{(i)} \cap T_s^{(i)} = \emptyset$, ($1 \leq (r,s) \leq \binom{N}{i}$, ($r \neq s$)). The last line is true because all $A_j^{(i)}$, i fixed, differ in at least one element and because the n-tuples considered contain all elements of the related $A_j^{(i)}$.

Similarly it is true that $T_r^{(P)} \cap T_s^{(m)} = \emptyset$ ($r \neq s$; $1 \leq P$, $m \leq r \leq \binom{N}{P}$; $1 \leq s \leq \binom{N}{m}$). The number of n-tuples of A that do not contain all elements of A equals

$$\sum_{i=1}^{N} \binom{N}{i} f_n(i)$$

This means: the number of n-tuples of A that contain all elements of A euqals:

$$f_n(N) = N^n - \sum_{i=1}^{N-1} \binom{N}{i} f_n(i) \qquad (I.1)$$

In another form:

$$f_n(N) = N^n - [N+\binom{N}{2}\cdot f_n(2)+\binom{N}{3}\cdot f_n(3)+\ldots \binom{N}{j}f_n(j)t\ldots$$
$$+\ldots\binom{N}{N-1}f_n(N-1)] =$$
$$= N^n - [N+\binom{N}{2}(2^n-2)+\binom{N}{3}(3^n-3\cdot2^n+3)+\ldots] =$$
$$= \sum_{j=0}^{N-1} (-1)^j \binom{N}{j}(N-j)^n =$$
$$= N^n + \sum_{j=1}^{N-1} (-1)^j\cdot\binom{N}{j}(N-j)^n. \qquad (I.2)$$

The last two lines are derived intuitively. They are proved in chapter I.2.

I.2   Proof of I.2

    N = 1:
        $f_n(1) = 1$ according to (I.1)
    N = 2:
        $f_n(2) = 2^n-2$ according to (I.1)

    N ε $\mathbb{N}$, N > 2:

It is assumed that (I.1) gives the correct value for $f_n(N')$, $N'\varepsilon \mathbb{N}$, $N'< N$.

$$f_n(N) = N^n- \sum_{i=1}^{N-1} \binom{N}{i}\cdot f_n(i) = \quad \text{(according to the assumption of the induction)}$$

$$= N^n - \sum_{i=1}^{N-1} \binom{N}{i} \cdot [i^n \sum_{j=1}^{i=1} (-1)^j \binom{i}{j}(i-j)^n]$$

$$= N^n - \sum_{i=1}^{N-1} \binom{N}{i} \cdot [\sum_{j=0}^{i-1} (-1)^j \binom{i}{j}(i-j)^n]$$

$$= N^n \sum_{d=1}^{N-1} [\sum_{\ell=d}^{N-1} (-1)^{\ell-d} \binom{\ell}{\ell-d}\binom{N}{\ell}]d^n \qquad (I.3)$$

In order to get (I.3) we put i-j=d and ℓ=j+d. The sum is then re-arranged.

For one term of the sum in (I.3) of the form

$$\sum_{\ell=d}^{N-1} (-1)^{\ell-d} \binom{\ell}{d}\binom{N}{\ell}, \text{ with } 1 \leq d \leq N-1$$

we receive with r: = ℓ-d and $\binom{d+r}{d} = \binom{d+r}{r}$:

$$\sum_{\ell=d}^{N-1} (-1)^{\ell-d} \binom{\ell}{d}\binom{N}{\ell} = \sum_{r=0}^{N-1-d} (-1)^r \binom{d+r}{r} \binom{N}{d+r} =$$

$$= \sum_{r=0}^{N-1-d} (-1)^r \frac{(d+r)...(d+1)}{r!} \frac{N...(N-d-r+1)}{(d+r)!} =$$

$$= \sum_{r=0}^{N-1-d} (-1)^r \frac{N...(N-d+1)}{d!} \frac{(N-d)...(N-d-r+1)}{r!} =$$

$$= \sum_{r=0}^{N-1-d} (-1)^r \binom{N}{d} \binom{N-d}{r} = \binom{N}{d} \sum_{r=0}^{N-1-d} (-1)^r \binom{N-d}{r} \qquad (I.4)$$

Considering the symmetry of the binomial coefficients:

$$o = (1+(-1))^{N-d} = \sum_{r=0}^{N-d} (-1)^r \binom{N-d}{r}$$

and with this

$$\sum_{(r=0)}^{(N-d)-1} (-1)^r \binom{N-d}{r} = \begin{cases} -1, \text{ if N-d even} \\ 1, \text{ if N-d odd} \end{cases}$$

If this is substituted into (I.4) and the result is substituted into (I.3), we get:

$$f_n(N) = N^n - \sum_{d=1}^{N-1} (-1) (-1)^{N-d} \binom{N}{d} d^n =$$

$$= N^n + \sum_{d=1}^{N-1} (-1)^{N-d} \binom{N}{d} d^n$$

With $d = N-j$, and $1 \leq j \leq N-1$ one gets

$$f_n(N) = N^n + \sum_{j=1}^{N-1} (-1)^j \binom{N}{N-j} (N-j)^n =$$

$$= N^n + \sum_{j=1}^{N-1} (-1)^j \binom{N}{j} (N-j)^n \qquad \text{q.e.d.}$$

I.3 Probability to test all elements

The classical definition of probability is used

$$p_c = \frac{\text{number of possibilities to draw each element of A during n runs at least once}}{\text{number of possibilities to draw tuples of n elements out of N elements}}$$

It assumed that during one run only one element is drawn. The test is with replacement. p_c equals the quotient of (I.1) or (I.2) and N^n.

$$p_c = \frac{N^n - \sum_{i=1}^{N-1} \binom{N}{j} f_n(j)}{N^n} =$$

$$= 1 + \frac{\sum_{i=1}^{N-1} (-1)^j \binom{N}{j} (N-j)^n}{N^n} =$$

$$= 1 + \sum_{j=1}^{N-1} (-1)^j \binom{N}{j} \left(\frac{N-j}{N}\right)^n =$$

$$= 1 - N \left(\frac{N-1}{N}\right)^n + \binom{N}{2} \left(\frac{N-2}{N}\right)^n - \ldots$$

$$\pm \binom{N}{j} \left(\frac{N-j}{N}\right)^n \ldots \mp N\left(\frac{1}{N}\right)^n \qquad\qquad \text{q.e.d.}$$

238

II   DERIVATION OF FORMULAE 5.8 THROUGH 5.11

Assumptions

IIa   Sequence and number of test cases do not influence the result of any single test (independency of test cases).

IIb   The probability of being selected during the test is equal for every program property.

IIc   The observation of the test is perfect, i.e. every fault that comes up is recognised.

Definitions

n   number of program properties that are tested during all test runs.

m   number of program properties that are recognised as being faulty.

p_o probability that one distinct but arbitrary program property is faulty.

p(n,m)   probability that m faulty program properties exist among m tested ones.

Derivation of (5.8)

$\binom{n}{m}$ number of cominatorial possibilities to have m faulty program properties among the n tested ones.

p_o^m probability that m tested program properties are faulty.

$1-p_o$ probability that one distinct but arbitrary program property is not faulty.

$(1-p_o)^{n-m}$ probability that n-m program properties are not faulty

$p_o^m (1-p_o)^{n-m}$ probability that one distinct but arbitrary combination of m faulty and n-m not faulty program properties is observed.

Since $\binom{n}{m}$ such combinations exist, we get:

$$p(n,m) = \binom{n}{m} p_o^m (1-p_o)^{n-m} \qquad (5.8)$$

Derivation of (5.9)

We set: $p_o = \lambda/n$. Starting from (5.8) we get:

$$p(\lambda,m) = \frac{n!}{m!(n-m)!} \cdot (\frac{\lambda}{n})^m \cdot (1-\frac{\lambda}{n})^{n-m} =$$

$$= \frac{\lambda^m}{m!} (1-\frac{\lambda}{n})^n \cdot \frac{n \cdot (n-1)...(n-m-1)}{n^m \cdot (1-\frac{\lambda}{n})^m} =$$

$$= \frac{\lambda^m}{m!} (1-\frac{\lambda}{n})^n \frac{1 \cdot (1-\frac{1}{n})...(1-\frac{m-1}{n})}{(1-\frac{\lambda}{n})^m} ;$$

$$\lim_{n \to \infty} (1-\frac{\lambda}{n})^n = e^{-\lambda};$$

$$\lim_{\substack{n \to \infty \\ m = const}} \frac{1 \cdot (1-\frac{1}{n})...(1-\frac{m-1}{n})}{(1-\frac{\lambda}{n})^m} = 1;$$

$$p(\lambda,m) = \frac{\lambda^m \cdot e^{-\lambda}}{m!} \qquad (5.9)$$

Derivation of (5.10)

The probability to have 1, or 2, or 3... faulty program properties is

$$p(\lambda,m \geq 1) = \sum_{m=1}^{\infty} \frac{\lambda^m e^{-\lambda}}{m!} = 1 - \sum_{m=0}^{o} \frac{\lambda^m e^{-\lambda}}{m!} = 1-e^{-\lambda}$$

The probability to have no faulty program property is

$$p(\lambda, m=0) = e^{-\lambda}$$

If we regard this as an hypothesis that is true at least with a certain probability P, we get:

$$p\,(p(m=0)) \geqq P$$

or

$$e^{-\lambda} \geqq P$$

For $\qquad$ P = 99 %, we get $\lambda = 4,6$

$\qquad\qquad\qquad$ P = 95 %, $\qquad\qquad \lambda = 3$ $\qquad\qquad$ (5.10)

Since $\qquad\qquad p = \dfrac{\lambda}{n_t}$, we get:

$$n_t = \frac{4,6}{p_o}$$

$$n_t = \frac{3}{p_o} \qquad\qquad\qquad (5.11)$$

III   PROOFS OF (5.14) THROUGH (5.17)

The proofs have been given by B. Krzykacz in [Krzy 82].

III.1 Expected value

r = expected value of L = EL

$$p\ (H=h) = \pi_h$$
$$E\ (L/H=h) = L_h \cdot p_h$$
$$EL = \Sigma\ L_h \cdot \pi_h \cdot p_h \qquad\qquad (5.14)$$

III.2 Confidence of the risk

Overview

The derivation of (5.15) starts from the binomial distribution, similar to the derivation of part II. Instead of p(n,m) the distribution of $p\ (n, \sum_{n=1}^{K} p_h \rho_h)$ is derived.

The part with the fraction stroke is for derivation of a confidence limit of the distribution (see e.g. [HeGa 72] and other commonly used books on statistics). Since the calculations are very long they are not replicated here. The results, however, are equal to those of part II, as is shown by the similarities of (5.16) and (5.11) and

In Detail

Let $H_1, H_2, \ldots$ be a sequence of independent random variables distributed like H. H_i represents the number of the stratum selected for the i-th replication of the test; $p(H_i=h)=\rho_h$. For a given stratum h let $X^{(h)}$ be the random variable which represents the result of one program run with input data selected at random from this stratum according to the input distribution in real operation, i.e.

Since $Y_1, Y_2, \ldots, Y_n$ are stochastically independent, Y has a binomial distribution with parameters n and

$$p = \sum_{h=1}^{K} \rho_h \, p_h, \quad i.e.$$

$$Y \sim Bin \, (n; \; p = \sum_{h=1}^{K} \rho_h \, p_h)$$

The derivation is similar to that of (5.30). If the test has been performed and been observed (e.g. Y=k the number of observed failures), one can obtain the upper 95 %-confidence bound $\hat{p}_{0.95}$ for p according to [HeGa 72].

$$\hat{p}_{0.95} = \frac{(k+1) \, F_{0.95} \, (2(k+1), \, 2(n-k))}{(n-k) + (k+1) \, F_{0.95} \, (2(k+1), \, 2(n-k))}$$

Since p can be expressed by r as follows

$$p = \sum_{h=1}^{K} \rho_h \, p_h = \sum_{h=1}^{K} \frac{L_h \pi_h}{\sum\limits_{i=1}^{K} L_i \pi_i} \, p_h = \frac{1}{\sum\limits_{i=1}^{K} L_i \pi_i} \sum_{h=1}^{K} L_h \pi_h p_h = \frac{1}{\sum\limits_{i=1}^{K} L_i \pi_i} \cdot r$$

one can obtain the desired confidence bound for r according to

$$\hat{r}_{0.95} = (\sum_{h=1}^{K} L_h \, \pi_h) \, \hat{p}_{0.95}$$

$$= (\sum_{h=1}^{K} L_h \, \pi_h) \, \frac{(k+1) \, F_{0.95} \, (\ldots, \ldots)}{(n-k) + (k+1) \, F_{0.95}(\ldots, \ldots)} \qquad (5.15)$$

III.3 Confidence of the risk if no failure occurred

If k=0: $\quad \hat{p}_{0.95} = \dfrac{F_{0.95} \, (2, 2n)}{n + F_{0.95} \, (2, 2n)}$

According to $\left[\text{HeGa } 72\right]$:

$$X \sim F \ (2,2n) > Z: \ = \frac{X}{n+X} \sim \text{Beta } (1,n)$$

i.e., if a random variable X has a F-distribution with (2,2n) degrees of freedom then $Z = \frac{X}{n+X}$ has a Beta-distribution with parameters (1,n).

Since Z is an increasing function in X over $(0,\infty)$, the 95 % quantile $Z_{0.95}$ of Z is given by

$$Z_{0.95} = \frac{X_{0.95}}{n+X_{0.95}}$$

where $X_{0.95}$ is the 95 %-quantile of X.

Since the cdf of Z is given by

$$F_Z(Z) = 1-(1-z)^n$$

the 95 %-quantile $Z_{0.95}$ of Z can be determined by solving the equation

$$1-(1-Z_{0.95})^n = 0.95$$

$$> \quad Z_{0.95} = 1-\sqrt[n]{0.05}$$

Hence

$$\hat{r}_{0.95} = (\sum_{h=1}^{K} L_h \ \pi_h) \ \hat{p}_{0.95}$$

$$= (\sum_{h=1}^{K} L_h \ \pi_h) \ Z_{0.95}$$

$$= (\sum_{h=1}^{K} L_h \ \pi_h) \ (1-\sqrt[n]{0.05})$$

Since $e^{-3} \sim 0.05$:

$$\sqrt[n]{0.05} = \sqrt[n]{e^{-3}} = e^{-\frac{3}{n}} \sim 1-\frac{3}{n} \text{ (for large n)}$$

$$> 1-\sqrt[n]{0.05} \sim \frac{3}{n}$$

This leads to (5.16).

III.4 Number of necessary test runs

To obtain the desired number n of program runs one has to solve the equation

$$\tilde{r} = (\sum_{h=1}^{K} L_h \, \pi_h) \; (1-\sqrt[n]{0.05})$$

and to apply the approximation $\ln (1-x) \sim x$ for small x.

This leads to (5.18).

$$X^{(h)} = \begin{cases} 1 \text{ if a failure has occured} \\ \\ 0 \text{ otherwise} \end{cases}$$

Because the input is randomly selected according to real operation

$$p\ (X^{(h)} = 1) = p_h$$

Let Y_i be the random variable representively the result of the i-th program run, i.e.

$$Y_i = \begin{cases} 1 \text{ if a failure has occured during the i-th program run} \\ \\ 0 \text{ otherwise} \end{cases}$$

Since the stratum is randomly selected according to the random variable H_i, Y_i can be expressed by

$$Y_i = X^{(H_i)}; \ i=1,\ldots,n.$$

The probability that the i-th program run will be faulty is given by

$$p(Y_i=1) = p(X^{(H_i)}=1) = \sum_{h=1}^{K} p(X^{(H_i)}=1/H_i=h)\ p(H_i=h) =$$

$$= \sum_{h=1}^{K} p(X^{(h)}=1) \cdot p(H=h)$$

$$= \sum_{h=1}^{K} \rho_h\ p_h$$

The number Y of all faulty program runs of the test is a random variable and can be expressed by

$$Y = \sum_{i=1}^{n} Y_i$$